THE SLOVENES AND YUGOSLAVISM

1890-1914

CAROLE ROGEL

EAST EUROPEAN QUARTERLY, BOULDER
DISTRIBUTED BY COLUMBIA UNIVERSITY PRESS
NEW YORK

1977

EAST EUROPEAN MONOGRAPHS, NO. XXIV

DB
34
S6
R63

Carole Rogel is Associate Professor of History
at The Ohio State University

To Philip and Iko

INTRODUCTION

The Slovenes are a Southern Slav people who currently number 1.8 million and inhabit the northern-most Republic of Yugoslavia. The boundaries of Slovenia reach Croatia in the south, extend to Hungary in the east, form the southern frontier of Austria in the north and reach the Adriatic Sea and the environs of Trieste in the west. Until 1918, when they were included in the newly created Kingdom of Serbs, Croats, and Slovenes (renamed Yugoslavia in 1929), Slovenes were subjects of the House of Austria. Inhabiting several of its alpine provinces and settled along the Adriatic Littoral, they did not constitute a political unity, and until the mid-19th century it barely occurred to Slovenes to engage in political activity. In the post-Napoleonic period, however, when the national consciousness of many peoples was awakened by the French example or by resistance to French expansion, Slovenes were also affected. From the beginning, however, it was obvious that Slovenes were operating under certain limitations.

Nation building is no game for the numerically small. It is particularly hazardous when engaged in simultaneously with larger aspiring nations. In winning Venetia from Austria in 1866 Italy absorbed some 27,000 Slovenes; the following year the creation of a Dual Monarchy in Central Europe left 45,000 Slovenes in Hungary. Earlier on Slovenes had found German nationalism a threat to their national aspirations. Germans in 1848 resisted granting autonomy to non-Germans living in territories of the old Empire. And in the next half century Slovenes saw their foothold in Trieste threatened by Germans who coveted a port on the Adriatic. As nationalism mounted among the Germans of Austria, Slovenes felt increasingly anxious about the imposition of German culture.

In the 19th century the Slovenes, predominantly peasant and Catholic, and ruled by Austro-Germans, were novices at politics. For the most part it was lawyers, writers, and priests, who spoke for the Slovene people and debated issues of cultural and political importance. It was among circles of intellectuals that the idea of a Slovene nation was first given form. After 1890 political parties also came to represent Slovenes in local diets and in the Parliament in Vienna. These parties often spent their energies emulating their Western European counterparts and engaging in traditional political battles rather than reflecting indigenous Slovene interests. Slovene

Liberals were preoccupied with attacking Slovene clericalism, while power-ful Clericals, like Mahnič, were ultramontane, forever defending Rome. Slovene Socialists fought both Clericals and Liberals and then battled one another over a number of issues, including the so-called Revisionism then being debated all over Europe. Eventually the parties conceded in their own way, in their own time, their neglect of the national question.

The small size of the Slovene nation led its would-be national leaders in the early 19th century to seek common effort with other peoples. Dur-ing the course of the century some Slovenes sought strength in Pan-slavism, others in Austroslavism. In the last two decades before the war, nearly all came to focus on Southern Slav unity, of which infinite varia-tions were offered. The chief difficulty was that neither Croats nor Serbs, within the Habsburg Empire or outside it, were eager to risk their own ad-vantages for the sake of Slovenes. They knew that because Slovene terri-tory stood between Vienna and the sea, Slovene autonomy, not to men-tion independence, was unthinkable so far as Vienna was concerned. Already in 1870 at a Ljubljana Yugoslav Conference it was argued by cer-tain Empire Serbs that a Yugoslav Program must exclude the Slovenes for the present, lest it involve South Slavs in a head-on confrontation with a German southward thrust. A similar reservation was made by Croat Rightists who were reluctant to commit themselves explicitly to Slovenes in spite of a party merger with the Slovene People's Party (Clericals) in 1912. R. W. Seton-Watson in 1911 in *The Southern Slav Question and the Habsburg Monarchy* noted that: "... urgent reasons of straegy and geo-graphy make it impossible for them [the Slovenes] to be included in any unified Southern Slav state in the immediate future."* Consequently he excluded the Slovenes from his study.

Given these limitations, Slovenes could not be daring and demanding in their nationalism. They had to allow for a variety of possibilities, while continuing to urge cooperation with other peoples, particularly South Slavic ones. Some Slovenes came to stress the value of Illyrism, or the cul-tural and linguistic unification of South Slavs, as a necessary prerequisite to Yugoslav political cooperation. Others urged political reform of Austria in order that Slovene and Yugoslav interests could be more equitably re-presented. All three political parties remained implicitly loyal to Austria, though all proposed alterations in the existing system. Only a handful of Slovene spokesmen, none proper politicians, advocated separation from Austria and that only after 1912. Most could not realistically preach sepa-ration until well into the First World War when major obstacles to an

---

*R. W. Seton-Watson, *The Southern Slav Question and the Hapsburg Monarchy*, 1911 (reprinted by Howard Fertig, New York, 1969), p. 2.

independent Yugoslav (i.e. Serb-Croat-Slovene) state had been removed. The study is concerned with the pre-World War I development of Yugoslavism among the Slovenes, beginning with a brief review of its 19th century roots and giving more detailed attention to Yugoslavism in the period 1890-1914. Each political party during those years developed an attitude toward both cultural and political Yugoslavism. Party programs and solutions offered by non-politicians, generally intellectuals, are discussed, and effects of Austrian policy regarding Southern Slavs and of events in the Balkans are considered. This investigation focuses on intellectuals and politicians. This does not mean that the people were not nationally conscious. They probably were, and many were certainly well informed of the issues, given the high literacy rate, the wide circulation of daily and weekly newspapers, and after the turn of the century the fact of a broadened franchise. Popular sentiment of this nature, however, is difficult to document, and it is here mainly discussed where it is known to have accounted appreciably for the strength of a particular party or program.

TABLE OF CONTENTS

INTRODUCTION   v

   I. BEFORE 1848: THE SEARCH FOR A NATIONAL IDENTITY   3

  II. 1848-1890: THE BEGINNINGS OF POLITICAL ACTIVITY   14

 III. THE SLOVENE PEOPLE'S PARTY:
      THE TRIALISTIC SOLUTION   28

 IV. THE NATIONAL PROGRESSIVE PARTY:
      SLOVENE LIBERAL NATIONALISM   40

  V. THE YUGOSLAV SOCIAL DEMOCRATIC PARTY
      THE SOCIALIST NATIONAL POLICY   51

 VI. 1908 AND 1909: THE RESPONSE TO THE ANNEXATION
      OF BOSNIA AND HERZEGOVINA   63

 VII. CULTURAL YUGOSLAVISM:
      THE REVIVAL OF THE VRAZ-PREŠEREN DEBATE   75

VIII. THE BALKAN WARS, 1912-1913:
      THE COMMITMENT TO AUSTRIA QUESTIONED   90

 IX. STUDENTS AND INDEPENDENTS:
      TOWARD A SOLUTION OUTSIDE AUSTRIA   102

NOTES   119

BIBLIOGRAPHY   153

INDEX   159

Before the twentieth century Slovenia did not exist as an independent national state. The Slovenes until 1918 inhabited several Austrian Habsburg provinces, which were regarded as individual administrative units; Slovenes lived in the duchies of Carniola, Styria, Carinthia, the county of Gorica, the Margravate of Istria, and in Trieste.[1] The very concept of a "Slovene" national unit did not exist until the 19th century and even then the very meaning of "Slovene" was not defined. In use the designation sometimes meant "Slovene;" at other times it was synonomous with "Slav." Germans often referred to these alpine Slavs and to Slavs in general as "Winden," as did the Slovene Primož Trubar, who during the Reformation period compiled and published the first Slovene grammar and early Slovene relgiious texts.[2] Most often, however, Slovenes were not called "Winden," but rather Styrians, or Carinthians, or Carniolans—after the provinces in which they lived. This explains why Slovene intellectuals of the late 18th and early 19th centuries referred to the Slovene language as the "kranjska špraha,"[3] or the language of Carniola, the Austrian duchy where Slovenes were clearly in the majority. The term "Slovenci," or Slovenes, was first applied to inhabitants of these provinces in 1811 by Kopitar and Vodnik (see below) in a joint linguistic study of the Illyrian Provinces.[4] However, it was several decades thereafter before the term was widely used with its present meaning.

The Slovenes were considered by many historians as one of the "nonhistoric" nations of the Austrian Empire, partly because they had no real history as an independent sovereign state.[5] More important, in modern times the Slovenes did not possess a nobility or a sizable middle class, and traditionally at least one of these is evident among "historic" nations. Such elements generally assume leadership of a people and ultimately determine whether it will be independent or at least whether it will enjoy a certain measure of autonomy. Without these upper class elements and because of their small numbers, the Slovenes were unable to preserve their independence in the early Middle Ages, nor were they able later to regain it. The Slovenes were an agrarian people, ruled by an Austro-

German nobility Their clergy was Roman Catholic and, particularly in the upper ranks of the church hierarchy, often German and sometimes Italian.

In the 6th and 7th centuries the Slovenes, coming as had other Slavs from north of the Carpathians, migrated to Carinthia. By the 9th century Slovene or Carinthian settlements reached their greatest expanse, stretching from the source of the Drava River in the west to Lake Balaton in the east encompassing much of what is now upper Austria and extending from present day Slovenia northward to the Danube toward Linz and reaching nearly to Vienna.[6] Carniola, Istria and other territories which were not a part of Carinthia proper, though settled by Slovenes, were marches of Carinthia. For this historical period the term "Carinthian" is used synonymously with "Slovene."[7]

When the Slovenes first came to Carinthia, they were independent and had a nobility which governed them; but this independence was short-lived. In Carinthia they established their own dukedom, headed by a duke (*dux*). He was elected by all freemen in the duchy, including former inhabitants of Carinthia, who, though they were not Slovene, figured prominently in the voting. The duke's election was followed by a unique enthronement ceremony; it was presided over by a simple peasant, and the duke himself was clad symbolically in peasant clothing when he took his oath as ruler of the Carinthians.[8]

In the mid-7th century the duke of Carinthia was a vassal to the ruler of Moravia which included Slavic tribes to the northeast;[9] yet the independence of the Carinthians, it seems, was not seriously threatened by this association. When the Franks moved eastward in the 8th century, they defeated the Carinthians and in 788 Carinthia's Duke came under Frankish domination; thereafter the Franks selected Carinthia's ruler. Carinthia became a part of the Empire of the West (later the Holy Roman Empire) and Carinthians found themselves subordinated to Germans, who soon imposed non-Slovene dukes upon them. The power and prestige of the ducal office was severely limited, and the Duke's enthronement ceremony at *Gosposvetsko polje* became a mere symbol of past independence.[10] With the Slovene Carinthian nobility diminishing in number and importance, by the 9th century the Carinthians had become a dependent people. The process of Germanization and Christianization was accelerated with the influx of German nobles, both secular and clerical; the area settled by the Slovenes had imposed upon it the life of medieval feudal Germany; and Carinthia with its marches was divided by German nobles and clergy into numerous and petty principalities. After 1273 Rudolf of Habsburg and his successors slowly consolidated control of these areas and they became part of the original crownlands of the house of Austria.

As a part of this Germanic world, the Slovenes were drawn into the Protestant Reformation. As elsewhere in Europe, this was not only a period of intellectual ferment, but also of peasant revolts, Turkish invasions, and intense social, economic, and political upheaval. The Church lost respect and prestige, and the secular nobles took advantage of growing dissension within the Church to augment their political powers. This was the case, too, in Slovene crownlands, where the Habsburg ruler—also Holy Roman Emperor—defended the Roman Church. Here the local nobility frequently joined the Protestant revolt as an act of defiance against the Emperor, whose power had been growing at the nobles' expense. Much of the population of the Slovene lands was in this way converted to Protestantism, and the beginnings of a national cultural awakening accompanied religious reform.

Among the Slovenes an early "national" awareness has been attributed to Primož Trubar, a Protestant reformer, sometimes called "the Slovene Luther,"[11] though in some respects Trubar's relgious convictions were closer to those of Zwingli.[12] Trubar was a cleric who felt called to write in the Slovene language so that those for whom he had spiritual responsibilities could find religious salvation. That his motives were primarily religious is evident from the materials he wrote or translated. Other than a Primer, which was necessary for practical purposes, all of Trubar's works were of a religious nature. Among these was a translation of the New Testament, which Trubar considered necessary for the spiritual redemption of his Slovene flock. But, though Primoz Trubar was primarily a religious reformer, Slovene national history has cast him in another image, as a cultural forefather of Slovene nationalism. He contributed to Slovene literary history its first printed book (1550), and he thereby laid the technical basis for the development of a "Slovene" language and of a Slovene literature. Trubar wrote much and translated much in the two decades after 1550—thirty-one items in all. His style left a good deal to be desired, and he did not labor long in search of a proper Slovene word if he could easily adapt a German one to his needs. He felt pressed for time and chose to produce his literary tools for religious salvation as rapidly as possible, giving little thought to the perfection of Slovene as a modern language.[13] But he did provide the foundation for it, and that in the Latin alphabet.

Trubar's work in the cultural sphere was carried on by Dalmatin, Bohoric, and Krelj, men of a more humanistic bent, who polished and refined the crude forms which Trubar had bequeathered them. Their most outstanding accomplishment was Dalmatin's translation of the entire Bible, completed in 1584. Some Catholic texts were written in Slovene before the Thirty Years' War; but, in general, one must attribute the development of an early Slovene literary language to the industriousness of these Slovene Protestant reformers. As the Catholic Reformation eradicated Protestantism in these Austrian provinces, the printing of Slovene books ceased altogether and did not recommence until the late 17th century. Even then the output was meager. For the most part, the cultural seeds of the 16th century lay dormant for two hundred years.

A genuine Slovene cultural awakening took place in the late 18th century. It did not, however, begin until Austria herself had experienced certain transformations—government centralization and secularization, during the reigns of Maria Theresa and Joseph II (1740-90). Efforts to modernize Austria altered the social and legal status of the Slovenes (most of them peasant-serfs), and required of them a measure of elementary schooling. In all this, Austria, in her eagerness to become more abreast of the rest of Europe, welcomed foreign examples and influences.[14]

Some Slovenes, no longer bound by serfdom, sought to understand the perplexities of the time. They sifted among imported concepts—generally derived from the Western European Enlightenment—and concluded that rational investigation of the society around them was a key to their queries. Among Slovene intellectuals there developed a great interest in local language, culture, and history. Their work was later given direction and purpose by Herder and those like him, who maintained that the people's culture expressed the real spirit of a nation—the creative genius of a collective segment of mankind.

This work was initiated among the Slovenes by a handful of men, often priests and monks, who took special interest in the local language.[15] Of these, one of particular significance was Marko Pohlin, a monk, whose *Kranjska gramatika* published in 1768 is generally considered the first real expression of a national awareness.[16] Pohlin entitled his work *A Grammar of Carniola* for he did not feel that the dialects spoken among Slovenes in Styria and Carinthia were the same as that used in Carniola. Yet many of his contemporaries, who were more influential than he, believed the linguistic differences negligible, and they began to think of the Slavic inhabitants of Carniola, Carinthia, and Styria as belonging to one language unit, as constituting one nation.[17] Of particular importance was the fact that Pohlin's grammar, as interpreted by his contemporaries, prepared the way for the development of a Slovene literary language aimed not at the peasant, as were the works of Trubar and the Reformation, but at the intellectual and the townsman, those most vulnerable before the forces of Germanization.

The task of investing the Slovene tongue with the refinements of a modern literary language passed from Pohlin to a group in Ljubljana known as the Zois circle. It was assisted financially by Baron Žiga Zois, the son of an Italian nobleman.[18] It was primarily intent on transforming Slovene into a medium of expression appropriate for Slovene intellectuals and townspeople, who found the Slovene peasant language deficient. The Zois circle promoted writing of history, drama, prose and poetry in Slovene, not in German as had been done in the past.

One of the basic works of the Slovene Enlightenment was a history which Anton Linhart (1756-1795) wrote while associated with the Zois group. *Versuch einer Geschichte von Krain und der übrigen südlichen Slawen Österreiches* (1788-91), though written in German, was vital for the further development of a "Slovene" national consciousness. This work, as Linhart himself indicated, was merely an "attempt" at conveying a history, and it emerged even less complete than intended due to the work of the censor. Linhart himself was somewhat of a liberal and sympathetic to the revolution in France; his work was essentially anti-feudal and anti-clerical. He wrote not in terms of rulers or crownlands, but rather of the people. His history was the first in which, irrespective of where they lived in the cluster of Habsburg domains, Slovenes were depicted as one national unit. Linhart thereby advanced the concept of a "Slovenia," while establishing the foundation of Slovene historical writing.[19]

Men of the Zois circle also produced some significant plays—two written by Linhart[20]—and some poetry, the contribution of Valentin Vodnik (1758-1819). Vodnik also edited the first Slovene newspaper, *Lublanske Novice*, published twice weekly, later once a week, from 1797 to 1800. It was discontinued in 1800 for lack of subscribers. However, by the end of the 18th century, the foundations had been laid. A Slovene grammar had been written, as had a history of the Slovenes: the concept of a "Slovene" nation was slowly taking form.

The impact of the French Revolution and of French expansion helped merge the idea of "nationhood" with the idea of "homeland;" the next logical step was to associate these with the concept of popular sovereignty.[21] Those who developed such trains of thought were few, and even before such ideas were fully conceived among politically aware Slovene intellectuals, Napoleon was at war with the Austrian Empire. He defeated Austria, acquiring some of her territory as spoils, and as a result, many of Austria's Southern Slavs were attached to the Napoleonic Empire in accordance with the Treaty of Pressburg (1805). At that time the French acquired Dalmatia, Venetian Istria, and other former Venetian possessions.[22] Four years later the Austrians lost again to Napoleon and were compelled to cede the county of Gorica, the city of Trieste, all of Carniola which lay on the right bank of the Sava, a part of Croatia, six Croatian military districts,[23] Fiume, Austrian Istria and various islands of the Adriatic.[24] All of these became a part of the French Empire, forming a separate political unit called the Illyrian Provinces. The population was chiefly Slovene and Croat; the capital was Ljubljana.

For four years, from 1809 to 1813, the French governed the Illyrian Provinces. The officials were for the most part young, idealistic Frenchmen moved by Enlightenment principles to adminster these lands with a genuine measure of benevolence and dedication. This was particularly true of Maréchal Marmont, Illyria's first governor. These administrators applied the Code Napoleon, centralized the court system, modernized the schools, and introduced the Concordat with Rome to the Illyrian Church. Many of the reforms were extremely unpopular, especially those dealing with taxation and military conscription, and, in general, the French regime encountered many obstacles. Because the period of occupation was short, little headway was made; from the French point of view the rule in Illyria was a failure.[25]

However, for some of the local population the very existence of the Illyrian Provinces as a South Slavic political unit came to mean something more than foreign military occupation, particularly after the French had retreated and Austrian rule was resumed. Unconsciously the French had done much to intensify national sentiment in the area, for aside from enlightened reforms which had exposed the Illyrians to new social and political concepts, two aspects of French rule were of particular importance— the resurrection of the name "Illyria," the other, the French encouragement of the national language.[26]

For Napoleon the name "Illyria" added to his Empire a hint of ancient splendor, for it recalled the original Illyrians, who had ruled in the area until conquered by Roman Emperors. However, for those 19th century Illyrians sensitive to new intellectual currents, it came to represent the resurrection of a Slaveno-Illyrian state, which had allegedly existed in the distant past. Actually the term had formerly been used to designate Yugoslavs and even Slavs in general, but it had not been so used since the Middle Ages. Napoleon became aware of this designation from a report he had commissioned to investigate the nature of these Southern Slavic lands. It is conceivable, though not probable, that Napoleon's choice of the term "Illyria" was not prompted by reveries of reassembling a Neo-Roman Empire, but came about because investigation revealed that the Southern Slavs thought of themselves as Illyrians.[27] Most relevant here is the fact that some Slovenes and Croats genuinely felt a oneness, a sense of identity, with Illyrians and Illyria, and this encouraged the development of a South Slav national sentiment which was to play a prominent, sometimes dominant, role in the future history of these people. An Illyrian national sentiment found expression, though it was not defined, and the Slovene priest

Valentin Vodnik sang praises to Napoleon in his *Ilirija Oživljena* (Illyria Reborn, 1811). This Illyrism was the first manifestation of a Yugoslav idea among the Slovenes, and it had authentic national political overtones.[28] Although at that time it was undeveloped and vague, it served to encourage the further definition of national character and national units. In the next two decades it generally aided in the formulation of Slovene or Croat national identity; later these were expanded into a broader Southern Slav consciousness.

The development of national self-awareness in Illyria was also furthered by the attitude of the French administration toward the use of the local language, which was either Croat or Slovene. Under Marmont a decree was issued providing for education in the national language for both sexes. Books were written in the vernacular to facilitate this.[29] Marmont also planned an "Illyrian," that is, Croat edition of the provincial newspaper, *Télégraphe Officiel des Provinces Illyriennes*;[30] however, it never materialized. The French showed a genuine desire to employ the national language in schools and in the courts, primarily because the local language was less objectionable than German, but these national languages were still primitive, undeveloped peasant tongues, deficient in terminology and not suited to French administrative purposes. Furthermore, the French soon realized that there was not one "Illyrian" language or dialect, but at least two.

By September 1813 when Austrian rule was reintroduced, Francis I, then Emperor of Austria, had come to abhor all that the French and their revolution stood for. His attitudes were significantly different from those of his immediate predecessors, his uncle Joseph II (1780-90), and his father Leopold II (1790-92), who were more receptive, even predisposed perhaps, to the predominant intellectual currents of the Enlightenment. Because Francis I was a legitimist and reactionary, Vienna promptly abolished all French reforms in Illyria, including those which had in one way or another favored the national languages. There remained in fact very little of the Illyrian experiment after 1815. Austria legally preserved the name "Illyria," and most of those territories which had been under French rule officially constituted the Kingdom of Illyria from 1816 to 1849;[31] in reality, however, the Habsburg Southern Slavs derived little "national" benefit from this.

The intangible spirit of the French period, though it was temporarily subdued (particularly during Austria's post-Napoleonic campaign against "francophils"), did not entirely vanish. Between 1815 and 1848 that spirit was continued in the cultural activities of the Zois circle and was directed toward further definition of national identity. Slovene intellectuals busied themselves with linguistic studies, which ultimately produced an acceptable orthography and some early literary works.[32] National activity of this nature was not prohibited by Vienna provided that the cultural boundaries were not transcended. Vienna in some cases even sanctioned the activities of cultural nationalists on the grounds that their aim and that of legitimists were one and the same—to preserve that which was traditional.[33] Sanctioning national cultural activity legitimized the work of conservative nationalists. Political and radical nationalism were, of course, disallowed.[34] But, this presented little problem since Slovenes hardly thought of political activity before 1848.

The cultural works of the Slovenes before 1848 were produced by a mere handful of men who did not always agree upon method and emphasis. One of these was Jernej Kopitar, who had been a member of the Zois circle before the French occupation. Already in 1808 Kopitar had published a monumental work on Slovene grammar.[35] It contained key fragments of his noted Pannonian theory upon which he later enlarged to support his Austroslavism.[36] Essentially, Kopitar had concluded from his linguistic studies that the Old Church Slavonic language had originated in Pannonia. He further reasoned that since Slavic Pannonia had constituted the core of Austria, Austria was basically Slavic. He counseled Austria to assume leadership of her Slavs, to establish a seat of Slavic learning at Vienna, to foster Austroslav unity, and to fortify it with Roman Catholicism.[37] He was anti-Russian because he believed the Russians had corrupted the Old Church Slavonic tongue and anti-German because Protestantism and romanticism flourished among Germans. He felt that Austroslav Catholicism could combat these evils, that it could, moreover, wipe out Panslavism, Orthodoxy, and Protestantism as well.[38] His wish was to join all Slavs together under Catholic Habsburg leadership. [39]

Kopitar is best known for his scholarly collaboration with the Serb Vuk Karadžić; together they produced invaluable studies on Serbian grammar. For his linguistic research this Slovene was and is highly esteemed among Slavic linguists. However, Kopitar was a controversial figure among Slovene intellectuals because as state censor in Vienna from 1810 to 1848 he often conflicted with contemporary Slovene writers whose works were inspired by Western Romanticism.[40] Basically, Kopitar was a Slovene cultural nationalist, who was staunch in his support of Austria and even approved of Metternich. He was a conservative, a traditionalist, who urged the development of a Slovene language, but for the purpose of safeguarding the legitimate institutions of the monarchy.[41] For that very reason Kopitar encouraged developing the idiom of the Slovene peasantry (also a legitimate Austrian institution), so that it in turn could buttress the monarchy and Catholicism. He eventually hoped to draw all Habsburg Yugoslavs into the circle of central European culture, but naively expected that they would, because of their staunch morals and natural intelligence, become the determining force of cultural development in the area.[42] Consequently, he resisted, and, as censor, was often severe with those who were attracted by Western European literary models, the virtues of which he never comprehended.

One who clashed frequently with Kopitar over this issue was Francè Prešeren (1800-1848), considered by many the greatest Slovene poet, and certainly the greatest Slovene poet of the Romantic period. Prešeren and a colleague, Matija Čop, were committed to the creation of a Slovene literary language which would provide those Slovenes who were not peasants with an adequate means of expression. Their intention was to transform the Slovene peasant idiom into a 19th century language which could compete with German and hopefully arrest the Germanization of town-dwelling Slovenes. Prešeren and Čop wished, in other words, to liberate the emerging Slovene middle class from its dependence on the German language—a goal not highly regarded by Metternich, who considered German an integrating factor in the monarchy and a thing worth preserving.[43] Vienna sanctioned Kopitar's work because he sought to unify, that is, to join the Slavic peoples of the monarchy on a religious basis in support of Austrian legitimism. Prešeren, because he was oriented toward the West, appeared to the authorities overly independent and even dangerous.[44]

Prešeren also had difficulties with some of the Slovene clergy.[45] The latter objected to the publication of non-religious Slovene literature and regarded the romantic poetry of Prešeren as immoral. Though the position of this clergy was much more extreme than that of Kopitar, the two sometimes made common cause against Prešeren and Čop, especially whenever they felt that the governmental or religious institutions of Austria were threatened. A definite break developed between the legitimists and those who advocated the establishment of an independent Western-oriented Slovene language and culture, though advocates of the latter had not yet applied their energies to political programs. These two trends—one culturally oriented toward folk idiom and politically legitimist, the other culturally cosmopolitan and leaning toward liberalism—were discernible in the 1830's.

About the same time certain cultural developments among Croats were directed toward the Slovene crownlands. In Croatia in the thirties an Illyrian or South Slavic cultural movement under the guidance of Ljudevit Gaj gained impressive support. In a way it had been encouraged by the Slovak Kollár, a Panslav, who had concluded in his research that there was, in fact, only one basic Slavic language, of which there were four dialects— Czech, Polish, Russian, and Illyrian.[46] The Croat Gaj agreed, and furthermore became convinced that *štokavian* was the dialect most appropriate for a common Illyrian literary language; all other sub-dialects would be secondary though they might be used privately.[47] For Gaj Illyrian or Southern Slav territory was that geographically contained within the triangle formed by the towns of Villach, Scutari, and Varna. The Slovenes obviously fell within these limits.

Gaj's Illyrism was basically Panslavic but rent by numerous difficulties—partly because of the romantic-idealist images which inspired it. It eventually became associated with Draškovič's program for Illyrian political union (1832), the first plan for South Slavic political unification.[48] Draškovič, and others after him, founded their political programs on the basis of Croat state rights, maintaining that the Croats had legal claim to autonomy. Vienna, unclear as to the nature of Croat South Slav national activities, felt politically pressed by these demands, and feared that the South Slavs were oriented toward Serbia. They attributed much of the political activity to Gaj's Illyrists and moved to control them. After 1843 the very use of the term Illyrian was officially forbidden; adherents thereafter began to use the word "Yugoslav," which at the time had primarily "ethnic" rather than political connotations.

In the mid-1830's and early 1840's efforts were made to extend Gaj's cultural Illyrian movement to the Slovenes. However, Illyrism failed to take root in Slovene lands, except in isolated areas, generally in Styria, where the Slovene dialect was closer to *kajkavian* Croat and where Slovenes constituted a very small minority in the towns and consequently felt under constant pressure from Germans.[49] Their only recourse, it seemed at the time, was to make common cause with other Southern Slavs. The only Slovene of note who accepted Gaj's Illyrism was Stanko Vraz, a Styrian, who wrote poetry in the *štokavian* dialect.[50] Other Slovenes, notably Prešeren, were directly opposed to the movement. Prešeren regarded the development of a "Slovene" language as the most pressing need of the time; the adoption of another language, be it German, Croat or any other—a language which the people did not understand—he considered a rejection of national heritage. Even Kopitar, who was at odds with Prešeren over the character of the Slovene cultural renaissance, agreed that Slovenes should first develop their own tongue. Kopitar rejected Kollár's views on the relationship of Slavic dialects to one another and denounced Gaj and the Illyrists as fanatics who sought to bring other nations under their control.[51] Consequently, Illyrism of the Pre-March (1848) period succeeded only in that it brought the Croat language closer to that of the Serbs through the adoption of *štokavian* as a linguistic base—ultimately preparing the way for a single Serbo-Croat literary language.[52]

In the 1840's Slovene cultural nationalism made slow, steady progress. The first Slovene public speech was heard and the first Slovene songs were sung in the theater in 1845. Slovene publications appeared: one was a literary journal, *Kranjska Čbelica* (1830-1848), the other a newspaper, *Kmetijske in rokodelske novice* (Peasant and Craftsman News), edited by Janez Bleiweis (1843-1902). The latter concerned itself with the practical, everyday concerns of the Slovene masses, and made a greater impact than the former, which was aimed at a more limited audience—the Slovene intellectual.

Intellectuals, be they priests or monks or lawyers (as was Prešeren), devoted themselves to the promotion of Slovene cultural development. They did not always agree as to the purpose of this culture: should it preserve the peasant tongue and produce works of a folk nature, or should it look toward the needs of the townsman. In either case both the conservatives, such as Kopitar and Slomšek (a Styrian clergyman whose love for the mother tongue prompted him to urge that Slovene be used in schools and local administration) and those more liberally oriented, like Prešeren, agreed that "Slovene" must be developed as a separate language. They rejected Gaj's Illyrism which proposed that Southern Slavs all adopt one idiom as the basis for a common literature. Slovene cultural development had come relatively far in the first half of the 19th century given the emergence of men like Kopitar and Prešeren and Gaj. Their teachings were all to be revived to one degree or another in the years before World War I.

During that same half century when cultural identity was being so intently pursued, political affairs were virtually ignored. When the revolution came in 1848, the Slovenes were more a nation than they had been—due to the work of the cultural nationalists—but they were not prepared for political action. Even the omnipresent and suspicious Austrian police, in their eagerness to eradicate Illyrism after 1843, reported that none existed in the Slovene provinces. In 1848 the Slovenes had to scrape and scurry in order to piece together a political program compatible with some of the cultural principles they had formulated.

CHAPTER II
1848-1890: THE BEGINNINGS OF POLITICAL ACTIVITY

News of the uprising in Vienna on 15 March 1848 reached Ljubljana on the 16th by the afternoon mail. The thirty-three year rule of Metternich, who was blamed by the revolutionaries for the bulk of Austria's ills, had ended abruptly. The Slovenes in their crownlands celebrated the news of the revolt. Already on the 16th white ribbons—"a sign of jubilation and nationality"—were pinned to the lapels of Ljubljana inhabitants. That same evening following a performance of rejoicing in the theater, street mobs destroyed a likeness of Metternich, and unruly gangs raided the home of the unpopular Mayor Fischer.[1] Activities of this nature continued for several days in Ljubljana, in Carniola in general, and in other Slovene areas. However, although many were clearly delighted that the old order had been overthrown, few had any clear notion as to what should replace it. Few Slovenes were fully aware of the issues involved; few even understood the leading political trends of the time.[2]

Slovenes soon learned that there was no simple choice between absolutism and constitutional monarchy though the Emperor had promised a constitution. It was soon learned that in the name of national self-determination German liberals, who were among the revolutionaries, were attempting to include Austria—that is, those Austrian territories which had been a part of the German Confederation—in a greater German union. Slovene territories, traditionally a part of the German Empire, were especially coveted; they could provide Great Germany with access to Trieste and the sea.[3] Slovenes would have to take some position not only in regard to their future with the Austrian Empire but also with respect to the Frankfurt Parliament and Great Germany.

The revolution, therefore, served to encourage political activity among Slovenes. Janez Bleiweis, the newspaper editor, became president of the "Slovensko društvo" in Ljubljana. Dr. Josip Muršec assumed a similar position in the Graz organization "Slovenija," as did the Slavicist Fran Miklošič in the Vienna society of the same name. All three organizations were formed after the revolution began and became centers of political agitation. Even small towns organized clubs, initially cultural in nature, which soon functioned as campaign centers for elections to the Vienna Parliament. Some also became centers of opposition to the Frankfurt Parliament and Great German aims.

The Viennese organization "Slovenija" was the first Slovene group with a political program in 1848;[4] indeed it was the first Slovene political program ever drafted.[5] Miklošič was its president, and the members were for the most part Slovene students studying in Vienna when the revolution broke out. A delegation from Ljubljana soon joined them (it had made the journey to Vienna to present Slovene demands to the Archduke John). Vienna's "Slovenija" called for: (1) a Unified Slovenia, that is, the administrative unification of all ethnically Slovene territories into one kingdom or crownland to be called *Slovenija*, with an assembly or diet in Ljubljana; (2) the introduction of Slovene in schools and in government administration (it demanded the establishment of a Slovene university as well); and (3) the independence of Austria from Frankfurt (that is, it opposed Austrian participation in the Frankfurt Parliament and therefore Austrian participation in a greater German union.)[6] Other Slovene programs in 1848 were essentially similar.

In July 1848 Ljubljana's "Slovensko društvo" began publishing the newspaper, entitled *Slovenija*, which was the first Slovene political publication. It championed the Unified Slovenia program of the Vienna organization, supported the claims of other national groups for autonomy—judging that national federalism was the solution for Austria—and opposed the movement for union with Germany.[7] Of the more important organizations in 1848 this Ljubljana group was probably the least radical. Its president Bleiweis, though an ardent proponent of Slovene cultural development, was a conservative; he backed the Unified Slovenia program only when Vienna seemed to encourage it.[8]

The program of the Ljubljana and Vienna Slovenes, essentially based on the idea of a Unified Slovenia, is sometimes referred to as the minimum program by Slovene historians.[9] The maximum program rested more broadly on political Illyrism or Yugoslav political union, and was somewhat less defined. In 1848 the appeal for political cooperation among Austria's Southern Slavs was based generally on the desire to consolidate forces against Germans or Magyars; some Illyrism was evident in both the Vienna and Ljubljana groups. The Ljubljana organization, for example, collected Slovene funds for Jelačić's campaigns against the Magyars; and in the thirteenth issue of Ljubljana's *Slovenija* Dr. Martinak wrote with reference to Slovenes combating Germandom: "It would, of course, be better if we could join with our brothers the Croats in a united state."[10] The Slovenes in Vienna had a certain sympathy for other Yugoslavs—significantly the

Croats—stemming from pre-1848 contacts; they were also sympathetic toward other Habsburg Slavs, especially the Czechs (who lived in lands of the German Confederation). These Viennese Slovenes welcomed an "Appeal" from Southern Slav brethren which urged their cooperation with Slavs from Croatia, Slavonia, and Dalmatia. Most prominent among those signing the "Appeal" was Ljudevit Gaj, often described as the father of Illyrism. The reception of this Illyrian appeal by the Viennese group was modified by a general expression of unity and brotherhood for other Slavs, indicating a measure of general Pan-Slav sentiment.[11]

The real stronghold of political Illyrism was the Slovene organization in Graz, another student center. It lay in the German and Slovene province of Styria which had had a recent experience of cultural Illyrism (the Slovene Illyrist Vraz was Styrian). As in Ljubljana and Vienna, members supported the unification of Slovene lands within Austria.[12] The Graz Slovenes also opposed sending representatives to Frankfurt, and they stressed the need for South Slav political cooperation against imminent Germanization and Magyarization. The Graz "Slovenija" organization sent one Dr. Kočevar to a Zagreb congress where he proposed the inclusion of a United Slovenia, as a federative unit, in the Triune Kingdom of Croatia, Slavonia, and Dalmatia. Graz also sent Stanko Vraz as its representative to the Prague Slav Congress.[13]

The strongest expression of Illyrism and by far the boldest Slovene political program in 1848, however, was not produced by any of these organizations. Matija Majar, a Slovene clergyman, whom Apih, historian of the Slovenes in 1848, depicted as "the leftist of that era," presented the most revolutionary program of all.[14] Majar accepted the principle of a Unified Slovenia, and approved of the existence of an Austrian Empire.[15] But he also made an appeal for close cooperation among Habsburg Yugoslavs and, further, among Habsburg Slavs in general. He counseled the regime to recognize that its Slavs belonged to one nation and urged it to grant them an all-Slav assembly in the Empire.[16]

The events of 1848 occurred rapidly, too rapidly for Slovene nationalism or for Illyrism—both of which were even in concept still new and disorganized—to plan political action. Those who participated most actively in formulating political programs were clergymen, or they were Slovene intellectuals, of whom there were few in 1848.[17] Some attempts were made at winning the peasants over to the idea of a Unified Slovenia, but those clergymen who circulated petitions for this purpose were effectively denounced by Austro-Germans and Slovene Germanophiles, with the result that the Slovene peasantry was alienated from that clergy. It was not able to regain peasant confidence for nearly ten years after the revolution.[18]

While the revolution was in progress, peasants were primarily concerned with the abolition of feudal dues, a demand soon granted.[19] As a consequence, revolutionaries were generally unable to mobilize much peasant support.

Of those Slovenes who were active politically in 1848 there was a general agreement that Austria should remain independent of Greater Germany, that unification of the Slovene lands was needed and that cooperation with other Yugoslavs or other Slavs might be desirable. Slovene liberals were generally Austro-Slav in sentiment, due to extended contact with Czechs. Those who campaigned against the Frankfurt Parliament used the same arguments as did the Czech Austro-Slav Palacky. However, there were prominent dissenters. Some were willing to accept union with Germany under certain conditions. Kavčič, who represented the Slovenes at the Kremsier Parliament, where the Empire's elected representatives were drafting their own constitution, was not opposed to the idea of a German union, provided Austria retained her sovreignty.[20] In towns and cities where the population was strongly German there was effective agitation for the union, and as a result, some Slovene provinces actually sent representatives to the Frankfurt assembly.[21] Slovene liberals in general found themselves in a genuine dilemma over the Frankfurt issue. They were torn between loyalty to a Unified Slovenia and a philosophical allegiance to liberalism, though German liberalism would deny the Slovenes their own national rights. The Slovene revolutionaries remained divided.

On the issue of a Unified Slovenia there were also strong and contradictory feelings. Many did not wish to see the old crownland units broken up or transformed.[22] Others such as Bishop Slomšek opposed both a Unified Slovenia and all forms of Illyrism on the grounds that language differences had resulted from man's sins, and that nationalism (the liberal variety) was essentially sinful too. Moreover, Slomšek, who had been active in Slovene cultural work before 1848, upheld the absolute authority of the Emperor and maintained that his power was of divine origin. Slomšek believed that authority could not possibly be derived from the people; therefore, all movements for national self-determination were ill-founded.[23] For some historians, dissenters from the "minimum" program stand out very prominently. Probably Slomšek and Bleiweis, the conservative who headed the Ljubljana "Slovensko društvo," represented the "grass roots" Slovene sentiment of the time. Most historians agree that the program for a Unified Slovenia had little popular support in 1848, and that a Yugoslav program had even less backing.[24]

It is not surprising, then, that the Slovenes, inexperienced in political affairs, few in number, and divided, made little headway in 1848. They participated in the Prague Slav Congress (June 1848), where they expressed a desire for a Unified Slovenia. At the Kremsier Parliament the Slovene representative Kavčič included the idea of a Unified Slovenia in his own overall scheme for a federalistic reorganization of the Empire.[25] But the plan for a Unified Slovenia was based on ethnic demands which in the long run were not accepted even by the 1848 revolutionaries. The plan for administrative reorganization of the Empire, adopted at Kremsier by revolutionaries themselves, retained the historic crownland units. The regime, by December of 1848, headed by a new Emperor and cleverly managed by Schwarzenberg, was even less willing to accommodate to the revolutionary yearnings of a handful of disorganized intellectuals. Moreover, the regime in the end had the power to impose its own preferences. Some revolts were put down by force; the Kremsier Constitution, creation of elected representatives, was discarded; and absolute rule was reimposed.

Although Slovene revolutionary activities in 1848 were limited and led by political amateurs loyal to Austria, the post-revolutionary regime treated Slovenes strictly. To those in power, all revolutionaries were a threat and all required watching. Austria's Minister of Interior, Alexander Bach—who so typified the government of the 1850's that his name came to designate the post-revolutionary decade—instituted repression throughout the Empire. Imperial controls were applied in their strictest form in the Bach era. Austria became a truly centralized state, some would say for the first and last time. This was accomplished by force and accompanied by a rather ostentatious display of police and bureaucratic power. In 1855 this mid-19th century absolutism was sealed by an anachronistic Concordat with the Roman Church. Allied with the Church, Austria felt more confident that movements from below could be contained.

For those Slovenes still intent on furthering national interests caution was the first consideration in the 1850's. Political involvement was, of course, out of the question. The minimum and maximum programs of 1848—a Unified Slovenia and the idea of a Yugoslav political unit—were temporarily set aside. Slovene national activities were confined to safe cultural pursuits. Nationalists of every potential hue concentrated on urging use of the Slovene language in schools and local administration. The conservative elements, such as the priest Slomšek, who had condemned the revolution and, with it, Slovene political programs in 1848, contributed most in the fifties to Slovene cultural development. Such individuals— though they considered popular political movements illegitimate—strongly believed that use of the mother tongue was intimately related to eternal salvation.[26] Such conservatives took up their cause intently in the decade after 1848; and because they were less suspect than political activists, they were able to reach a wide audience. They consequently made important advances in stimulating a sense of national identity among the people.

The cultural activities of the 1850's continued into the sixties. This was the era which saw the spread of reading rooms to all Slovene territories,[27] and it saw the establishment of important publishing houses as well. The *Dru*ž*ba sv. Mohorja* (Celovec/Klagenfurt) began in 1852 and the *Slovenska matica* (Ljubljana/Laibach) established in 1864, headed by Bleiwiess conservatives, both printed and distributed Slovene books. In this early period publication of *belles-lettres* was secondary to the output of more practical works destined for broad Slovene audiences.

Cautiously the Slovenes also resumed their political activity in the 1860's. The fact that there was no retaliation from Vienna was interpreted as encouragement. But the Imperial government's failure to curtail Slovene developments in the early sixties was not due to Vienna's approving such stirrings, but because Austria was in desperate troubles. The Habsburg power had miscalculated its strengths in Europe. In the mid-fifties it was dealt a serious affront by the European powers who neglected to invite Austria to the Paris peace conference, though as a great power she assumed a right to participate and had an interest in the lands concerned. Soon thereafter Austria became entangled with Sardinia and Prussia, both building "national" empires on the edges of her own state. Two wars, one with the Italians in 1859, one with Italy and Prussia in 1866, lost Austria prestige and territory, and meant the abandonment of leadership in Central Europe.

All these pressing concerns forced Austria to alter her policy at home. In the 1860's the regime embarked upon a series of experiments regarding the constitutional structure of the Empire, hoping to hit upon a plan mutually acceptable to the rulers and the ruled. The government had come to feel that the obstinacy of the national groups had contributed to domestic difficulties as well as to defeats and setbacks in Europe.[28] It was during this period of constitutional revisionism that the Slovenes resumed their political activities, resurrecting 1848 programs and adapting them to the needs of the sixties.

The October Diploma of 1860, the regime's first attempt at a new constitution, was still-born and came to naught; but Schmerling's February Patent of 1861 was put into operation, requiring that elections for local diets and the Imperial Parliament be held. These were the first elections in the Empire since 1848 and they naturally produced political activity. In 1861 Slovene candidates were poorly organized, each running as an independent agent. During the period of the Schmerling government, Slovene representatives, moreover, did not belong to any one political club, nor did they vote as a unit. They avoided stressing radical political goals,[29] but agreed that Slovene language rights must be promoted strongly.[30]

In spite of the lack of parties and political programs Slovenes did work out a program of sorts by 1865. Its tone and scope were moderate and practical. Men like Matija Majar and Andrej Einspieler, who were liberal revolutionaries in 1848, retreated from demands for ethnic rights (a Unified Slovenia) and tried instead to present a case for Slovene historic claims. This seemed to be a sensible approach, given the fact that the regime itself had in the October Diploma (1860) put forth a federalistic constitution based on old crownland autonomies. The fact that the October Diploma had been superseded within a few months by the centralistic February Patent did not divert Slovenes from their search for legal, historic bases to support their demands. The February Patent had been poorly received by the non-German nationalities, and many were convinced that before very long it would be withdrawn. Moreover, Slovenes were confident that a federation based on historic units, not unlike that proposed in the October 1860 document, or by Palacky in 1848,[31] would eventually be accepted. Therefore it seemed advisable to prepare a legal argument for Slovene autonomy within such a federation. When Belcredi replaced Schmerling in 1865, Slovenes were confident that their labors had not been in vain. They were soon disappointed.

In the early sixties the Carinthian Andrej Einspieler was one of the first to make proposals along the lines of historic federalism. Einspieler, a rightist liberal in 1848, had thereafter retreated steadily toward a more conservative position—due largely to pressures from German liberals in his own province.[32] In 1861 he began publishing a journal entitled *Stimmen aus Innerösterreich* in which he urged the creation of a federation for Austria based on her historic components; the Slovene unit, to be composed of those provinces inhabited by Slovenes, might be called Inner Austria (*Innerösterreich*). By 1865 a precise plan for such a component was outlined in collaboration with Matija Majar and came to be known as the Maribor Program of 1865. Basically it proposed to unify the Slovenes by joining together two historic units of Europe—the Kingdom of Illyria and the Duchy of Styria.[33] At the time both Einspieler and Majar agreed that it would be unwise to call the unit "Slovenija," for this, with its implications of national sovereignty, might frighten the regime. Einspieler therefore proposed the term Inner Austria, while Majar, already an Illyrist or Yugoslav in 1848, preferred to call it Illyria. The latter term would partially satisfy those with national aspirations,[34] and Majar felt the regime, too, could not possibly object to it, since the Emperor had since 1816 held the title of King of Illyria. The Maribor Program was never adopted. Even its supporters soon abandoned it in favor of reviving the Unified Slovenia Program of 1848. The Maribor plan was indicative of Slovene cautiousness in the early sixties. After 1866, when a series of crises shook the Empire, it was deemed too moderate.

It is appropriate at this point to say a few words about Slovene political alignments of the period. The traditional view has been that conservatives (*staroslovenci* or Old Slovenes) dominated the twenty years from 1848 to 1868 and that liberals (*mladoslovenci*, Young Slovenes), succeeded them, holding primacy until 1895[35] A number of points have been made about the inaccuracy of this periodization. For one thing, these divisions were presented in a study of Slovene cultural history and were based on an understanding of philosophical positions assumed essentially by intellectuals. Such periodization is not necessarily appropriate for Slovene political history.[36] It has also been noted that the Old Slovene (*staroslovenci*)— Young Slovene (*mladoslovenci*) designations, the same as those used for Czech political history of the time, are also inappropriate. In the Czech case there was a real generation difference, which did not exist among the Slovenes. Differences, if anything, were of world view or philosophical approach, and it has been demonstrated that both "Old Slovene" and "Young Slovene" types could be found throughout the period from 1848 to 1895. Furthermore it cannot be said that "the Old" or "the Young" truly dominated any particular period politically.[37]

Evidence invalidating the traditional periodization of Slovene history comes particularly from the 1860's and the political activity of Slovenes in the era of constitutional experimentation. Studies of electoral campaigns, election results, and the subsequent performance of those elected have proved enlightening. From these it is clear that until 1867 Slovene delegates to local diets and to the Parliament in Vienna did not gravitate toward opposing political associations and did not yet reveal either a clerical or liberal stamp; in fact, all seemed judiciously to avoid being labeled politically. Moreover, before 1867 they achieved a certain unanimity, jointly promoting Slovene cultural interests. All cooperated so effectively in the 1867 elections that they even doubled the number of Slovene representatives elected.[38] Political divisions began to emerge only after the 1867 elections (January), when in March of that year Slovene political types sorted themselves into liberal and clerical camps over an issue relating to the Concordat with the Roman Church.[39] A movement in the Imperial Parliament against the Concordat forced Slovene clericals into a conservative position and Slovene liberals responded with an appropriate counter-commitment. Some would contend that even after 1867 clerical-liberal lines were not hard and fast; they were clearest whenever the Church issue arose.[40]

The period from 1865 to 1871 was a very active one for Slovenes politically. The Maribor Program of 1865, with its legal argument for

Slovene autonomy within Austria, was no sooner drafted than abandoned. The regime's response to it had been disappointing; the new head of government, Belcredi, was unimpressed. In 1866 came defeat for Austria in the war with Prussia and Italy. Then in 1867 the Austrian regime made its peace with the Hungarians, instituting a major constitutional reorganization of the empire, the so-called Compromise of 1867 which legally created an Austria-Hungary. The Slovenes were very directly affected. When Austria lost Venetia in 1866, about 27,000 Slovenes were left in Italy; and the 1867 Compromise relegated 45,000 Slovenes to the Hungarian half of the monarchy.[41] For a nation of merely one and a half million, just beginning to put together a national program, these losses were catastrophic. Furthermore, the success of both Italy and Prussia at Austria's expense in 1866 convinced Slovenes that the national principle was meant to prevail. By 1870 during the convulsions of the Franco-Prussian War, many became certain that the triumph of national forces outside the Empire was imminent and they seriously doubted that the Austrian state would survive the major European upheaval. Therefore from 1866 onward Slovenes pursued their national interests with an increasing sense of urgency. It was not a time for moderation or legal programs; drastic measures seemed to be in order.

Since 1848 the central concern of Slovene leaders had been to bring all Slovenes into one unit. In 1848 they expressed this in terms of ethnic rights, in the fifties they dared not voice any political opinions at all, while in the early sixties they attempted to give historic validity to their claims. Until 1866 the larger political framework of the Austrian Empire was assumed a constant factor in their planning. But thereafter, due to the developments discussed above, this was no longer the case. The Slovene liberals or *mladoslovenci* (Young Slovenes) publicly revived the Unified Slovenia program (1866), and they seriously began considering the likelihood of Austria's demise. Should the latter occur, they felt a Slovene national program must be founded on ethnic principles.[42] Indeed, whether Austria survived or not, the ethnic rights program would be most appropriate, given the desire to recoup losses of Slovenes to Italy and Hungary in 1866 and 1867. In the next five years, as Austria's overall situation grew more precarious, many Slovene conservatives came over to the ethnic national program as they had done in 1848. Indeed the Carniolan diet, where after 1867 Slovenes constituted a majority of the representatives, went on record in favor of working toward a Unified Slovenia.[43]

Singular accord was chieved in support of the Unified Slovenia program between August of 1868 and August of 1870 through the *tabors*. These *tabors*, or mass political rallies (held outdoors), took place in all Slovene lands. They reached a large audience in both towns and countryside and are considered the first real example of popular Slovene political activity. Some would regard these *tabors* as a kind of national plebecite in favor of a United Slovenia.[44]

While Slovene leaders rallied national support for their own unification program, they speculated on how they could best mobilize allies. Because they were weak numerically, Slovenes concluded that outside support was imperative. Emulating the Czechs, whose position in the Habsburg Empire was somewhat analogous to theirs, some looked to Russia for reassurances. A few traveled to Moscow to the Slavic ethnographic congress in 1868, others drank toasts and sang hymns to the Russian tsar,[45] and certain *mladoslovenci*—often those associated with the new liberal Slovene paper *Slovenski narod* (begun in 1868)—conjured up images of a benevolent Russia.[46] In a time of crisis, with the possibility of Austria's collapse becoming ever more probable, Slovene liberals were comforted by their reveries of a mighty Russia watching tenderly over her Slavic brethren. These were, however, reveries, and most were quickly sobered by the realities of tsarist autocracy.[47]

A Southern Slav alliance, on the other hand, seemed to make eminently good sense, particularly after 1868. Gestures toward Yugoslav cooperation had been made in 1848, and when faced again with a national crisis, Slovenes almost intuitively turned in this direction. Slovene appraisal of the situation was, moreover, highly realistic, given the fantasies they indulged in where Russia was concerned. The likeliest candidates with whom to make common cause were the Croats for many obvious reasons, but particularly because the Hungarian-Croat Compromise of 1868 had made Croats determined opponents of their association with Hungary. Yet many Slovenes had grave doubts about Croat political motives. True the Croats after 1868 seemed more eager for Slovene-Croat cooperation, yet Slovenes suspected this was due to their anti-Magyarism, rather than from any genuine urge for Southern Slav solidarity. Slovene liberals in particular were uncomfortable in the feeling that Croats were not really "Slavic" enough in their loyalties and that many Croats were even anti-Serb. Some Slovenes, therefore, opposed any common effort with them, while others were ready to attempt a joint Yugoslav program.[48]

This Yugoslav activity reached a peak in the second half of 1870. M. Mrazović of the Croat National Party, which had rejected the Hungarian-Croat Compromise of 1868, wrote a letter proposing a congress of Southern Slavs from the various provinces of Austria-Hungary—a congress which would be representative of four million people.[49] *Slovenski narod*'s editor, Anton Tomšič, who received the Croat invitation, traveled to Sisak in early

November 1870 for preliminary discussions.[50] No Serbs attended this meeting. Several other Slovenes were among the thirty who gathered at Sisak. The Slovenes agreed that their conationals should be granted a separate national administrative unit (as stipulated in the Unified Slovenia program), and they discussed the possibilities of joining with the Croat lands in a confederation, most probably within Hungary. No final provisions were made to this end at Sisak; rather another congress was scheduled for the following month, where related concerns could be debated in greater detail. This meeting was held in Ljubljana from the first to the third of December 1870 and resulted in a Yugoslav program.[51]

There is much that remains unclear about this Ljubljana conference which historians still debate with great spirit.[52] Even the preliminaries to the congress have raised historical disputes. The Sisak meeting, its origins, its conclusions, the selection of Ljubljana for a second meeting place, are veiled by lack of reliable evidence. What is certain is that the European crisis of a Franco-Prussian war had thrown the Southern Slavs of the Empire, already discontented and insecure, together. By autumn of 1870, French defeat was imminent, and it was generally believed that the victorious Prussians in creating a German Empire (accomplished soon thereafter on 18 January 1871) would incorporate Habsburg lands—or, certainly those lands formerly within the German Confederation. The Austro-Hungarian Empire was likely to collapse. That the Habsburg Slavs wished to prepare for such developments is certain; but they had difficulty settling on a common program in 1870. There are no published minutes from the Ljubljana congress. The content of debates, the positions taken by national groups and political factions, are difficult to determine with any precision.

About 100 Slovenes, Croats and Serbs—though the latter had not been at Sisak—participated in the congress. At its conclusion they presented a vague statement of South Slav solidarity, pledging as goals cultural, economic, and political cooperation. The vagueness of the document, many feel, attests to the wide variance of views represented, though perhaps it was imprecise because illegal aims had been frankly considered. The program was least explicit in its statement of political goals, though it had been agreed that Yugoslav political unity was universally desired.

At the congress the participants clearly had four political alternatives from which to choose. (None of these was specifically designated in the final statement of the conference). South Slav unity might be achieved (1) in Austria, (2) in Hungary, (3) in the Empire (autonomous with respect to Austria and Hungary), or (4) outside the Empire. If the latter had been agreed upon, it certainly could not have been publicized.[53] The Croat participants definitely leaned toward unification within Hungary; the Mrazović faction (Croat National Party) certainly had promoted this plan at Sisak. The Serbs present, headed by Miletić, probably preferred the fourth alternative, unification outside the Empire.[54] Slovenes on the other hand probably were divided. The liberals who had attended the Sisak meeting in November did not participate; the Sisak proposal for unity within Hungary did not appeal to them; they may even have been quite radical in their views.[55] The Slovene conservatives who did attend the congress probably understood the program as being in favor of union within Austria.[56]

What complicated matters at the congress (for the Slovenes in particular) were certain firm convictions among the Serb delegates regarding the outcome of general European developments. The Serb Miletic believed that Prussia would triumph in her war against France, that Austria thereafter would collapse, and that the South Slavs should salvage what they could from the imperial wreckage. This, however, in Miletić's view involved leaving the Slovenes stranded, though temporarily. He felt that the new German Empire would covet Slovene lands because of their access to the Adriatic. He was sure furthermore that if Habsburg Southern Slavs, or even Serbia, attempted to liberate Slovenes they would find themselves in a suicidal war with Germany. Consequently, Miletić urged that the Slovenes be abandoned until Russia could come to the rescue. Miletić, the Serbs, and other liberals believed in an ultimate confrontation between Germandom and Slavdom. The Slovenes, Miletić argued, would have to put off the fulfillment of their national aspirations until that time.[57]

The program of the December 1870 Ljubljana congress was ambiguous, its further definition awaiting the turn of general European events. The outcome of the Franco-Prussian war, though it resulted in the creation of a Prussian-centered German Empire, had no immediate harmful effects on Austria. Emperor Francis Joseph had feared it would and dismissed a liberal ministry which might have been favorably disposed to union with Germany. The Emperor's subjects, too, waited anxiously expecting Bismarck to turn his imperialistic designs southward. But what was feared did not take place. Bismarck soon guaranteed Austria's integrity and thereafter got on uncommonly well with the Habsburg foreign minister Andrassy. For the Slovenes there was less cause to worry that their lands would be incorporated into the new Empire to the north; there was less need after 1871 for the implementation of a Southern Slav political program. Moreover, the Croat National Party of Mrazović, with whom Slovenes might have collaborated as Yugoslavs, finally accepted the Hungarian-Croat Compromise of 1868, thereby ending its official opposition to the existing arrangement. As a consequence the Slovenes had little choice but to accommodate as best they could to dualism.

From 1871 to 1879 the Auersperg-Lasser government dominated the Cisleithian half of the empire. Its tendencies were German liberal, anti-clerical and centralistic; therefore, it pressured non-Germans to conform. Slovene liberals, who stayed with the Unified Slovenia program, experienced difficulty expressing their position; they were even forced to cease holding *tabors* (mass meetings) on behalf of unifying ethnic Slovene territory. At the same time the Slovene conservatives, who in 1870 had briefly made common cause with the liberals, reverted back to supporting a plan for historic federalism. In this they cooperated with the feudal and clerical elements in the Empire.[58] In the 1870's the conservatives (Old Slovenes) and the liberals (Young Slovenes) organized politically, assuming positions most appropriate for their respective political views. In 1873 for the first time each presented separate lists of candidates for elections. In general, however, Slovene political activity was very limited with both conservatives and liberals focusing on cultural pursuits. In this regard, the liberal or Young Slovene achievement was extraordinary; they alone were largely responsible for a great flowering of a modern Slovene literature.[59]

The Yugoslav sentiment, which had ebbed after 1871, experienced a resurgence in the mid-70's, really for the last time until after the turn of the century. The immediate occasion was news of the Russo-Turkish War (1876-78), which was in many ways a battle for Slavic national liberation. Slovene liberals, who idealized Russia, made much of the "Slavic" factor, and rather hoped that Serbia would acquire the Bosnian Ottoman territories. The conservatives preferred that Austria, though she had played no part in the war, should have them; they noted that in 1875 Francis Joseph, traveling in Dalmatia, had received appeals for protection from Bosnian Slavs whose Turkish province was then in a state of revolt. When in 1878 Austria assumed a protectorship over Bosnia and Herzegovina, many Slovenes were pleased. They subscribed to the contention that Austria had a civilizing, Christianizing mission in the Balkans, that Austria because of her advanced state of development could dispel the religious hatreds raging in Bosnia and bring enlightenment to the deprived Southern Slav peoples.[60] Slovene liberals were suspicious of Austria's intentions in overseeing the affairs of Bosnia, yet hoped Austria would not use her Slavs against Russia. In any case the new relationship between Bosnia and Austria did afford one advantage: more South Slavs in the Empire might strengthen the bargaining position for Yugoslav national programs.

With the Congress of Berlin and the occupation of Bosnia and Herzegovina came the end of German liberal rule in Austria. In 1879 a conservative coalition assumed power. It included clericals, crownland federalists, and Slavs. The coalition remained in power until 1893. The Old Slovenes or conservatives, who since 1871 had supported historic federalism, and who were becoming increasingly Catholic-oriented (they were often referred to as "Clericals" already), fitted nicely into this alliance. Slovene liberals, though far from compatible philsophically with the Taaffe coalition, chose to cooperate with it.[61] Indeed both conservatives and liberals belonged to the conservative Hohenwart Club during this period. For the Slovene liberals this move was a matter of choosing the lesser of evils. They had learned in the seventies that their greatest enemies were German liberals, who desired above all to centralize the Empire under German leadership and had no sympathy for non-German movements for national autonomy.

What the Slovenes achieved during this Taaffe era was minor, but even the liberals did not look for significant political advances. They cooperated with Taaffe and thereby painstakingly extracted from the government permission to use Slovene in schools and administration, where population figures warranted it. In the eighties and nineties Slovenes were regularly appointed as public officials and teachers, particularly in Carniola where Slovenes constituted more than 90% of the population. Elsewhere, in provinces such as Carinthia, where there were few Slovene schools or none at all, private ones were opened and supported by contributions from the national community.

In the end, however, Slovenes were not satisfied with such pittances. By the 1890's it was also clear that Germans were not willing to continue relinquishing administrative and educational positions to Slovenes.[62] Even Slovene conservatives found it more difficult to cooperate with German conservatives (Catholics, Christian Socialists), who were becoming more centralistic. Both Slovene conservatives and liberals found themselves growing uncomfortable in the Taaffe alliance. They wanted a revitalization of the national programs—Slovene and/or South Slav. This was sometimes difficult to achieve since there were many diehards in both parties who were content to continue "fortwürsteln" (muddling along).[63] But in the early nineties a break with this type of politics was accomplished by a new generation of Slovene leaders.

CHAPTER III
THE SLOVENE PEOPLE'S PARTY: THE TRIALISTIC SOLUTION

Slovene politics in the quarter century before the World War was strongly dominated by Slovene Catholic politicians. Collectively they are best known by their 1905 designation, the Slovene People's Party (*Slovenska ljudska stranka*).[1] Officially the party, organized as the Catholic Political Society (*Katoliško politično društvo*) in 1890, became the Catholic National Party (*Katoliška narodna stranka*) in the mid-nineties. In 1909 the name was further modified to All Slovene People's Party (*Vseslovenska ljudska stranka*).[2] In 1912, in order to express unity with the Croat Rightists, the party for a short time became a component of the Croat-Slovene Party of Right (*Hrvatska-slovenska stranka prava*).[3] Here, in the interests of clarity, the 1905 name, Slovene People's Party,[4] will be used; or, more simply, party members will be referred to as Clericals.[5]

The party emerged as a distinct political organization in the 1890's. The Clerical element had, like the Liberals, presented a separate list of candidates for the 1873 election,[6] but at that time differences between the two were virtually negated by Austrian politics. Then and for some time thereafter Austro-German liberalism was the primary enemy for both (for Slovene Clericals because these Germans were secular and liberal, for Slovene Liberals because Austro-German Liberals were "German" and centralistic.)[7] Therefore during the Taaffe regime (1879-93) Slovene leaders often worked together within the system, bargaining for minor ethnic and cultural privileges, cooperating with Taaffe to keep the German Liberals isolated.[8]

In the early nineties when Taaffe's coalition met with increasing difficulties, Slovene politics experienced a major transformation. The Catholic-oriented leadership achieved a certain political sophistication by the close of the Taaffe era. In a rapid, almost kaleidoscopic, fashion it sifted through several possible approaches, committing itself finally to a program which with minor modification would serve it well until 1914.

When these changes were taking place the head of the party was Karel Klun, a cleric of the old school. Klun, who had found congenial the atmosphere of Taaffe's "Iron Ring," lived beyond his time. He regretted the shuffling in personnel and the revising of ideology which had come to characterize the movement. By the time Klun died in Budapest in 1896 the Taaffe regime had fallen, "opportunistic" Slovene politics had been relegated to the past, and the Clericals had consciously worked out a modern national political program.

What prompted a new course was the growing realization that Slovene politics in the Taaffe era had led nowhere. *Rimski Katolik* (The Roman Catholic), a monthly which began publication in 1889 and lasted until 1896, took the initiative. Repeatedly it stressed that "Catholic" politics was a prime requisite for the well-being of both Slovenes and Austria, that without the definitive identifying factor of Catholicism neither could survive.[9] Therefore only professed Catholics, be they clerics or laymen, should represent Slovenes in provincial diets or in the Vienna Parliament. *Rimski Katolik* was so adamant on this point that it took to task *Slovenec*, the daily which claimed to speak for Slovene Catholics, and which carried the clerical party's motto, "All for religion, home, and Emperor."[10] The commitment of *Slovenec* and of the Clericals to Catholicism during the Taaffe reign was not sufficiently zealous, implied *Rimski Katolik*. It took even Karel Klun, then head of the *Katoliško politično društvo*, to task for displaying those opportunistic, compromising attitudes which allegedly had disgraced Slovene Catholic politics under Taaffe.[11]

Rimski Katolik deplored vagueness and vacillation among Catholic politicians as damaging to both Slovenism and Catholicism. For *Rimski Katolik* unquestioning commitment was primary; principles were to be expressed in journals and newspapers and then determinedly pursued. In this vein *Rimski Katolik* proposed that Slovene Clericals follow the example of Czech Catholics, who had recently broken with Old and Young Czechs alike on the grounds that these national parties had become indifferent, even hostile to true religious ideals. Emulating Czech Catholics, *Rimski Katolik* asserted, would profit Catholicism in general, and Austria and the Slovene nation in particular.[12]

The moving force behind *Rimski Katolik* was Anton Mahnič, a noted theology professor from Gorica. His purpose in publishing the journal was to establish a strong bond between Slovene Catholics and Rome, hence the title of *Rimski Katolik* (The Roman Catholic). This ultramontane sought in Rome a mighty force against liberalism, to him a hateful creed which since 1789 had been undermining religion everywhere. Mahnič maintained that to serve the Slovene nation best one had to preserve its religious and cultural heritage; a people deprived of its faith lost its real identity to say nothing of its prospects of eternal salvation.[13] Alone no nation, particularly a small Slovene one, could combat the liberalism which had already corrupted and made politically impotent the so-called "liberal Catholics."[14] A strong centralized church demanding unquestioned obedience to Pope and bishops was basic to the overall welfare of nations, more specifically to the Slovene nation.[15] Mahnič opposed any attempt to curtail or interfere with the Church's affairs in any way.[16] He saw liberalism, in collusion with free masonry, as precisely bent on just such a curtailment of the Church's influence; moreover, he contended, Liberals had been uncommonly successful in Austria, even during Taaffe's anti-liberal ministry.[17] They were so determined in their purpose, Mahnič asserted, that they misused the appeal of nationalism to assist in their destruction of the Papacy; if their first concern really had been the good of the nation, they would have seen to it that the people's religion thrived.[18] Mahnič felt that liberal nationalism was destructive, even sinful, setting one people against another, even Catholics against Catholics, in order to achieve its ends. Therefore, if it was a choice between nationalism and Catholicism, there was no question which was preferable.

Mahnič and *Rimski Katolik* during its eight years of publication had a major effect on Catholic politics, particularly on the younger generation. Constant pleas for an aggressive Catholic program, distinct from the coalitions and compromises which had characterized Slovene politics for a quarter century, were taken seriously. Largely due to Mahnič's untiring efforts, a Catholic congress of Slovenes from all Austrian provinces met in the summer of 1892.[19] The Catholic Party, formed in the early nineties, then gradually extricated itself from coalitions, developing first a separate organization (clearly separate by 1897) and then, as Mahnic had argued, a program of its own. The program itself, however, bore few of Mahnic's markings. The opposition to liberalism was there, as was the concept of Slovene culture as essentially a component of Western Christian (Catholic) civilization,[20] but the tone and stress were less extreme, much less like a call to arms than the exhortations of Mahnič.[21] More important, the ultramontane message—the crux of all Mahnič's writing—had been virtually ignored. Slovene Catholic leaders, because their commitment was first to Austria, or because they preferred to focus primarily on social and economic problems, were not especially attracted to the idea of subservience to Rome. By 1896 with the era of Klun and Taaffe come to an end, Mahnič, too, had lost his influence. He left his professorial post in Gorica and took over the bishopric of Krško. Other men were to define a Catholic program for the Slovenes.

In 1897 a new learned journal of Catholic persuasion, *Katoliški Obzornik* (Catholic Review),[22] appeared. It lasted until 1906, when it was succeeded by *Čas* (Time) which was published from 1907 to 1942. Aleš Ušeničnik, a philosopher, theologian, and professor, edited both, and together with the priest Janez Evangelist Krek, who contributed regularly to these reviews, led the way in Slovene Catholic thought in the years before

World War I. Catholic politics was in many ways a working out of the ideas developed in these journals. The pivotal figures in the party were Ivan Šušteršič, a lawyer, and again, Krek. The former was more a politician than an ideologue (though the Catholic ideology suited his purpose); while Krek was an idealist, a Catholic theologian, a well-loved and charismatic figure. With Ušeničnik and Krek shaping Slovene Catholic thought (the two were also active among Catholic youth groups), and Šušteršič and Krek directing Slovene national politics, a Slovene program that was nationalist, but strict in its Catholic orientation, emerged. Both the Catholicism and the nationalism also merged easily with the Austrian idea.

From approximately 1896 to 1913, when open disagreement developed within the Slovene People's Party over Austria's Balkan policies, the Clericals presented a remarkably united front. Moreover, the leadership of the Church had little difficulty approving Clerical programs and politics. Clerical ideologues defended the cause of the Church and of Austria in Catholic journals. Clerical politicians upheld the Church's claims in Vienna. In turn the clergy gave open support to Catholic politicians. This cooperation was best seen in the mutual confidence expressed at Slovene Catholic congresses (1892,1900,1906,1913), where Šušteršič and other political spokesmen gave major addresses and churchmen voiced their loyalties to Austria and to the Slovene nation.[23] Therefore, bearing in mind that varying points of view did exist and that the potential for disagreement was present, it can be said that the Clericals and the clergy acted as a united body in Slovene politics.

The greatest individualist in the party—one who fought determinedly for innovation—was Dr. Janez Evangelist Krek. He came into conflict in the early nineties with Klun, who balked at Krek's Christain Socialism, vowing to resist it as strongly as Mahnič had resisted liberalism. Krek's work later among Slovene workers and peasants in Carniola accounted for much of the overwhelming popularity of the Slovene People's Party. A great asset to the movement, he could not be eased out of it. After Klun's death (1896), when Šušteršič and Krek came to share the leadership of the party, Krek proceeded to work for the social and economic reforms he had urged at the 1892 Catholic Congress. In 1894 he founded a Slovene workers' association (*Slovenska katoliška delavska društva*),[24] and thereafter worked untiringly to alleviate the lot of Slovene workers in the towns. Other members of the party were inclined rather to be more concerned with extending economic assistance to, and founding cooperatives among, the rural population. Krek also organized a Christian Socialist society among Slovene workers (1897). He was especially active in the building of cooperative workers' housing. He gave particular attention to the tobacco workers, whom he had helped organize.[25] Meanwhile Šušteršič, though he sometimes claimed credit for the successes of the cooperative associations, founded and sustained by Krek,[26] occupied himself more exclusively with politics. Krek was left to his interests, Šušteršič to his. Krek worked largely in Carniola, while Šušteršič spent most of his time in Vienna.[27] Even if their respective views differed significantly after the turn of the century, and they probably did not, the two men rarely came face to face long enough to discover serious incompatibilities. Paradoxically, Krek, the clergyman, was the less clerical of the two, associating closely with laymen within the party.[28] Šušteršič, the lawyer, was more representative of traditional conservative interests.[29] What most got Krek into difficulty was his notion of creating among Slovenes an inter-confessional party that would welcome anyone willing to fight German influences.[30] This was regarded by his more cautious associates and by church officials as strangely unorthodox behavior.

No one in the party was so strongly inclined toward Christian Socialism as Krek; it was an orientation acquired in his university years in Vienna (1888-92) after study of the social impact of industrialism.[31] Krek developed a special concern for the town laborers of his constituency, though he felt that peasant society was also very troubled. He was imaginative in his social thought, making perhaps the most original contributions to Slovene social and economic theory in the pre-1914 period. His economic thought is intimately related to his attitudes toward Christianity and toward nationalism.[32]

In 1901 Krek published *Socializem*.[33] Clearly, Krek found socialism eminently compatible with Christian principles.[34] To Krek harmony in society was essential and attainable, but liberal capitalism with its acquisitiveness and its corruption of the concept of individualism, had destroyed all balance and well-being.[35] For Krek liberalism was a product of sixteenth century rationalism and had led to the secularization of society and to the misconception that power was derived from the people.[36] Basically, he saw two kinds of socialism. The first was fundamentally materialistic and communistic and a foe of established Christianity. The second was that of Pope Leo XIII, whose *Rerum novarum* of 1891 acted as a strong buttress to Christian Socialist doctrine. Simply, what divided the first form of socialism from the second was the latter's basic acknowledgement of the absoluteness of divine power. For Krek, God was all powerful; God determined the nature of man and society, and God invested men (monarchs and/or groups of men) with temporal power.[37]

In Krek's mind, God intended man to live in society with class divisions based on differing rights and responsibilities and in the state which was God-ordained and without which no man could achieve his ends.[38] In this society the traditional family unit was absolutely essential for the freedom and natural development of individuals, but it was threatened by liberalism.[39] Civil marriage, secular education—bringing women into factories when they should be performing their maternal duties—all were indicative of the fact that society was in a state of dreadful disorder.[40] Krek did not feel that one could reverse economic and social change brought about largely by industrial development; one could not return to the past. But Krek was certain that the ways of liberalism were also doomed and that socialism was the blueprint for the future.[41] Democracy, too, Krek felt was appropriate,[42] for those imbued with the spirit of God would vote correctly. God and Christianity pervaded all human relationships.

Mahnič has been credited with compelling Catholic politicians to assume a clear and defensible political position in the 1890's; but to Krek must go credit for the popularity and imaginativeness of Clerical politics thereafter. For Krek, though he may have differed with Mahnič ideologically, did agree that success required a firm commitment. For him this involved a primary concern with the economic developments of the age, how these might affect Slovenes, and finally how Clericals might resolve existing inequities. All of this in Krek's mind became inextricably tied to nationalism (brought to the foreground by external developments and internal pressures); and again, by and large, it was Krek who formulated the national program for his party.

For Krek the nation was an extension of the family unit within which the essential God-given dignity of each human being was nurtured;[43] that is, the nation was composed of that society of worker and peasant families for whose well-being Krek showed his deepest concern.[44] He feared for their spiritual health and for their economic security, concluding that pursuit of a common cause (also the national cause) was the only solution. In defining what benefited the Slovene nation, Krek came to oppose the influence of both Russia and Germany, the first because of its Orthodoxy (a heresy), the second because of its Protestantism (likewise a heresy, but also linked with the development of liberal rationalism and capitalism) and for its imperialistic designs on Trieste and the Slovene sea coast.[45] At the same time Krek concluded that the well-being of Slovenes rested upon the continued strength of a Catholic Austria and the further broadening of the national "family" to include all Catholic Southern Slavs who lived in the Habsburg Empire.

With respect to Russia and Eastern Orthodoxy, Krek's attitudes were developed when he was quite young and are to be distinguished from his feeling for the Russian people, which was distinctly warm and fraternal. Indeed, Krek throughout his life, but particularly in his late teens and twenties, was a romantic and a bit of a Pan-Slav. He demonstrated this in his gymnasium and university years by avidly learning all Slavic languages,[46] and by promoting close association of Slavic theological students, among whom he furthered the study of Slavic tongues and culture at the Augustinian seminary in Vienna.[47] Slavic culture, for Krek, however, was a component of Western Christian (Catholic) development. Rome had been chiefly responsible for the high level of Slavic culture; moreover, it also had permitted the freest individual national expression. In other words, Krek believed, Western Christianity was conducive to the national autonomy and natural cultural development of its component parts.

Krek and other Clericals took pains to discredit Orthodoxy, particularly Russian Orthodoxy, because Slovene Liberals had raised the issue by idealizing "Mother Russia" and implying that Slovenes should rely on Russia for national salvation. *Čas* frequently stated the anti-Orthodox position which Krek espoused. Its central contention was that the Eastern Church, after its break with the West, had fallen into a state of cultural deprivation.[48] The culprit was Byzantinism, characterized by the absolutism which had pervaded Greek Orthodox culture and had given it an essentially despotic base.[49] As such it was transported to the Balkan and Eastern Slavs, producing a religious expression fundamentally alien to and unworthy of the Slavic peoples, for it was shallow and based merely on external ritual.[50] The Russian church and the Russian imperial regime had forced this inferior culture upon those Slavs who had become Orthodox. Krek and *Čas* were particularly horrified by Russian treatment of the Catholic Poles.[51] For the Clericals the clear solution was to extend the benefits of Western Catholicism with its superior culture and high degree of civilization to the deprived Orthodox. This was only proper and natural where Slavs were concerned: had not the Slavic apostles Cyril and Methodius originally received sanction from Rome?[52] Fear of the spread of Eastern Orthodoxy mounted among Slovene Clericals in the first decade of the twentieth century when Russian imperialists seemed to focus their attention on the Balkans, thereby threatening Austrian interests there and endangering the spiritual future of South Slavic brethren.

Krek's opposition to Germany, bastion of Protestantism, was more complicated. Protestantism, especially German Protestantism, was, of course, intolerable to Slovene Catholics; but it need not have presented Slovene clerics with any serious political concerns, since its adherents in Cisleithian Austria were few.[53] What caused the Catholics real anxiety was the Protestantism of Bismarck's Empire and of German liberalism generally and the appeal this might have for Austrian German liberals.[54] More to the point, Bismarck and German liberals in both Empires had revealed themselves enemies of Catholicism.[55] Bismarck had waged a *kulturkampf* against German Catholics, and Slovene Clericals sensed it might be transmitted easily across the frontier through Pan-German propaganda. Would not German Liberals in Austria themselves independently engage in such cultural expression were it sufficiently in their power to do so? In fact, Krek believed the Austro-Germans, encouraged by Bismarck's example were tallying alarming successes in their "los von Rom" movement; liberals among Czechs, Poles, Croats, and Slovenes were even joining their ranks.[56] Austrian enemies of Catholicism were increasing their numbers, and could count on sympathizers in the German Empire and in Transleithian Austria, that is, Hungary.

For Krek, Germany also symbolized that offshoot of liberalism, capitalism, with its greed, its perversion of individualism, its mockery of human dignity.[57] The centralized secular state (which German liberals, including those in Austria, advocated) had become a political goal of capitalism, and capitalism in turn employed it to further economic gain, reducing individuals to mere cogs in a brutal system. Men, moreover, could no longer act cooperatively or feel secure; the state had abolished the autonomy of societal units; it had assumed complete power over every individual. Traditional institutions, such as the Church, were logical targets for capitalist liberal nationalists who wished to build centralized states.[58] Slovene Clericals believed what had happened to Germany could happen to Austria; if the Austrian liberals did not effect it on their own, the "Prussians" would eventually impose it. German capitalists, the Clericals felt, would sooner or later conclude that Austria's Adriatic coast with its lengthy sea front—though populated largely by Southern Slavs—was indispensable to the continued development of Germany's economy. At the same time many Slovenes were laying national claim to the valuable port of Trieste, the Austrian Empire's leading coastal city, though the Italians had impressive national claims to it as well.[59] Nevertheless Krek feared German liberal capitalists would soon incorporate Trieste and other Slovene territory into the German Empire.[60]

To counter these German and Russian threats Slovene Clericals developed a pro-Austrian Southern Slav national program. This approach was based on the contention that national rights, not "liberal" national ones, but rather rights of the people—the real nation, the majority—must be championed. Clericals who had found that the spirit of the age required a nationalist point of reference, concluded that they had been nationalists all along. For to be occupied with total well-being of a people, particularly with its spiritual good, was to be in the most meaningful sense a defender of the nation; in other words, Slovene Clericals came to regard themselves as more nationalist than the "nationalists" (Liberals). To assure national well-being in the future, Clericals maintained traditional ties to Catholicism and Austria must be strengthened. For these in the past had been vital in shaping the nation and were inseparable from the concept of Slovene nationality. National security, greatness in the future, would have therefore to be pursued within the limits of these traditonal strengths.

The key for Krek and the Clericals was Austria. Austria was Catholic and had, moreover, been traditionally the defender of Catholicism on the borders of Western civilization. Her rulers had led in fighting Reformation heresies and more important in stopping the Ottoman infidel. It was in battling the Turks, Clericals wrote, that the Austrian idea really evolved. Austria's purpose, her mission, became vitally linked to that of Western Christendom; Austria's "raison d'être" as a great state had become: "The defense of European (i.e. Western) Christianity against Ottoman coercion."[61] Or, as one Clerical put it in 1904: "*The Austrian state idea from the beginning was that she protect European nations from the Turkish threat.*"[62] Austria's defense of Christianity in South Eastern Europe gave that collection of disparate states under Habsburg domination a common purpose; in fighting the Turk, the Austrian peoples, including the Slovenes,[63] were bound together and united in the Austrian mission.[64]

Unfortunately, Austria had not been acting recently as if she were sufficiently aware of her mission. The struggle for dominance in Germany had distracted her, Clericals felt; and for them the very conception of Austria as essentially a German power was destructive of Austria's strength, for it not only compromised her with German Liberals, but it had precipitated a dualistic ruling arrangement with the Magyars. All this ran counter to Austria's tradition, of unity of peoples in defense of Christianity in the Balkans.

Therefore the Clericals urged Austria to resume her mission to the Southeast. She could begin by driving out the remaining Turks.[65] Once liberation had been achieved Austria could extend the benefits of her advanced civilization to the South. Clericals, for example, frequently expressed concern for the welfare of Bosnians whose future they felt could be safe only within such a highly civilized and religiously enlightened state as Austria. They greeted the occupation and later annexation of Bosnia and Herzegovina as a positive step toward the fulfillment of Austria's destiny.[66] Similarly, Clericals were encouraged by the Montenegrin declaration of war in the Balkans in 1912; and, they urged Vienna's support or even leadership of this struggle to liberate the Christian provinces of European Turkey.[67]

Liberating Balkan Christians from Turkish rule would not end Austria's mission, for the Slovene Catholics believed it required her to bring the true Christian faith to these peoples. Because the Balkan people most immediately concerned were Slavic—specifically South Slavic—the Slovenes and other South Slavs in the Empire could be of special service. The Empire's Slavs could act as intermediaries with the Balkan Slavs; that is,

Austro-Slav Catholics could exert their influence on the Orthodox Southern Slavs to reunite with Rome. For Slovene Clericals this was clearly the natural orientation of Balkan Slavs; the Byzantines, then the Turks, had deprived them of the true faith.[68] In pursuit of these ends Austria must not permit her "German" reveries to distract her, she must not shirk her responsibilities in the Balkans, for this would be tantamount to surrender to Russian interests in the South and thereby to Orthodoxy.

Slovene Clericals began to gravitate toward this position in the 1890's. By the mid-nineties, evaluating their strength in terms of numerical force, they concluded that allies were needed. By 1897 they had largely agreed that the best advised association was with Croats of the Empire.[69] These were Austrian and Catholic historically, contiguous to Slovene areas geographically, Southern Slavic in origin—therefore of kindred spirit. In addition, Croats were very unsatisfied with their lot, for the Magyars of Hungary had not been at all sympathetic to their rights, much less their demands.[70]

In their desire to make common national cause with the Croats, Slovene Catholics juggled their own claims vis-à-vis Austria to accommodate to the program of Croat state rights. This trend was evident by 1898;[71] by 1912 Slovene Clericals even effected a tenuous merger with the Croat Party of Right.[72] Essentially, the position of the Croat Rightists was that the Croat states—Croatia, Slavonia, Dalmatia—had a legal right to exist separate from Austria or Hungary, unified in a distinct kingdom which would be autonomous within the broader Imperial structure.[73] Practically what the Rightists were proposing was that a third unit, consisting of the Empire's Croat peoples—and those Serbs who resided in the Croat lands—be given autonomy and equal status with Austria and Hungary within the Empire. Slovene Clericals in the late nineties concluded that their own views were largely compatible with those of the Croat Party of Right and that the Croat state rights position was flexible enough to include Slovenes as well. Moreover, there had been some legal precedent for such cooperation.[74]

What the Slovene Clericals and the Croat Rightists had in mind here was what has been loosely referred to as trialism. Generally, trialism might be defined as a program for union of the South Slavic territories of Austira-Hungary, for the purpose of creating a third large administrative unit in that Empire. Thereafter attempts at further description of trialism break down. The respective positions of Croats, Slovenes, and those Serbs involved have not been adequately examined to present a definitive analysis. It is clear that within each national group, aside from stated party resolutions, views differed from person to person and changed with time. More important, the position of the Archduke Francis Ferdinand in regard to trialism was always deliberately vague.

The unit was to be historic and include South Slavic lands. But which lands and which peoples should this involve? Certain Serbs of the Empire wished to be included. Slovenes were not opposed to this, nor were the Krek people in 1912 against according Serbs religious (Orthodox) equality. But, a wing of the Croat Rightists (Frankists) opposed this on principle and subsequently broke with the main branch of the party. Slovenes wanted to have their lands included, so did some Croats of Dalmatia and certain Croats and Serbs of Bosnia and Herzegovina. The Hungarian Croats, however, were disinclined to commit themselves to any trialistic program which required the inclusion of Slovenes or any non-Transleithian South Slavs; the Croats believed that the Archduke's trialism was founded chiefly on his desire to diminish Magyar strength, which could be achieved simply by removing South Slavs, largely Croats, from the Hungarian or Transleithian part of the Empire. There was no reason to believe that Francis Ferdinand would wish thereafter to further the cause of South Slav nationalism by joining Transleithian Yugoslavs with Cisleithian ones or even including Bosnians in the plan.[75] Such a move would tend to fortify the Southern Slav power and could pose problems for the Habsburg Empire similar to those involving the Magyars. Croat Rightists, suspecting they had a better chance for autonomy if they left their demands vague, hesitated in commiting themselves to a program involving non-Transleithian Southern Slavs.

But what of Slovene trialism? Pleterski, writing most recently on the subject, prefers to call it the "Croat-Slovene program" or the program for "Yugoslav unity," terms most frequently used by its adherents, and which more accurately expressed their point of view, intrinsically Yugoslav and nationalistic. It is distinguished from the Archduke's plan, which was dynastically and clerically oriented and designed primarily to fortify the Habsburg power. The very term "trialism" was employed by Francis Ferdinand and more precisely described his own orientation.[76] One thing that is quite certain, however, is the fact that Slovene Clericals before World War I had not perceived any serious discrepancies between their trialism and that of the Archduke. When Korošec, a prominent clerical, tried to approach the Archduke on the subject, all he learned—and that from a secondary source—was that Francis Ferdinand had said, "I have great plans for the Yugoslavs."[77] Such a statement was ambiguous, yet welcomed and reassuring, so Slovene Clericals sustained great faith in the Archduke. They refused to waver from the conviction that Francis Ferdinand thought of Slovenes, too, when he thought of trialism. This confidence was the key ingredient in Clerical Yugoslavism, and it was maintained with virtually no modification until the outbreak of the war.[78]

By the turn of the century Slovene Clerical leadership had developed the philosophical basis of a national program which would serve the party adequately until 1914, when the Archduke's assassination shattered their illusion of trialism. Founded on the belief that the Slovene national mission had evolved as part of the Austrian Catholic one—one historically oriented toward the Balkans—Slovene Clericals proposed to resolve contemporary problems by revitalizing and reemphasizing that mission. Members were divided as to approach, though not irrevocably so before the war; the Krek people, generally Christian Socialists, preoccupied with economic concerns and social problems, were most democratic, while the Šušteršič faction approached trialism from the more traditional, conservative, dynastic position. What was best for Slovenes, they agreed, was Austrian Catholic commitment to a positive Southern Slav policy. This involved treating the Southern Slavs, especially within Hungary, with consideration. This, in order to make the Austrian Empire attractive to South Slavs generally. Before the Archduke's death his approach to trialism and the popular one of some Slovene Clericals were not clearly incompatible.[79]

Whenever official Austrian interest in the Balkans increased, Slovenes were encouraged that Austria was responsive to their wishes and their counsels. They were elated, convinced in 1908, when Bosnia-Herzegovina was annexed, that Austria was expressing a sense of its true destiny in the Balkans. (See below, Chapter VI) All Slovene Clerical activities in these early years were based upon the strong belief that Austria and the Church were "in their camp."[80]

CHAPTER IV

THE NATIONAL PROGRESSIVE PARTY:
SLOVENE LIBERAL NATIONALISM

In the last decade of the 19th century the Slovene Liberals,[1] like the Clericals, had come to constitute a separate political party. Since 1873 they had been offering their own lists of candidates for election to provincial diets and to the Vienna Parliament. Essentially, however, if one examined programs and tactics, Liberals—particularly the "elastics" or "opportunists"[2]—were virtually indistinguishable from Slovene Clericals. Until 1890 it was deemed in the interest of the nation that both elements cooperate in Vienna with the Taaffe administration though the rewards were minor.[3] By 1890, however, involvement in coalition politics was no longer attractive to Slovene Liberals. Many German clerics and crownland federalists, who had once been willing to make common cause with Taaffe and the Slavs, were becoming, like the German liberals, increasingly nationalistic and centralistic.[4] Slovene Clericals had organized a party of their own and its ultramontanist wing was about to launch an energetic campaign against all liberalism, irrespective of national origin. In addition, Taaffe himself was experiencing difficulties holding together his disparate group. The Young Czechs, for whom Slovene Liberals had an affinity, were blazing a trail away from coalition tactics. They had won impressively in the 1889 provincial elections (and also in the 1890 Reichsrat election). Slovene Liberals attributed the success of the Young Czechs to their obstructionist practices.[5] Therefore Slovene Liberals, who had been loosely joined in the *Slovensko društvo* (Slovene Society), responded to such political developments by founding their own party, the *Narodna napredna stranka* (National Progressive Party), in 1891.

Liberal politics of the 1890's are a very complicated matter. For in spite of the fact that a party had been organized, a unified program and policy were still lacking. Residual enmities between Liberal "opportunists" and radicals (the more anti-German, nationalistic element) accounted for some of the confusion. There had already been disagreement over cooperating with Vienna in the 1880's and renegade Liberals had sporadically challenged the mandates of those with official backing.[6] After Clericals and Liberals formally went their separate ways in 1890, a good many Liberals felt so anxious about the split that in time they crossed over to the Clerical camp. One "opportunist" Liberal who found a comfortable niche in the Slovene People's Party, while also forwarding his own political career, was Fran Šuklje. As a Clerical he sat in the Carniolan provincial diet from 1906 to 1911, was appointed its head (*deželni glavar*) in 1908, and also sat in the Vienna Parliament from 1903 to 1910.[7] Real party solidarity emerged only gradually, becoming evident during the 1890's in connection with elections for provincial diets (in Carniola 1895, in Styria 1896, in Gorica 1899).[8] The key factor in the growth of Liberal unity was Clerical opposition—particularly in Carniola, where ultramontanist Mahnič had really stirred up a good deal of anti-Liberal, anti-capitalist, anti-secular sentiment. In the face of such attacks Slovene Liberals had no choice but to unite and defend themselves. Liberal relations with individual Clericals improved somewhat after 1896 when Mahnič assumed his bishopric in Krško and ceased publishing *Rimski Katolik*. But Clericals and Liberals never again worked as closely as they had in the Taaffe period.[9]

Whereas Clerical political strength was founded on support from the Slovene countryside, the Liberal political base was the middle class. In the quarter century before 1914 Liberals, who represented Slovenes in provincial diets or in the Imperial Parliament, usually came from towns, having been chosen by either the town or general electoral curias. They were especially strong in the Carniola diet until 1910 and they dominated the Ljubljana town government. Furthermore the post of Ljubljana mayor was monopolized by the two leading Liberals of the period: Ivan Hribar from 1896 to 1910, Ivan Tavčar from 1911 to 1921.[10]

These Liberal mayors set about the task of creating a modern capital for the Slovene middle classes. Hribar maintains in his memoirs that the central purpose of his fourteen year tenure as mayor was to expand and beautify the town.[11] The town's physical appearance was in fact altered appreciably with housing and electrification, a public bath house, a gasworks, an electric railroad, a bridge over the Ljubljanica (built for the 50th anniversary of Francis Joseph's reign), and a number of public monuments to Slovene national and cultural forefathers.[12] Both Tavčar, a lawyer, and Hribar, a banker, were concerned that the Slovene townspeople prosper financially. They promoted tourism and improvements in transportation (especialy the railroad), and they helped promote Slovene business, extending contacts with other Slavic peoples both within and outside the Empire. They also did much to develop Slovene banking institutions. Hribar was among the founders, and president from 1900 to 1916, of the Ljubljana Credit Bank (*Ljubljanska kreditna banka*). It operated in affiliation with the Prague-based *Živnostenka banka* (three Czechs were on the Ljubljana Bank's twelve-member directory) and it had its own branches, including one in Split.[13]

All of this served to create the foundation for a Slovene middle class capitalism. And this was precisely the Liberal intention. Liberals believed that only a thriving commercial class could command respect and make realistic political and national demands in a modern world. Therefore Liberals on principle opposed socialism and Clerical cooperatives.[14] They strongly resisted attempts to extend the franchise to the masses, lest Liberal efforts and middle class power be overturned by the Clericals who had overwhelming support among the numerous peasantry.[15]

This Liberal concern for the development of a Slovene middle class was in keeping with the tradition of Prešeren and Čop, who in the second quarter of the 19th century had sought to avert the Germanization of Slovene townspeople by cultivating a modern Slovene literary language. Though Hribar and Tavčar worked most vigorously to strengthen that middle class economically and politically, both were profoundly concerned, as had been Prešeren, with the spiritual and cultural well-being of the Slovene individual. More immediately, the Liberals of the 1890's were heirs to the Young Slovene movement of the sixties, seventies, and eighties, sharing with it a world view that was essentially rational, secular and freethinking (*svobodomiselno*). Much like the Young Slovenes, who produced the classics of modern Slovene literature, Hribar and Tavčar sought to nurture the ideal of a rational, creative man, one who expressed his freedom through literary efforts. Both were active journalists and also belles-lettrists of sorts; Tavčar's prose works filled six volumes and have gone through several editions. Hribar wrote for and Tavčar edited the daily paper *Slovenski narod* (1868-1945)[16] which became the voice of the National Progressive Party, and they co-founded the weekly journal *Slovan* (1884-1887) in which the prose pieces, though often political, were still in the Young Slovene tradition.

Slovene Liberals admired and drew upon Western European intellectual tradition. Ivan Hribar in his memoirs states that as a student he avidly read and absorbed the thoughts, among others, of Rousseau and Kant.[17] Yet at times Hribar seems to boast too much of being liberated from the chains of irrationalism. His boasting account of cool-headedness in the face of natural disaster illustrates this point. During Easter Week of 1895 Ljubljana experienced a serious earth quake. All in the Hribar household, awakened by the first tremors, were frightened and could think only of fleeing the house immediately—all but Hribar. The future mayor calmly and with deliberation gathered together his thoughts and his warmest clothing— remembering that science had proven second tremors, should they occur, were never as severe as the first, and that spring nights in Ljubljana were cool, damp, and unhealthy. Later in a town square in which much of the Ljubljana populace had assembled, Hribar passed, he writes, from family to family urging each to return home for warm clothing, assuring everyone that the worst of the quaking was over. His trust in the authority of reason permitted him to sleep at home undisturbed the next day, though irrational impulses troubled many others for some time to come. He did move his bed near to an exit on the first level of the house, but only, he maintains, to calm the hysteria of the ladies terrified that another quake would occur.[18] It seems, however, that Hribar protesteth too much—like one to whom the rational approach came not quite naturally. Hribar's coolheadedness in that spring of 1895, however, did afford him important political advantages. For subsequent to the earthquake, which had damaged many buildings, Hribar promoted town renewal projects and proposed tax exemptions for those repairing damaged structures. He attempted also to secure Imperial funds for this purpose and, when these were refused, arranged for a Viennese firm to set up a lottery for the benefit of earthquake-stricken Ljubljana. These concerns seem to have impressed the townspeople, for in the following year they elected Hribar mayor.[19]

What perhaps best describes the Slovene Liberal outlook are the terms found in the party name, "national" and "progressive," terms derived from Enlightenment rationalism, Romantic nationalism, and French Revolutionary jargon.[20] In Liberal minds the fortunes of progress and the nation were dependent on the exercise of free thought so dear to Young Slovenes. As Hribar put it, free thought was basic to the growth of knowledge, without which progress—either general or national—was impossible.[21] In promoting progress and the national good Liberals put a heavy premium on secular national education. They demanded that Slovene children receive quality instruction in their own language—a goal largely achieved in Carniola. Outside that province Slovene minorities were being pressed into German language schools; therefore the Liberal Cyril-Methodius Society, established in 1886, funded private schooling in the national language. Liberals also favored the founding of a Slovene University to counter Germanizing pressures on Slovene university matriculants and to afford them equal opportunity with Germans for teaching posts.[22] They fought opponents vigorously, largely in Liberal journals as was the tradition, but unfortunately their arguments were almost wholly negative.

To be anti-German was only natural. German Liberals after 1848 but particularly during the Auersperg ministry in the 1870's became unrelenting propagators of German culture. In a world where men had become conscious of what the nation could contribute to mankind, Austro-Germans offered to the underprivileged the advantages of German civilization. Some Slovenes accepted the offering, or even became ardent converts.[23] Most Slovene Liberals, however, viewed Germanizing as a violation of natural freedom, most explicitly of free expression. For them man progressed and was free only when communicating in the language of his forebears, for it expressed the purest substance of a man's being. Hence in the second half of the 19th century Austrian domestic politics often centered on debates over language use. Slovene Liberals contributed their share to these debates, urging not only the establishment of Slovene schools and theater, but also the use of Slovene in government administration. During his mayorship, as Hribar proudly points out, the official "inner language" of the town administration which had been German became Slovene, and was used among governmental employees themselves for oral and written communications. The "outer language" was also Slovene, but in the Empire it was customary that the language used to communicate with the public be the language of the people.[24] Hribar was not successful, however, in introducing Slovene street signs in Ljubljana, though a substantial majority of the population was of Slovene nationality.[25] Slovene street markers were erected in 1908—most spontaneously—only after the shooting of two young Slovenes by German soldiers had aroused the populace.[26]

Liberal anti-Clericalism was a more complex matter for it involved combat with fellow Slovenes, most of whom also professed to serve the nation. Elsewhere in Europe, liberalism regarded the Church as a reactionary institution and had been traditionally anti-clerical. But among Slovenes until the late eighties Liberals had gotten on well with Slovene Clericals. Moreover, after 1890 certain clerics were still highly regarded by Liberals. The poet priests, Aškerc and Gregorčič,[27] and the Croat Bishop Strossmayer, who had refused to comply with the 1870 Papal Proclamation of Infallibility, were not considered enemies, for they resisted rigid, Vienna-oriented conservative clericalism and the ultramontanism of Mahnič.[28] Moreover, when Jeglič[29] who had worked in Sarajevo under Archbishop Stadler, a friend of Strossmayer, was named the new Archbishop of Ljubljana—replacing the deceased Missia, a patron of Mahnič—Hribar traveled to Dubrovnik to greet him even before Jeglič assumed his post. Hribar's purpose, he states, was to save Jeglič from Šušteršič clericalism, and indeed Jeglič began his tenure with an apparently tolerant attitude toward Liberals. He even attended performances in the "Narodni dom" (National home), a Liberal gathering place—until, according to Hribar, the risque dress of a singer offended his sensibilities.[30]

That "liberal" clerics were acceptable to Slovene Liberals is clear. Yet inordinate cleric-baiting ("farška gonja") did go on in the Liberal paper *Slovenski narod*. The resulting personal feuds often lasted for decades.[31] *Slovenski narod* also indulged in sometimes crude mockery of parish clergy, typically laced with innuendo about the priest and his housekeeper. *Narod*'s editor, Tavčar, instituted these practices, partly in response to the determined challenge of the ultramontane Mahnič, yet continued them well beyond the Mahnič era.[32] The threat of growing Clerical political strength made Liberals fear for their own political prospects. So overwhelming was this anxiety, that Liberal anti-Clericalism even tempered the Liberals' anti-Germanism in Carniola, where leaders of the National Progressive Party chose to work with the German large landowner element against the Slovene People's Party. Needless to say, neither the agreement with Germans—for practical purposes effective for twelve years (1896-1908)—nor the cleric-baiting of *Slovenski narod* increased the popularity of Liberals. Ultimately it diminished rather than strengthened the Liberal position.[33]

In the 1890's, much like their counterparts in 1848, Slovene Liberals counseled Austria to resist a "German" orientation. The National Progressive Party urged a Palacky-like transformation of the Austrian Empire into a federation of equal national units. (A Unified Slovenia would, of course, constitute the basic administrative unit for the Slovenes). Such a reform would fortify Austria, giving strength in union to her numerically small nations, and would serve to stave off the aggressive impulses of giant powers such as Russia, but especially Germany.[34] Slovene Liberals, however, became frightened, increasingly so after the turn of the century, that Austria was becoming more thoroughly tied to Germany than ever. Most ominous was the fact that Austria in the 1890's became Germany's closest ally. Liberals believed such a partnership could only bode ill for the small developing nations of East Central Europe.

Slovene Liberals, allied in Carniola with German landowners until 1908, indulged only rarely in open criticism of Germans or of the German-Austrian alliance. But when in September of 1908 two Slovene student demonstrators were shot in Ljubljana by German soldiers, Hribar helped lead a mass anti-German national protest.[35] The coalition of Slovene Liberals with local German landowners was not renewed and Francis Joseph declined to confirm Hribar's reelection in 1910.[36] The Ljubljana shooting supported suspicions that Vienna was assuming a more aggressive, decidedly pro-German stance. This was seemingly confirmed several weeks later when Austria annexed the Balkan Slavic provinces of Bosnia and Herzegovina without consulting the peoples affected or preparing states with interests in the area, notably Serbia and Russia. Some Liberals concluded that official Austria had become anti-Slavic: her troops were shooting Slovenes in the Empire and her diplomats were seizing Balkan Slavic territories, which, for ethnic reasons, more appropriately belonged to Serbia.

For Slovene Liberals the Triple Alliance constituted a German conspiracy against Slavdom.[37] So did Austria's attempt to deny Serbia access to the sea in 1912-1913 by promoting the creation of an independent Albania.[38] Even Tsar Ferdinand of Bulgaria was dubbed a tool of German imperialism, when, complying with Austrian wishes, he turned against the Serbs in 1913. But then what could one expect from a former "German" prince? Pan-Germanism had become the outstanding enemy; its forces had to be routed if the Slovene nation were to survive. "We Slovenes," claimed *Slovenski narod* in 1912, "have a universal historical role to fulfill, to prevent Germandom from reaching the Adriatic and the Balkans."[40]

This was brave language for spokesmen of a nation numbering about one million, particularly for Liberals, whose constituency—the Slovene middle class—was so limited. But if Slovene Liberals were in many ways naive, in their bold anti-Germanism they at least recognized a way to win allies. For the most part, they sought this broader support in greater Slav solidarity, a course that proved neither realistic nor particularly fruitful.

Slovene Liberal Slavism was Russophile. The intellectual foundations for this had been established by Prešeren in the 1830's and 1840's. In their search for national identity, Slovene Panslavs had always taken pride in being members of a greater Slavic family, and they were fond of evoking Prešeren's words: "more children hear the Slavic tongue than any other."[41] Within that family, it was clear the Russians were most advanced, the Russian language achieving exceptional heights of creative expression which less developed Slavic brethren might hope to emulate. In following the Russian example, in taking courage from Russian literary accomplishment, and in acknowledging a kinship with all Slavs, the small Slavic peoples could insure their freedom from bonds of German culture.

This was essentially the rationale behind Slovene Liberal Pan-Slavism. Young Slovenes and later Slovene Liberals idealized Russia; as students they gathered in Russian "circles" and urged new students to learn the mother tongue (Russian).[42] Such Slovenes wrote about Russians and other Slavs in *Ljubljanski Zvon* (The Ljubljana Bell, 1870-1941) and in *Slovan* (1884-1887), the journal founded by Tavčar and Hribar; and they traveled widely in Slavic areas. Trips to Russia were particularly popular toward the end of the 19th century.[43] Most returned from Russia lyrical about the land's beauty, the warmth of the language, the nobility of the people.

What Slovene Liberals had in mind politically with regard to Slavic solidarity was never explicitly stated. It seems that they envisioned a federation of Slavic states, where the common official language would be Russian, but in which the equality and dignity of each nation would be affirmed in order that the progress of each, and therefore all, would be assured. In pursuing this end Liberals found Czechs most sympathetic;

other Slavs in the Austrian Empire were not as accessible either because they were isolated by Magyar administrators or because they had little "liberal" inclination. In any case, Slovenes and Czechs of a Panslav bent maintained close relations, exchanging cultural delegations, attending Slavic journalistic congresses, and developing strong ties between respective Sokol gymnastic groups.[44] The problem with Panslavism was that its adherents found it difficult to reconcile their "Liberal" principles with the realities of tsarist Russian politics. Many Slovene Liberals returned from Russia disillusioned with the pervasiveness of the autocracy. Moreover, they had found European middle class liberalism virtually non-existent in that Empire.[45] The implications for a Russian-dominated Great Slav federation were obvious; the Liberal Panslav experienced real anxieties as a result.

Panslavism, under the designation Neoslavism, nevertheless underwent a revival in 1908.[46] Encouraged by constitutional changes in Russia and by an improvement in Russian-Polish relations, Panslavs hastened to resurrect plans for a Slavic federation in East Central and Southeastern Europe. Austrian Slavs were particularly anxious to encourage better relations between official Austria and Russia as a means toward forwarding the greater Slav cause and weakening Austria's ties with Germany; they viewed not only Russia but Austria as a "Slav" state. Hribar, with the Czech Karl Kramař, promoted an All Slav Congress for 1908,[47] and the two led an Austrian delegation to a preliminary May meeting in St. Petersburg which was addressed by Piotr Stolypin, the Russian Prime Minister.[48] At the Prague congress in July 1908 all went even better than expected, for the Russians and Poles in attendance got on uncommonly well. Within a few months the euphoria was abruptly dispelled by Austro-Russian conflict in the Balkans over the Bosnian annexation. The Panslav meeting in Sofia (1910) failed to rekindle the optimism of Prague; the proposed Belgrade congress did not meet; and by 1912 and 1913 Balkan Slavic states were at each other's throats in a war over Ottoman spoils.

Slovene Liberals, however, continued to hope for better Austro-Russian relations. On the very eve of World War I the Liberal paper was still calling for an Austro-Slav federated state and for Austro-Russian friendship.[49] Officially, the Liberal party deftly skirted treasonable suggestions; it remained in principle committed to Austria. But within the party some engaged in serious flirtations with Russia. Hribar, still bitter about his loss of the Ljubljana mayoral post, resumed his activities as a banker, traveling widely particularly in Slavic lands, and it would seem that some Slovene Liberals had commercial as well as spiritual cause for courting their Slavic brethren. In 1909 Hribar journeyed to St. Petersburg, to Prague, to Serbia and to Bulgaria, investigating a number of trade possibilities.[50] Throughout much of the winter and early spring of 1913-14 he was on the road again pursuing the viability of a joint "Slavic" banking venture. Several times in those months his business led him to the audience chambers of Izvolsky (then Russian Ambassador to Paris) and Sazonov (then Foreign Minister). In his memoirs Hribar reveals a Russophilism remarkably blind to the particulars of tsarist autocracy and one verging on the treasonable where Austria was concerned. To Sazonov, in explaining the advantages of commercial exchange with Slovenes, Hribar stressed Slovene ethnic possession of the northern Adriatic, specifically the Trieste area, suggesting that such a Southern Slav port could serve as a strong Adriatic foothold ("krepka oporišče") for the Russian navy![51] During those last visits to Russia in 1914 Hribar remained a remarkable romantic; he breathed more freely, more deeply, as his train crossed from Germany into the tsarist Empire; hearing the spoken Russian word was like listening " . . . to the singing of angels."[52]

Within this Panslavism, liberal Yugoslavism based on an alliance with Croats, immediate neighbors of the Slovenes and themselves South Slavs, would seem to have been logical. But until about 1904 or 1905 Croat leadership was predominantly clerical or conservative, and not at all philosophically compatible with Slovene liberalism.[53] Consequently, well into the first decade of the 20th century the latter continued to cling to a vague Panslavism, maintaining friendships with Czechs, and idealizing Russia.

Strong ties between some Slovene Liberals and individual Croats nevertheless existed in the late 19th century. Most noted were the associations established with men like the historian Franjo Rački (1828-1894) and the churchman Strossmayer (1815-1905). Both were men of a liberal hue;[54] both, though they were clerics, deplored clericalism and the widespread ultramontanism of the age; both were also Panslavs, meaning most importantly that for them Serbs, in spite of their Orthodoxy, were brothers and equals. Indeed, Strossmayer led ecumenical efforts, though in vain, to reunite Eastern and Western churches in order that Slavic brethren would no longer be divided by details of doctrine. The liberalism, the anti-Papal stance, the reverence with these two Croats had for the cultural development of Southern Slavs in general,[55] made them most appealing to Slovene Liberals, Hribar reports. Hribar first met Bishop Strossmayer when he traveled in 1884 to Djakovo, seat of the episcopal diocese, to sell the bishop insurance.[56] He was immediately taken by Strossmayer's imposing figure and by his prediction that "the star of the Slavs was rising."[57] Hribar found he shared with Strossmayer many beliefs and preferences. He welcomed his advice on political and cultural matters, and the two corresponded regularly thereafter.

But about the time Slovene Liberals had established an organization of their own, pursuing distinct party politics, Strossmayer was old and frail (he died in 1905 at the age of 90). The bishop's advisor Rački died in 1894. For Slovene Liberals with inclinations toward an "Austrian" Yugoslav policy, there really were no "liberal" Croats of stature with whom to work.[58] The Great Croat state rights politics of Starčević and his attacks on Serb Orthodoxy, which Slovene Liberals preferred to Catholicism, were regarded by Slovene Liberals as "operetta politics."[59] It was not until a decade after Rački's death that Slovene Liberals again found Croat politicians whose basic views were compatible with their own.

In October of 1905 two declarations, one signed in Rijeka (Fiume), the other at Zadar (Zara), by Croats and Serbs respectively, signaled the advent of a new politics. The resolutions were in large measure opportunistic and intended to express support for Magyar Opposition parties in an immediate Hungarian struggle with Vienna, but in these resolutions, principles relevant to the Yugoslav issue were enunciated. Serbs and Croats were declared one nation by blood and language, cultural-religious differences were minimized, and in general liberal and egalitarian views were stressed. That same winter a Croato-Serb political Coalition was organized to stand on those principles.[60] Slovene Liberals were therefore greatly encouraged, hoping that Croat-Serb differences could be resolved, that thereafter South Slavs of the Empire could together effect a "liberal" Yugoslav program. But the new Coalition ignored Slovenes. Croato-Serb liberals had little intention of risking what they had gained; and working with Slovenes would have involved the Coalition in futile combat with both Italians and Germans over Trieste. Nevertheless, when members of that Coalition in 1909 were falsely accused of treason and put on trial as a kind of sequel to the Bosnian annexation crisis, Slovene Liberals staunchly defended the accused and Masaryk who came to their defense.

This new trend in Croat-Serb politics after 1905 was encouraging to Slovene Liberals despite its insularity, and, together with other developments, caused them to look increasingly toward some form of Southern Slav alignment, both within and outside the Empire. They particularly looked toward Serbia, for the 1903 royal assassination had brought to the throne Peter Karageorgević, who had passed his time in exile translating John Stuart Mill. Hribar received the coveted Order of St. Sava II from Peter in 1906 and describes that ruler as "democratic in spirit." Hribar maintains that after 1903 he himself was convinced that the future of Slovenes would be somehow tied to that of little Serbia.[61] With the emergence of "liberal" Croats and Serbs in the Empire, with a "democratic" king reigning in Serbia, with Slavic Bosnia and Herzegovina "liberated" from the Turks after 1908.[62] and with Slavs of the Balkans about to drive the Turks out of Europe altogether—what else could be in the offing but unity, liberty and a promising future for the South Slavs?

Slovene Liberals were bound to be disappointed. They put too great a store in the appeal of Slavic brotherhood. For among Croats Great Croatism continued to take precedence over cooperation with Orthodox Serbs. Moreover, during the First Balkan War, when Slovene Liberals fully expected the foundations of democratic federalism to emerge from the common struggle,[63] Bulgars and Serbs clashed violently over claims to Macedonia. Slovene Liberals attributed this to "German" manipulation of Bulgaria's Tsar Ferdinand—himself a former "German" prince.[64]

By the eve of the war Slovene liberalism and its Yugoslavism could muster little support. Its Slovene adherents had been whittled away by Germanizing pressures outside Carniola and in that province by its own social conservatism and anti-clericalism. Perhaps because they had little faith in the future appeal of liberalism among Slovenes, Liberals espoused more tenaciously those attitudes which had brought them some measure of support in the past; their anti-clericalism became ever-stronger, their anti-Germanism more uncompromising. Liberals also promoted the cause of Yugoslav unity, but within the Empire. South Slavs with whom they had philosophical affinity—those of the Croato-Serb Coalition—continued to show little interest in Slovenes. As a result the Liberals, after alienating the masses at home and being snubbed by the Empire's Serbs and Croats, had to look elsewhere for a solution. Their predicament led them to flirt again with Panslavism (Neoslavism), winking at the omnipresence of Russian autocracy. After 1908, however, few Slavs could or would rise above their particular national interests in order to further the ephemeral Greater Slavic cause. In the end all the Slovene Liberals could do was choose a conservative course. Officially, the National Progressive Party threw its weight behind Austria, ultimately criticizing all alternatives suggested.[65] Hribar, independently, chose to court Serbia and Serbia's patron Russia; but he did this so clumsily that he ended up in an Austrian prison soon after the war began.[66] It would seem that Slovene Liberalism suffered from serious weaknesses, rendering it incapable of accommodating to new circumstances and new needs. In the end it seemed out of necessity less dependent on the aspirations of South Slavs as brothers than on the benevolence of Austria and on wishful thinking about the creative intentions of autocratic Russia.

CHAPTER V

THE YUGOSLAV SOCIAL DEMOCRATIC PARTY:
THE SOCIALIST NATIONAL POLICY

The Yugoslav Social Democratic Party (*Jugoslovanska socialnodemo-kratična stranka*, hereafter JSDS) was the last of the three pre-World War I Slovene parties to organize. It came into formal existence only in 1896, though Socialists had established a following among Slovenes as far back as 1869.[1] Its rank and file and its leadership were workers who had organized into syndicates or unions according to trade and had grown steadily in numbers.[2] They were most heavily concentrated in the mining districts of Idria, Southern Styria (the Trbovlje-Hrastnik-Zagorje coal area), Southern Carinthia, Trieste and Ljubljana. In the latter towns they were printers or tailors, cobblers, bakers, or railroad workers, and in Trieste many were employed by the Austrian Lloyd shipping company.[3] By the 1880's their concern seemed less with the overthrow of the capitalist system than with extracting greater benefits from their employers—improved working conditions and higher wages. By the 1890's they struck regularly for an eight hour working day. They also began demanding the vote.[4]

Little is known about the movement's specific aims and activities in the 1870's and early eighties, though socialist leanings seem to have been encouraged by contact with workers from outside the alpine provinces—particularly with Germans and Italians. Migrant laborers, skilled and unskilled, were crisscrossing the Empire in search of jobs. From Vienna, Lower Austria, and sometimes from Czech industrial centers, itinerants brought word of labor trade unions and Socialist activity; Slovenes worked intermittently in Westphalian mines. Socialist newspapers, though censored, kept many Slovene workers conversant with developments within European Socialism generally. Some elements were distinctly anarchistic. Fran Železnikar, one of its early adherents, a veteran of the Paris Commune, was prone to advocate terrorism as well as the pursuit of the class struggle.[5] By the late 1880's the movement had mellowed, partly as the result of material gains, partly because of repressive police action against its extremists in 1884.[6]

With the founding of the Austrian Social Democratic Party (Sozial-demokratische Partei Oesterreiches-SPÖ) in 1888-89 Slovene organizers had the option of working within that larger organization. Karl Kordelič, a cobbler, who later co-edited the Slovene Socialist paper *Delavec* (1893-

1898), attended that Hainfeld meeting where the Austrian party outlined its initial program.[7] One other Slovene participated as an observer. But in spite of the fact that Victor Adler, the Austrian-German Socialist leader, demonstrated his personal good faith by sending these two home from Hainfeld with funds to begin a Slovene language publication,[8] contact with the Austrian party organization was poorly maintained. Though Slovene Socialists subscribed in general to Hainfeld principles, their activities were dictated by their more immediate concerns; they sent Slovene spokesmen only irregularly to Austrian Social Democratic meetings.[9]

The Yugoslav Social Democratic Party, much like the Austrian Party, emerged out of a struggle extending over several decades among trade unionists, syndicalists and anarchists and the respective clashes of these groups with the police.[10] It emerged, too, at a time when in Europe Socialism itself had achieved some measure of respectability,[11] even the Vatican having tempered its position, though it did not accept Marxist materialism. The emergence of a Slovene party organization also coincided with an infusion into the movement of a new kind of leadership. Workers such as Karl Linhart (1882-1918), one time secretary of a Trbovlje miners' organization who had five years education at a Ljubljana real school (*realka*), and Albin Prepeluh (1881-1937), a school mate of Linhart and a government clerk, still filled upper echelon positions. But men who were intellectuals, not proletarians, were being attracted to the movement and they quickly came to man the editorships of the various Slovene Socialist papers and journals.[12] After 1896 Slovene Socialists needed to apologize no longer, as they had in 1889, that their paper's editor did not "have enough schooling" adequately to sustain a regular publication.[13]

In 1896 when the Yugoslav Social Democratic Party was organized Etbin Kristan (1867-1953) assumed leadership. He was an intellectual and a writer (he translated Ibsen into Slovene). He had pursued a formal gymnasium education in Ljubljana—the Clerical party's Krek being one of his school colleagues there—then in Zagreb. He founded in 1898 *Delavec-Rdeči prapor*, which became the leading Socialist newspaper and he edited and wrote regularly for the Austrian party's paper, *Arbeiter Zeitung*. After the founding of the Yugoslav Social Democratic Party, party policy was delineated chiefly by intellectuals like Kristan,[14] whom the workers, according to the Trieste Socialist, Rudolf Golouh, were very proud of having in the party, precisely because he was an intellectual.[15]

Several factors accounted for the gravitation of intellectuals to a party which for two decades had been exclusively one of workers. The National Progressive Party to which they might have normally been drawn had become intellectually barren. It seemed smugly content with its local political successes and was apparently unconcerned with pressing societal needs. Association with the Slovene People's Party was, of course, repugnant because of that party's clericalism. The intellectuals looked instead to their academic mentors for guidance. Many young Slovene intellectuals in the late 1890's had studied in Prague and were students of the popular philosophy professor, Thomas Masaryk. They came away from Charles University spiritually imbued with Masaryk's positive approach to national and social problems. The "Masarykites" (*Masarykovci*)—Dragotin Lončar (1876-1954), Anton Kristan (1881-1930), and Anton Dermota (1876-1914), to name the best known—resolved to attack social problems through intellectual dialogue. In 1902 they founded *Naši zapiski*, a "social" review, in which they debated contemporary issues.[16] One by one that generation of Masarykites felt obligated to take a political stance. They joined the best vehicle at hand, the Yugoslav Social Democratic Party. Ultimately, *Naši zapiski* became a "Socialist" journal (1913) and many Masarykites also began writing for *Rdeči prapor-Zarja*, though they were not won over to a strictly materialist position, and therefore provided the party with a broader intellectual base.

The influx of Slovene Masarykites into the party was prompted in part by fundamental changes in European Socialism, particularly in Austrian Social Democracy. Though the leadership of that party, and of the Slovene party as well, was still strongly orthodox in its Marxism, maintaining that the workers would triumph only when the bourgeoisie and the capitalist system had been overthrown, its methods had changed noticeably. It eschewed appeals to violence to work for immediate ameliorative reforms. Moreover, though the leaders remained as firmly opposed to Socialist "cooperation" with bourgeois governments (i.e. accepting governmental ministries), they sought office at all levels of government as representatives of the working class. Ebtin Kristan, founder of the Slovene party,, sometimes referred to as the "Slovene Bebel,"[17] was an orthodox Marxist who became a regular Socialist candidate for office.[18] Preoccupation with everyday concerns and electoral campaigns made any resort to the barricades less meaningful, indeed extremely remote. When in 1907 universal manhood suffrage was introduced in Cisleithania these Socialists concluded, not unlike Bebel and other German Marxists, that it was not unlikely that in time the masses would simply vote the capitalist system out of power.[19] With that, though it did not concede the point, orthodox Marxism put a virtually unbridgeable gap between itself and resort to sudden and violent overthrow of the existing order.

Moderate tactics appealed to Slovene Masarykites. But even more attractive than this "reformist" approach was the revisionism of Eduard Bernstein. At first summarily dismissed by Marxists, it made rapid inroads in all European Socialist parties in the last decade of the 19th century. In some instances the erosion of orthodoxy was so marked that revisionists came to dominate the party. Such was the case with the J SDS after Masaryk-ites joined the organization, according to Dušan Kermavner, historian of Slovene Socialism.[20]

Like their mentor, the Czech philosophy professor, Slovene Masarykites were encouraged by Bernstein's reinterpretation. They respected Marx's insights, but they felt Bernstein's analysis of society as "evolving" toward social democracy was more convincing than Marx's contention that vio-lent revolution would impose a new order. Their observations told them that even in a bourgeois capitalist state, the political power of the working class was increasing and that operating within the system could forward the proletarian cause.[21] As intellectuals they were especially drawn to Bernstein's modification of Marxist economic determinism. Historical causality, Bernstein had maintained, was a complex matter; economic factors could not be singled out as the sole determinant of historical dev-elopment. That latter point convinced even the most reluctant Masaryk-ites—who shunned philosophical materialism—that they could function within a Socialist party.[22] They could not stomach Slovene Liberalism. Now revisionism had built them a bridge to Socialism.[23]

When the JSDS organized in 1896 it took most of its cues from the Austrian party, for Etbin Kristan its organizer had learned his Socialism in Vienna and was spiritually tied to the Vienna organization. Slovene Soc-ialists therefore accepted that party's Hainfeld program as its own, and soon after, when an Austrian (Cisleithian) party federated by nationality was proposed, Kristan led his delegation to the first *Gesamtpartei* gather-ing in Brno (1899). Slovenes remained members of this larger organization throughout the pre-war era, even after many Czechs had seceded from it.[24] This was partly because Kristan remained loyal to the Vienna-based party and partly because the Slovene organization was financially depend-ent upon that larger unit.[25] The Czechs, on the other hand, could in a pinch supply their own funds.

Though Slovene Socialists used Hainfeld principles as a starting point,[26] they were not bound to these by any hard and fast lines. They were a small group, founded upon a limited proletarian base, yet they engaged in the same doctrinal squabbles that rent larger and more powerful parties. They debated the issues of orthodoxy and revisionism, of political action and cooperative organization. Etbin Kristan was the agitator and worked for revolution, Anton Kristan (no relation to Etbin) was an organizer, a revisionist, promoting the betterment of worker welfare through trade union, banking and cooperative organizations. Etbin founded *Delavec-Rdeči prapor* (1898), Anton published *Naprej* in the Idria mining district after 1903. After his challenge to Etbin's leadership, abortive attempts were made to shut Anton out of the party; he had too formidable a support.

After 1903, according to Henrik Tuma who joined the party five years later, there were two branches to Slovene Socialism,[27] though some contend that differences between the two Kristans were resolved at a party council in 1905.[28]

Most Masarykites—even when they joined the party after the turn of the century—remained somewhat aloof from these debates. The dialogue seemed to them to stress crudely only the economic or political status of the worker, while Masarykites were concerned with his moral regeneration: they proposed to act as educators of the masses. They functioned briefly on the periphery of Slovene Social Democracy in this capacity. Their approach was reminiscent of the Russian *narodniks* who also "went to the people." Both were naively optimistic and similarly ineffectual in their endeavors.[29]

In some ways the most practical suggestions for Slovene Socialism came from two party members who were "mavericks." One, Albin Prepeluh (1881-1937), a clerk from a poor Ljubljana working family, who wrote under the pseudonym Abditus, cofounded the Masarykite journal *Nasi zapiski* and defended revisionism against Etbin Kristan. The other, Henrik Tuma (1858—1936), son of a Czech cobbler and a generation older than most Masarykites, was schooled in the Young Slovene tradition. He pursued a legal career in the Gorica-Trieste area, ran for office as a Liberal, but was ever-attracted to new intellectual movements. (He also, according to his memoirs, thoroughly displeased the old Emperor Francis Joseph, when the latter in 1900 attended a celebration commemorating four hundred years of Habsburg rule in Gorica; Tuma, knowing that Francis Joseph was a fast eater, resolved not to put down his utensils as was customary, when the honored guest completed his meal. Tuma remembers with great satisfaction the look of reprimand the Emperor gave him on this occasion.)[30] In the period 1903-08 Tuma sampled Masarykite and Socialist thought.[31] He ultimately joined the JSDS, but neither he nor Prepeluh, whose impact on the party pre-dated Tuma's by a few years, fit neatly into any of its factional categories. Both valued the Masarykite confidence in the moral dignity of man, but concluded that that dignity required economic independence or at least a measure of material security. What troubled them most was that most Social Democrats were insufficiently peasant in their outlook, Slovenes belonging, after all, to a backward society.

Both Tuma and Prepeluh addressed themselves to this reality. For Tuma it was inconceivable that an alleged proletarian party eliminate from its purview the "agrarian" proletariat; he urged the party to amend its outlook, but to little avail.[32] Independently he worked to bring socialism to peasants in Gorica. Prepeluh was more adamant than Tuma that the agricultural laborer should not be excluded from Socialist party considerations. He even debated the issue with Karl Kautsky.[33]

Prepeluh's thoughts are not always easy to follow; his argument at times seems to travel in circles. Essentially, what he concluded was that Slovene peasants were proletarians, too, and that Slovene Social Democrats must develop a program for them. Prepeluh had reached this position by noting the rapid growth of clerical socialism under the inspiration of Krek. This phenomenon, for Prepeluh, betrayed an underlying class conflict; the peasant was obviously being exploited economically, else why would he organize. In a similar way socialism had grown among town workers who were being oppressed by industrial capitalists. This train of thought then carried Prepeluh to nationalism. For if one observed carefully one could see that Slovenes were either peasants or workers, while their exploiters were non-Slovene. The whole nation was composed of proletarians, gravitating toward socialistic organizations; their individual efforts had in fact become a national effort. In other words nationalism, for Prepeluh, was synonymous with the Slovene class struggle against the non-Slovene oppressor.[34]

Prepeluh found it difficult to convert party colleagues to this view. Moreover, his proposals for implementing a "native" Slovene Socialism, particularly among the agricultural proletariat by supporting existing peasant cooperatives, led him to offer defenses of Christianity, embarrassing to many in the party. For Prepeluh Christianity was "native" and fundamental to the peasants' cooperative instinct. The Party leaders did not accept this argument, though at least one Masarykite defended Prepeluh's right to his opinion.[35] Most Social Democrats simply concluded that Prepeluh had become in effect a Christian Socialist and that he might be happier if he joined the Slovene People's Party. But no real pressure was put on him either to alter his views or change his political affiliation.[36] The JSDS was not monolithic; it was not well-disciplined; instead it was in many ways a forum for those who could not or would not conform to traditional liberal or conservative party allegiances. Its views on the nationality question illuminate the diversity of its thinking.

As part of the Austrian party, the JSDS initially resolved to keep its sights fixed on the attainment of Socialist internationalism. Slovene Socialists maintained that they felt decidedly uneasy whenever they took up "bourgeois" national questions; after all these were not proper concerns for an international proletarian organization. But in the quarter century before the war the Slovene Socialists had no more success than other European Socialists in remaining aloof from such issues. Already in the 1870's and eighties German and Slovene Socialists found themselves engaged in unbecoming debates over which language worker singing societies should use in their performances.[37] Thereafter, if Slovene Socialists did not become nationalistic, the movement at least reflected increasing concern for national questions. Socialists, of course, properly rationalized their preoccupation with the nationality question within a Marxist philosophical framework.

Some of the concern with nationalism came as the legacy of associating with the Austrian party. At Hainfeld the national question was touched on only indirectly. The program stated that its central goals were to be pursued irrespective of national affiliation, race, or sex, and that, as an internationalist party, Austrian Social Democracy regarded national rights in the same way it looked upon natural ones, that is, to be defended against all forms of exploitation.[38] The congress avoided committing itself more specifically. But soon the very multinational character of the party (though between 1889 and 1899 it was run centralistically and dominated by Germans) forced it into recognition of national differences. With relation to the Empire itself, Social Democrats assumed a remarkably conservative stance.

At the Brno Congress in 1899 the Austrian Social Democratic Party was converted into a federated unit, constituted from the national Social Democratic units in Cisleithia; thereafter these would share a common program and a common executive organization. This diminished somewhat the organization's internationalism, though temporarily it did ease minority fears, particularly among the Czechs, about a strong German centralistic tendency in the party. Nevertheless Victor Adler, head of the Austrian German Socialists, was fond of referring to the Austrian party as the "Little International," suggesting—perhaps not unlike certain Russian Socialists who believed that because of the existence of peasant communes, Russia could skip the "capitalist" stage of history—that Austria might avert national conflict because of its multinational (or international) character. In the end Adler was clearly proven wrong. Not only was the Empire destroyed by nationality conflicts, but the Austrian Social Democratic Party itself already at Brno took to discussing the national question with greater involvement than before. Conscience-stricken delegates were moved to insist that national sentiment was after all "bourgeois," and not becoming to true internationalists, but such arguments carried little force.[39]

The most astonishing decision made by the party at Brno was that it favored preserving the Austrian Empire. This conclusion was reached by delegates taking different routes, but the final justification was always the same—it would benefit the Empire's proletariat. This was after all Socialism's aim. The party did not, of course, approve of the existing governmental apparatus; dualism was especialy abhorrent. It proposed instead to work for the restructuring of the old Empire along the lines of democratic federalism. And then another surprise: by the time the resolutions had been made, debated, and amended, and the votes taken, the Socialists at Brno had committed themselves to work for a federalism based on "national" units. Again the essential argument was that such a plan best served the interests of the proletariat, for middle class capitalist nationalism was needed to spark proletarian class consciousness. In other words, the nationality problem had to be solved first; social progress would follow inevitably later.[40]

Slovene Social Democrats attended the Brno meeting and participated in its decisions. Slovenes led by Etbin Kristan, however, offered an alternative to the final program; it was one which Otto Bauer and especially Karl Renner developed further in post-Brno years. At Brno Kristan proposed that the Austrian Social Democratic Party work toward a two-level federalization of the Empire. One would be purely administrative, the other national and relating to cultural matters. The latter involved the so-called "principle of personality," which has since been widely associated with Renner, though Hans Mommsen recently traced and attributed it to Kristan.[41] Though perhaps not sufficiently defined, that principle aspired to protect the national cultural rights of each individual no matter where in the Empire he lived, while leaving other matters to the administrative units of the territorial federation. Such a solution, which was widely supported by Austrian Social Democrats and especially Slovene Socialists after Brno, though never officially adopted by the party, seemed more in keeping with Socialist internationalism. It acknowledged cultural national rights, but rejected political nationalism as "bourgeois."

In keeping with the spirit of Brno, Slovene Social Democrats remained Austro-Marxist, to the point that on the very eve of the war they even seriously considered issuing a statement expressing deep sympathy on the death of the Archduke at Sarajevo.[42] One exception to this Austro-Marxism was the noted writer Ivan Cankar, who ran as a Socialist candidate in 1907, but by 1913 was making treasonable speeches for which he was quickly interned.[43] As with other Slovene parties, the program and ideology of the Social Democrats—though by no means unanimous on specifics—assumed a Yugoslav orientation. The party itself strong in the nationally mixed Trieste—Littoral area had organizational ties with Socialists in Istria and Dalmatia. According to Etbin Kristan who spent formative years in Zagreb, it also hoped to associate with Croats in Transleithania. In fact, though it remained essentially Slovene, the party had included the term "Yugoslav" in its title precisely in order to attract Transleithian Croats.[44] To this end Slovene Socialists also agitated regularly for an end to dualism in order to facilitate closer cooperation of all the Empire's South Slavs.

In assuming this Yugoslav orientation the party also began to look beyond the frontiers of the Austrian Empire. Behind it was the notion that Austria's fate lay in the Balkans. But in no instance did the party venture disloyalty to the Empire. When in 1907-1908 some non-Socialists began referring to Serbia as a Yugoslav Piedmont, Albin Prepeluh, as a Socialist, quickly scoffed at the suggestion. The Yugoslav (and therefore the Slovene) question, he wrote, could only be resolved within Austria. Serbia was economically unstable and politically weak; its army was only large enough for a small parade.[45] Austria, on the other hand, had the stability Serbia lacked, and it was certainly more advanced socially and economically by any Marxist criteria one might apply. Socialism, in other words, had greater potential for development in Austria than in Serbia.

A most interesting Slovene variation on this Yugoslav Austro-Marxism was produced by Henrik Tuma in *The Yugoslav Idea and the Slovenes* (*Jugoslovanska ideja in Slovenci*), in 1907.[46] Tuma who joined the party one year later, moving gradually thereafter from a revisionist to a revolutionary Marxist position, was struck in examining the national question by what he considered inescapable geographic and economic realities. He concluded that the territories inhabited by South Slavs had unique economic potential. They were destined to be the chief outlet for Middle European industry and commerce. German industrial goods would be transported via Austria through Trieste to the Adriatic, or via Budapest and Belgrade to Salonika, or by way of Sofia to Constantinople. Italians, Tuma pointed out, had already perceived this potential and were preparing to extend their influence into Albanian areas by training engineers in Trieste and establishing commercial and trade schools there.[47] For Tuma it was quite clear that Slovenes were assured a bright future; Trieste was the Empire's major northern port and it, or at least its hinterland, was Slovene.[48] Tuma urged that Slovenes cultivate Trieste as their own; he advocated, for example, the founding of a Slovene-Italian university in that city in order that a Slovene cultural as well as economic claim might be established.[49] This was intended, however, as a detail of what Tuma foresaw as an Austrian mission. He believed the Austrian Empire constituted a natural geographic-economic unit which had, in comparison with Southeastern Europe, achieved impressive social and economic advances. To destroy this unit would be historically regressive; what was required was its expansion. Economic and geographic factors pointed logically Southeastward where it was Austria's obligation to civilize and to bring economic progress. Ultimately, the whole Balkans, Tuma foresaw, would be joined to Austria in federation. In preparation for such a time Tuma counseled Serbs and Bulgars to keep their eyes on Salonika and

Constantinople, whose ports would be vital to the future Austro-Balkan unit.[50] In sum, Tuma was urging Austria to unify Southern Slavs, including Bulgarians, by expanding southward. For Tuma, South Slavs belonged together, not for nationalistic reasons, but for economic ones; for those same reasons their association with Austria had to be maintained.[51]

In all this Tuma did not lose sight of Socialist goals. He merely concluded that commercial and industrial progress would introduce those conditions necessary for Socialism's development. And a Danubian-Sudeten-Adriatic economic unit would create the optimum situation for such advances.[52] That the South Slavs would also be united nationally was incidental to the plan.

Tuma's influence on the JSDS was second only to that of the two Kristans. His notion of a "Mitteleuropa"[53] Austro-Balkan federation, which would transform much of Central and Southeastern Europe into a formidable economic unit, though not officially subscribed to by the party, was nonetheless important. It reserved for Austria a central role but it also provided for dynamic expansion to the South, and as such it could appeal to Slovene Austro-Marxists. That Bosnia and Herzegovina were annexed to the Habsburg Empire shortly after Tuma introduced his widely-read thesis, made his thoughts all the more pertinent. In any event by 1909 Austro-Marxist Yugoslavism, until then intellectually confined to the boundaries of the old Empire, began to venture its thoughts beyond those frontiers. Tuma himself had advised in 1906 that "loyalty to Austria should not intimidate one from thinking beyond the boundaries of that Empire;" expansion need not compromise allegiances to Austria.[54] He was, of course, wrong. Given the direction assumed by European politics in the ensuing decade, it became ever clearer that Austria and Serbia could not co-exist in the same federation. Slovenes, even Socialists, who permitted their thoughts to wander beyond the boundaries of the Empire—no matter how loyal to Austria—ultimately would have to choose between Austria and Serbia.

The JSDS had made its official commitment to a Yugoslav position when it first organized in 1896 by including the term "Yugoslav" in its title. In 1909 that "Yugoslav" orientation which had been until then Austro-Marxist, took on a new emphasis. In November of that year, Slovene Socialists met in conference at the Tivoli Hotel in Ljubljana, in response to the Bosnian annexation, so that they as Slovenes and Socialists could assess its relevance to themselves and to the Empire.[55] They concluded—Tuma was one who helped draft the Tivoli resolutions—that, because of the annexation, the future of Austria had come to focus (as Tuma had recently speculated) on the fortunes of the Southern Slavs. The annexation had made it clear that it was here that Austria's destiny lay. The conference therefore called for electoral reform in Transleithania in order to bring democratic institutions to the Croats, an autonomous diet for Bosnia-Herzegovina, and immediate federalization for the Empire.[56] Having implemented such reforms for her own South Slavs, Austria presumably could proceed with her natural historical mission to the South. Tuma's preferences are clearly reflected in these opening conference resolutions.

At that same conference Etbin Kristan sought more cautiously to confine Slovene Socialism's national concerns. Many Brno Austro-Marxists had after all concluded that national questions should be regarded by Socialists as cultural ones. But even Kristan was unable to resist projecting beyond the frontiers of Austria. He authored the controversial, though central, resolution at Tivoli which called for "*the complete national unification of Yugoslavs,*" irrespective of name, religion, alphabet, and dialect or language.[57] However, in attempting to stem Tuma's expansionist "Yugoslavism," with its dangerous implications for the party, Kristan riled the JSDS Masarykites, who subsequently spoke and wrote eloquently on the need for Slovene linguistic and cultural individuality.[58] Masarykites thereafter tended to agree more with Tuma, that the Yugoslav question was essentially an economic and political one.

The Bosnian annexation had confirmed the opinion of Slovene Socialists that Austria's historical mission lay to the South. Moreover, though they opposed the method of annexation, particularly Austria's subsequent imperialistic manipulation of Serbia,[59] Socialists welcomed the crisis, for crises provided the climate in which social advances were made. After 1909 Socialists began to address themselves more regularly to questions relevant to Yugoslavs. They spoke more vigorously against non-Socialist national programs; they dismissed Clerical "trialism" as "mountain Croatism;"[60] they rejected Liberal proposals for an Austrian federalism based on national units as "bourgeois."[61] Dualism, of course, was already obsolete, given the fact that Bosnia and Herzegovina had not been made a part of either Austria or Hungary. To many Socialists the march toward Social Democracy had begun and it would emerge from the resolution of the Yugoslav question.

Not all went smoothly, however. War erupted in the Balkans in 1912 and though Slovene Socialists denounced war as a product of imperialistic meddling in the area—particularly by Russia, but also Austria—they rather approved of the First Balkan War.[62] It meant that South Slavs were liberating themselves from the Turks, that popular will was dictating the course of affairs to the South. The second Balkan war troubled them, not only because Serbs and Bulgars fought one another, but because Austria was suspected of encouraging Bulgaria in that conflict.[63] They felt Austria should remain above Balkan conflicts, doing all in her power to promote cooperation in the area, in order to help effect Austro-Balkan friendship. The Serb-Bulgar encounter and Austria's involvement in it generated a sentiment for an independent Yugoslavia among some Slovenes.[64] Though Ivan Cankar shared that sentiment and Tuma turned against the Bulgars in championing the Serbian cause, most other Socialists only reluctantly ventured any comment; their ties to Austria were too strong.

The JSDS, like the other two Slovene parties, though advocating reform of the government system, officially went little beyond the position of Austro-Marxism. Cankar was really the only bold one, but then his own impoverishment and bohemian life style lent itself to the daring and impulsive gesture. That he seemed to hit upon the ideal resolution of the problem is beside the point. All others seemed to feel that the Yugoslav question was somehow inextricably bound up with the future of Austria. Even at the Belgrade Social Democratic Conference in January of 1910, where Slovenes reiterated Kristan's plans for the cultural unity of Yugoslavs, they still conceived of it being implemented within an Austrian state. If Slovene Socialists talked about independent Socialist republics, not federation with Austria,[65] they saw no basic conflict between the two approaches. For them, in spite of the mounting intensity of Serb-Bulgar and Serb-Austrian hostilities—or alternately, because of these—the future continued to point toward an Austrian Yugoslav solution.

CHAPTER VI

1908 AND 1909: THE RESPONSE TO THE ANNEXATION
OF BOSNIA AND HERZEGOVINA

By the turn of the century Slovenes had come of age politically. In the nineties three distinct political parties had been formed to which men with clear professional party interests belonged. Among these there were still men of literature and clergymen, like those who had played leading, though short-term, roles in 1848 and again in the sixties and the seventies. But by 1890 lawyers and bankers had come to constitute the core of political organizations. They were elected to the local diets or sent as provincial representatives to the Vienna Parliament. In Carniola Slovene politicians dominated local affairs. By 1883 they had take control of the Carniolan diet,[1] and after 1888 the mayor of Carniola's capital, Ljubljana, was a Slovene.

Through periodic extension of the franchise in the Cisleithian half of the Habsburg Empire, more and more Slovenes became eligible to vote. The adoption in 1907 of universal manhood suffrage for elections to the national Parliament encouraged many Slovene Socialists to believe their goals might be realized through parliamentary means. Indeed in the last two decades before the war the position of the Slovenes within the Empire improved steadily. Compared with the Croats their lot was enviable. The Slovenes attributed Croat misfortunes to Hungarian intransigence, while their own experience seemed to attest to Vienna's good faith even though Vienna's hands were somewhat bound where Hungary's South Slavs were concerned. Slovene politicians believed that Vienna was favorable to the realization of Slovene national aspirations. Any setbacks could usually be traced to the pernicious pressure of German national elements, but Slovenes believed that in spite of these pressures Vienna's authority would prevail and eventually champion their cause.

Because they believed this, Slovene politicians drafted their national and Yugoslav plans with an Austrian context ever in mind. The motives behind these plans might vary, but in some way each was based on the premise that Austria was needed, that she had a special mission to fulfill. The Clericals promoted the conversion of the Empire into a trialistic state, one providing a separate administration for South Slavs. This plan would not have ruled out the eventual implementation of federalism for the whole empire, which both Slovene Liberals and Socialists proposed. None of the plans would have excluded outright territorial expansion into the Balkans by extending federalism to South Slavs there.

Whenever the future of Austria was threatened, Slovenes registered concern. This had been the case in 1848, in the late 1860's and again in 1870. After 1871, however, when the new German state proved compatible with continuance of the Austrian Empire, Slovenes felt more secure. Between 1871 and 1908 no international developments seriously challenged Austria's existence and Slovenes pursued their national programs legally, temperately, and with patience. There was a vague stirring of Southern Slav sentiment during the Russo-Turkish War in the mid-1870's and again in 1903 when Peter Karageorgević succeeded the assassinated Alexander Obrenović in Serbia,[2] but in neither case did Slovenes really feel that their future or the future of Austria was at stake. A sense of urgency was markedly absent from their politics. After the autumn of 1908, however, the picture changed.

In October of 1908 Bosnia and Herzegovina were annexed to the Habsburg Empire. This event, discussed below, heightened the national awareness of South Slavs, both in the Empire and outside it. Moreover, Slovene national sensitivity had already been aroused by the shooting of two Slovene youths by soldiers in Ljubljana on the 20th of September. The two were killed after a week of sustained conflict between Slovenes and Germans, which had erupted both in Styria and Carniola. The initial confrontation occurred on a train carrying Slovene representatives of the Society of Cyril and Methodius to a meeting scheduled for the 13th of September in Ptuj (in Styria). Slovenes, anticipating difficulties in predominantly German Styria, had requested police protection for the society's members. None was extended, and the Slovenes traveling to Ptuj were assaulted by Germans and Slovene Germanophiles.[3] Tension mounted in Styria and spilled over into Carniola where a sympathetic protest demonstration was scheduled by Slovenes for the 18th. On that day anti-German rioting resulted in the breaking of windows of German shops. The police subdued the rock throwers, but the military was called in to prevent future disturbances. The presence of soldiers in Carniola's capital,[4] however, merely provoked the more militant nationalists. Their demonstrations led to the shooting on the 20th. Dead were Rudolf Lunder and Ivan Adamič; many were wounded.

This incident aroused even docile Slovenes. Overnight German and bilingual signs were torn down and replaced with Slovene ones. German merchants were boycotted, and Ljubljana homes and shops were draped in black. The funeral of the victims was attended by thousands. Throughout the Slovene provinces commemorative ceremonies were held. Lunder and Adamič had quickly become national martyrs.

The three Slovene political parties were united in their reaction to the shooting. They interpreted the regime's handling of the Slovene-German conflicts in Styria and Carniola as provocatively anti-Slovene. The Liberals were perhaps most concerned, since the Ptuj confrontation had taken place in connection with a Liberal gathering (Society of Cyril and Methodius). Indeed the Liberal paper *Slovenski narod* in late September repeatedly demanded what amounted to revenge and retaliation. Clericals and Socialists were equally indignant. Both participated in demonstrations after the shooting, and the Clerical leader Ivan Šušteršič telegraphed Baron von Schonaich, then Minister of War, demanding an investigation of the military which could permit such irresponsibility.[5] Representatives from each of the parties delivered eulogies at the graveside of Lunder and Adamic, and a joint council (*Združeni narodni zbor*) arranged for immediate erection of cemetery monuments. The Liberal mayor Hribar and the town council promptly provided financial aid for those wounded in the skirmish on the 20th. Liberals referred to it as the Slovene St. Bartholomew's Eve.[6]

Slovene daily papers were still reviewing these events when the annexation of Bosnia and Herzegovina on the 7th of October 1908 directed Slovene attention to developments in the South. The joint Ministry of Finance of Austria and Hungary had been administering these lands since 1878, when at the Congress of Berlin the Habsburg Empire had been assigned administrative custody. The Austrians had come to regard this arrangement as temporary, to be altered at Austria's discretion, while Serbia—then the only independent South Slavic state and contiguous to Bosnia-Herzegovina—became increasingly convinced that these South Slavic provinces belonged to her by national right. In any case Austria took action, perhaps fearful that if she did not the Young Turks, who had revolted in the summer of 1908, would reclaim these former Ottoman territories.

The Serbs were, of course, furious, as were the Turks. The Russians too—sometimes patrons of their less experienced Serbian kin—denounced Austria's unilateral act as an inexcusable affront. But the Slovenes, that is the Slovene political parties, reacted rather favorably, feeling that the annexation signaled an advance toward a positive Austrian Yugoslav policy. Carefully monitering Balkan events, the Clericals and the Liberals in their daily journals had anticipated the annexation for at least a week before it occurred. Indeed when on October 5th Bulgaria announced her independence both *Slovenec* and *Slovenski narod* acknowledged it as a corollary to Austria's Greater Balkan policy, it being widely accepted that Austria exercized great influence in Bulgarian affairs.[7] Each Slovene party interpreted the annexation as a positive evolutionary step, leading toward the fulfillment of its own particular political goals.

The Clericals, spokesmen of the strongest Slovene party, welcomed the annexation with virtually no reservations, going to great lengths to justify Austria's claims and to explain away any violations of the 1878 Treaty of Berlin. The Clericals, less Panslav than the Liberals, were not seriously disturbed by ensuing complications in Austro-Russian and Austro-Serbian relations. Moreover, because Austria had annexed Bosnia, Clericals were convinced that Vienna had at last realized Austria's purpose as a state, as Clericals construed it of course.

In expressing his approval party leader Ivan Šušteršič also presented a Clerical plan for the future governing of the annexed territories.[8] First he demanded democratic institutions for Bosnia and Herzegovina, which together should be joined to the Croat Triune Kingdom (Croatia, Slavonia, and Dalmatia) in one administrative autonomous unit.[9] This initial development was to be followed by a second administrative reshuffling, one which would unite all the Yugoslav lands of the Habsburg Empire. In other words, Clericals used the occasion to promote their program of trialism. Clericals presented their plan within a day or two of the annexation and they continued for the next few months to urge its implementation. This was done against a background of mounting international crisis accompanied by real resistance to the annexation from important elements within the Empire, notably the Hungarians, whose relationship with South Slavs worsened daily because of it. Certain additions, clarifying points and justifications were appended to the initial Clerical appeal for trialism thereafter. Šušteršič reiterated his pleas;[10] Krek spoke of a Constitution for Bosnia and of a Yugoslav unit for the South Slavs of the Empire. He said in a speech on December 23 that the Slovenes had never before the annexation felt so strongly that they belonged to a South Slav unit which included Croats and Serbs. Both stressed Austria's dependence on her Southern Slavs in achieving, as Šušteršič put it, *"a Balkan federation under the leadership of our monarchy."*[11]

With quiet mobilization begun, and with much rumor of an impending Austro-Serbia war,[12] Slovene Clericals increased pressures as the year drew to a close for adoption of their plan. On 16 December Šušteršič urged the Austrian Parliament to give its priority to resolving this Yugoslav question.[13] But neither the Parliament, nor the regime, was very responsive. Bienerth, then Prime Minister, refused to be rushed by emotional pleas.[14] though he assured Šušteršič that the matter was being studied carefully. Essentially, all the regime came up with was an offer to create the post of "Yugoslav Minister" to act as a liaison between the regime and the South Slavs. The Clericals rejected this as a half measure, facetiously advising the regime that it need not make such staggering concessions until drastic solutions were really in order.[15]

When the Carniolan diet met on 16 January 1909 for its first session since the annexation, the South Slav question was prominent on the agenda. The Clericals reaffirmed their approval, lauding annexation as "the first step toward the unification of all South Slavs of the monarchy in an independent states rights unit under the auspices of the Habsburg dynasty." Krek later elaborated on the historic and legal reasons for such an association, tracing genealogical tables to the Middle Ages in order to establish family ties between the rulers of Bosnia and the noble family of Celje (Cilli) in Southern Styria. He spoke of Bosnia and Herzegovina as an extension of "our homeland and our people." But Krek was unhappy with the regime's handling of the situation, he was growing more impatient for a prompt implementation of trialism, and he concluded that the Magyars were the principal obstacle. In concluding his talk to the diet he said, "I hope the time will come, when the Yugoslav will take a map into his hands and say to the Magyars: 'Where is Hungary? I cannot find it!'"[16]

Neither the Liberal nor Socialist Party response was that of the Clericals. The nationalistic Liberals moved to strong Panslav impulses in times of crisis, were frankly paralyzed by the Autumn 1908 developments. The Liberals did not wish to abandon Austria; rather they hoped a federation of sorts could be worked out in such a way that Austria and other Slavs—most importantly the Russians—could cooperate in self-defense against Germandom. These Liberals idealized Russia and had fond associations with South Slavs in the Balkans; but the Austrian annexation had offended both, and had, perhaps irreparably, damaged Austria's relations with Slavs outside the Empire. Their answer to this dilemma—with Austria, their real homeland, and Russia, their spiritual homeland, hostile to one another — was to appeal to Christian charity and brotherly love to help avert war. To present their case they quoted appropriate passages from Tolstoy.[17]

Not unexpectedly the Liberals failed to produce any workable new approach. Perhaps they were waiting to see what turns the crisis would take; but in any case it must have been mentally crippling for them to have to choose between the two pillars of their national program—Austria and Russia. Three months after the annexation, at the 16 January 1909 meeting of the Carniolan Diet, the Liberals were still clinging to the fundamentals of their pre-1908 program, hoping the crisis would subside. In that diet Liberals welcomed the addition of South Slavs to the Empire, but they harshly reprimanded the regime for its methods. They maintained that concerned states—not only Russia, but the Ottoman Empire, Serbia, and Montenegro—should have been consulted. The Clerical Šušteršič was more realistically of the opinion that such consultation would have resulted in a negative response from all.[18] Though the Liberals saw the obvious bargaining advantage of having more South Slavs in the Empire and welcomed the union of Habsburg Slavs with Balkan ones, they feared that without Russian friendship and brotherhood, the South Slavic cause would be lost.[19]

The Slovene Socialists, as might be expected, denounced the actual act of annexation. In terms of their own ideology, it was a typical act of capitalist, imperialist aggression. It was accompanied also by an intensification of militarism which increased taxes and the likelihood of war. Moreover, it had increased international hatreds and aggravated the whole Southern Slav question. The Socialists expressed open sympathy for Serbia, whom they depicted as a helpless pawn at the mercy of Austria's imperialistic whims.[20]

Although the Socialists reacted adversely to Austrian tactics, they actually welcomed the incorporation of Bosnia and Herzegovina into the Empire. Their reasoning was of course left-handed, having to do with their understanding of the forces of history. Essentially they judged that the annexation, though initially embodying unwholesome features, created a situation which made a prompt solution of the South Slav problem imperative It had produced a real crisis in Austro-Hungarian dualism, and the Socialists felt that because of this, a federalistic reorganization of the Empire must soon result. Indeed, the Socialists contended that the regime had already destroyed dualism by permitting Bosnia to exist independent of either Austria or Hungary. In the event this arrangement were to endure for some time, they were convinced that Bosnia would achieve a great measure of autonomy.

Yet the Socialists did not expect that this situation would be at all permanent, for the same reasons that they were critical of the Clerical program of trialism. Essentially, they felt, other national groups in the Empire would not accept autonomy for Bosnians or South Slavs unless it were granted to themselves. The Czechs were cited as certain to object to a trialistic structure, unless they obtained their own autonomy.[21] Furthermore, Bosnian autonomy, particularly if it moved to expand northward to include Hungarian Croats and/or Austrian Slovenes, would raise strong opposition from the Magyars and the Germans. In both cases land and populations would be lost to the South Slav unit, and if national self-determination succeeded in asserting itself, Vienna and Budapest would be deprived of access to the sea. The Socialists believed that the regime would never permit this to happen.

For the Socialists the future course of events was clear. Bosnia could not be allowed to exist as a separate unit of the Empire, for the regime would certainly then be overwhelmed by South Slav sentiment for unity. Yet the Bosnian Slavs could not be incorporated into Cisleithian Austria either; the German elements would not permit such a deluge of Slavs. The most probable and most practical immediate solution, in the opinion of the Slovene Socialists, was to attach Bosnia to Hungary. Moreover, the Socialists themselves were partial to this plan, certain that the increase of population in the Transleithian half of the Empire would force introduction of universal suffrage there. From that juncture the steps to democratic federalism and ultimately to socialism would be very short.[22]

Clearly the Slovene Socialists were not radicalized by the Bosnian annexation. They still planned within the concept of an Austrian framework; what annexation did was encourage them to believe that social democratic federalism was evolving within that structure. They were convinced that their goals could be achieved through constitutional reform and universal suffrage, especially in Hungary, and after October 1908 they promoted these changes more vigorously.[23] Their desire to keep the Empire intact was due partly to the nature of the party, which was strongly influenced by centralistic Austro-German Marxists, and partly due to Marxism itself, which predicted socialist successes for advanced industrial states. Therefore in spite of strong sympathy for Serbia and for other South Slavs (including the Bulgarians), Slovene Socialists favored a solution to the Yugoslav question within Austria, where historical development was more conducive to the establishment of socialism than it was in the backward Balkans. The Socialists, however, did feel that since things were moving rather quickly in the South, they needed to plan their strategy more precisely. They clearly were embarrassed that the Clericals, not they, were first with a program in 1908.[24] To remedy that deficiency the Socialists planned a conference for late 1909.

The general European crisis lasted some six months. Other than the Bulgarians, who had declared their own independence from the Turks in conjunction with the annexation (probably even at the urging of Austria), no country was pleased with what Austria had done. Britain, France, and Italy disapproved. Even Austria's ally Germany was disturbed that the annexation had been undertaken without Germany being consulted. The Serbs, the Montenegrins, Russia and the Turks were infuriated. Serbia sent troops to the Austrian frontier; Austria threatened to attack Serbia; but in the end war was averted. The Ottoman Empire, which could do little about the violation of its sovereignty, due to urgent internal problems, finally gave up claim to Bosnia, with ten million dollars paid by Austria to the Turks helping facilitate this decision.[25] Germany also played her part in containing the crisis by intimidating the Russians so that Serbs stood alone against Austria, with no choice but to give in. On 31 March 1909 Serbia officially accepted the annexation and removed troops from the frontier. For the Serbs at least, the confrontation had not been averted; it had merely been postponed.

Within the Empire during the crisis the ruling nationalities, the Germans and particularly the Magyars, had been infected with a growing fear that their own Yugoslavs were conspiring against them on behalf of Serbia. This assumption was not new; even before 1848 the regime was often concerned with the dangers of Panslavism. But in 1908 and 1909 fear of the Habsburg Slavs operating in collusion with Serbia reached panic proportions. Serb sympathizers were hunted as traitors to the regime. Most South Slavs in the Empire were suspect to some degree. The fear was greatest in Hungary and focussed on the Transleithian Serbs (of Croatia). At the height of the annexation crisis, in January 1909, fifty-three Serbs were arrested and accused of belonging to a pan-Serb revolutionary organization. Their trial, which dragged on into October, began in March in Zagreb, just a few weeks before Serbia acknowledged Austria's incorporation of Bosnia.

The fity-three were formally charged with treason, that is, of collaborating with a Serbian nationalist organization in Belgrade, called *Slovenski Jug* (The Slav South), one whose aim was to destroy Austria. The prosecution's chief witness was one George Nastić, whose own past was notorious and elusive; it seems that he made a career of spying and informing, appearing from time to time in various Balkan capitals, transporting bombs or preaching revoluion. Nastić in August of 1908 had published a pamphlet entitled *Finale* in which he maintained that treasonable pan-Serb organizations existed in the Habsburg monarchy among the Empire's South Slavs. His report was based, he said, on inside information. But at the Zagreb trial, Nastić's testimony, which was based on the *Finale* allegations, was far from incriminating for the accused and full of serious loopholes. In fact, it became quickly apparent that Nastić was an unsavory character employed by the regime as an *agent provocateur*. His pamphlet indeed had been released in August of 1908, shortly before the Bosnian annexation, precisely in order to prepare the public for that event. In the end the prosecution's case was so weak that twenty-two of the fifty-three charged were dismissed. The light prison terms given the remaining thirty-one—in a state where treason was punishable by death—was tantmount to admission of gross error. A Court of Appeal in the end nullified the trial, and a retrial, though designated, was not held.[26]

Before the Zagreb trial ended, another was impending. The regime in attempting to indict the Empire's South Slavs enlisted the aid of the prominent historian Heinrich Friedjung and of the Viennese journal *Reichspost*. Again the government's involvement soon became apparent. Both *Reichspost* and Friedjung were supplied so-called privileged information and both wrote of pro-Serbian conspiracies in the Empire, implicating the Croat-Serb party. Several libel suits resulted. Masaryk intervened and was able to prove that the "privileged information" was based on forged documents which had been fabricated in the Austrian Embassy in Belgrade with the assistance of the Habsburg foreign minister, Count Forgach. However, in spite of this clear indictment of Forgach and Friedjung, neither was damaged by complicity in the affair. Freidjung indeed was absolved; it was said that he had not been aware that his information was based on forged materials. But Aehrenthal later told Redlich that he had requested that Friedjung "collaborate" in a case against the Serbs, to which Friedjung presumably agreed.[27] The South Slavs in the end won their case, but the accusers went unpunished.

All these developments—the shooting in Ljubljana in September 1908, the annexation crisis, the Zagreb trials, and the Friedjung-*Reichspost* affair—made Slovenes very anxious. Until 1908 their confidence in Austria had been great, though all political parties certainly agreed that reorganization and constitutional revisions were in order. Most importantly, none really expected hostility from Vienna to Slovene (or to South Slav) aspirations. The events of 1908 and 1909, though they did not substantially alter existing Slovene positions, definitely brought Slovene national thinking to a more realistic plane. Programs until 1908 had been romantic projections, resting on confidence in an Austrian ideal; but as events in those crucial months developed, incompatibilities between the ideal and the real became painfully evident.

The Slovene parties became uneasy about the regime's intentions. They witnessed attacks not only on South Slavs outside, but more important, within the Empire. And though Slovenes themselves were not prominently victimized in the period after the annexation, they were conscious of their scant numbers and of the shootings in Ljubljana of just the year previous. It was difficult for them to comprehend that not only Hungary, but Vienna, too was a partner to the anti-Yugoslav activities; yet it was increasingly clear that this was so.

Throughout 1909 Slovene party spokesmen—particularly Liberals and Social Democrats—sharply criticized Austria's treatment of her South Slavs. The Liberal dilemma after the annexation had been complicated further by the trials of 1909, when the loyalty of the Croat-Serb Coalition party members had been seriously questioned. It was as if the loyalty of the Slovene Liberals was also doubted. The Socialists were similarly troubled; they wrote that the trials had confirmed their opinion of the regime's corruptness, of its moral bankruptcy. Writing about the Friedjung trial, Anton Dermota bitterly assailed the clerical and aristocratic circles of

Vienna, whom he held responsible for the singularly reactionary character of recent politics.[28] *Rdeči prapor*, the Socialist newspaper, even began employing "nationalistic" rhetoric, urging that something positive be done about Yugoslav unity.[29] Among Liberals and Socialists one could detect real excitement when Masaryk came to the defense of the Croat-Serb Coalition members and proved the Friedjung documents forgeries. But in their minds the regime became an ever greater puzzle.

The Clericals, too, became increasingly concerned about the regime's good will. They were not excessively dismayed at the attack on Croat-Serb Coalition members. These in 1905 had projected a program philosophically incompatible with that of the Clericals; and some of the extreme Rightists in Croatia, with whom certain Clericals were more in tune, actually cooperated with Magyars in the Zagreb trial. But even Slovene Clericals by the summer of 1909 were writing in their daily paper of "new German-Magyar malicious intentions toward the Slavs."[30] Such statements by Clericals appeared more frequently as the history of *agent provocateur* Nastić was unraveled. When Nastić's *Finale* was first published (August 1908), Clericals objected to his attacks on Serbs. When they learned his pamphlet had been intended to pave the way for the annexation, a goal they approved of, Clericals reconsidered. But during the Zagreb trials they again revised their thinking, fearing that the regime's real intent was to reject trialism completely. They came to feel that the regime's ultimate plan was to divide South Slavs even more—into at least three separate units—to prevent them from ever achieving a common Yugoslav state. The notion moved party leader Šušteršič to send to the Archduke Francis Ferdinand in mid-summer 1909 details of the Slovene Clerical trialist program.[31] The receipt of Šušteršič's message was acknowledged, but the Archduke expressed no further interest in it.

One last item which needs to be discussed in connection with the events of these two critical years is the Social Democratic Congress held in November 1909. It took place within weeks of the Zagreb treason trials but actually had been suggested shortly after the Bosnian annexation as a direct response to it. The Slovene Socialists, who were strongly influenced by (and financially tied to) Austro-German Socialists, had not really revised their party program for nearly a decade. Moreover, that program was essentially Austro-Marxist in character, resting on the Brno resolutions of 1899.[32] Until 1908 most Slovene Socialists were willing to suppress specific nationalist concerns in order to pursue that greater goal of social democracy. But the annexation moved them to reconsider, and they promptly concluded that the Bosnian crisis had radically shifted the focus of Austria's relationship to the fortunes of the South Slavs. As South Slavs and Socialists they felt obliged to reassess their policy in terms of recent developments. In this way the Slovene Socialists (Yugoslav Social Democratic Party) came to immerse themselves in the Yugoslav question, giving nearly undivided attention to "nationalistic" problems, which in the past, as Marxists, they felt were not their proper concern.[33]

Meetings were held on the 21 and 22 of November 1909 in Ljubljana's Tivoli Hotel, which gave its name to the conference resolutions. Slovene delegates were, of course, active participants, and official representatives from Croatia, Slavonia, Dalmatia, and the newly annexed Bosnian lands also attended. Czechs, Italians, Austro-Germans and Serbs came as observers. The conference membership quickly disposed of fundamental preliminary questions, affirming first, the reality of Southern Slavism as a vital force, and second, the legitimacy of Socialist concern with it. Debates then turned to more specific issues. Conclusions were then incorporated into the Tivoli resolutions.[34]

At first established Socialist positions were restated, earlier policies reaffirmed. For example, the conference characterized the Bosnian annexation as imperialistic and designed to exploit the impoverished Balkan masses. Furthermore, it condemned Austro-Hungarian dualism as absolutistic and feudalistic, proposing in its place democratic federalism for those within the bounds of the Empire.[35] Most immediately it proposed to agitate for electoral reform in Transleithia and for an autonomous diet for Bosnia. The delegates felt that the existing boundaries of Austria, however, were required for the state's economic stability. And although no statements were made with regard to the dissolution of the Empire, some would regard the general sentiment of the conference as revolutionary, perhaps even treasonable.[36]

What was most radical about the Tivoli program, and also the most controversial, were its specified cultural goals—*"the complete national unification of all Yugoslavs, irrespective of name, religion, alphabet and dialect or language."*[37] The resolution, elaborating on this point, included Serbs, Croats, Slovenes and Bulgarians in its definition of South Slav, conceiving of all of these as belonging to one nation. Moreover, at Tivoli delegates urged serious discussion with regard to a common language and common orthography for all South Slavs.[38] Whether the delegates considered such Yugoslav national identification in political terms is not known. The resolution restricted itself to the cultural aspects of the problem. One cannot, however, believe the political implications eluded those present.[39]

Although the Tivoli resolutions did not evoke official opposition or even serious concern among other Slovene parties, the proposal for Yugoslav cultural unity precipitated a heated conflict within the party. The controversy centered on the problem of cultural unity as opposed to cultural diversity; the bulk of party members, led by Etbin Kristan, supported unity, while the Masarykites connected with the journal *Naši zapiski* stood opposed to cultural merging. The followers of Masaryk felt that Slovenes and other South Slav groups should develop language, literature, orthography—culture in general—independently. Drafters of the Tivoli document focussed on goals of cultural unity; Masarykites pursued economic and political ends, judging cultural leveling artificial and not necessarily conducive to political unification.[40]

In early January, six weeks after the Tivoli meeting, a Balkan Social Democratic Conference was held in Belgrade. South Slav Socialists of Austria-Hungary sent representatives. Henrik Tuma, one of those who helped draft the Tivoli program, represented the Slovenes.[41] At Belgrade again the spirit of Tivoli seemed to prevail. Yugoslav cultural unity and national autonomy were championed, and a preference for the Austrian framework was expressed. The slogan of the Belgrade Conference, "the Balkans for the Balkan nations in a federal republic," clearly left room for Austrian-Balkan cooperation. Yet warnings were issued to the effect that Austrian negligence with respect to the South Slavs might mean Austria's destruction.[42] Meanwhile *Rdeči prapor* at home reminded the regime that, "Whoever wishes to play a leading role in the Balkans, must never swim against the Yugoslav current."[43]

By the end of 1909 the Slovene Social Democrats, not unlike Clericals and Liberals, had come to focus on nationalistic issues. They defended the Southern Slav cause not as "nationalists" *per se*, but as those concerned for the plight of the proletariat. During the annexation crisis they had come to believe that out of the misery of the Yugoslav masses would arise those historical forces necessary to produce revolutionary transformations in both Austrian and Balkan societies. Oddly enough, however, the party core chose to stress cultural factors rather than political or economic ones, the latter certainly being more legitimate Socialist concerns. Indeed the Tivoli exchange for and against South Slav cultural unity reads like a debate engaged in by liberal European intellectuals. The arguments pro and con were mere reiterations of the Prešeren-Vraz (Slovene-Illyrian) debate of the 1830's and 1840's. In fact the debate soon thereafter captured the interest also of Liberals, Clericals, and politically non-aligned Slovenes. The cultural implications of Yugoslavism were thoroughly reexamined in the next few years.

CHAPTER VII

CULTURAL YUGOSLAVISM:
THE REVIVAL OF THE VRAZ-PREŠEREN DEBATE[1]

For centuries the Slovenes had been inhabitants of a multi-national Austrian state, including Slavic and non-Slavic peoples. The administrative structure of the Empire, however, permitted Germans and Magyars to dominate. In the half century before the world war Slovene political leaders pondered this reality and concluded that they were not fundamentally opposed to an association with Austria, but that a more equitable distribution of rights and powers would have to be effected. By 1910 all three Slovene political parties—Clericals, Liberals, and Social Democrats—were expressing a need for some form of political Yugoslavism. They agreed that a million Slovenes could not survive as an independent political entity unless they had allies. Consequently each party came to work for political reorganization within the Empire and each included other South Slavs in its plans.

Political Yugoslavism had to face the problem of a multiplicity of languages. The Habsburg Empire was grappling with language controversies, and the Slovenes realized that some of these would be transplanted to any Yugoslav administrative unit which might be created. Some Slovenes put forth programs of cultural Illyrism. But whereas most could agree upon the need for Yugoslav political unity, cultural solidarity repelled many because it aimed at assimilation. Slovenes became sharply divided and even political parties split over the issue.

There were several themes which dominated this controversy. One was the nature of the nation and of the language. Some maintained that there were four separate Southern Slav nations—each with a language of its own (related, however, to the other Yugoslav tongues)—while others insisted that there was in reality only one Yugoslav nation, which, because historical developments had caused it to be divided, expressed itself in four different dialects. Those who adhered to the concept of one Yugoslav nation composed of several dialect groups held that cultural and linguistic unity could easily be realized. The contrary was true of those who distinguished among four Southern Slav nations and four separate languages. Cultural heritage also became controversial with Western Catholic often pitted against the Eastern Orthodox culture, the gap between them regarded by some as unbridgeable. The Clericals, for example, looked upon Western

Yugoslavs as a superior cultural unit to which others would have to adhere. Masarykite Social Democrats acknowledged the cultural differences, but maintained that linguistic and cultural consolidation could not and, moreover, should not be implemented. Liberals, on the other hand, generally dismissed as insignificant the differences between Western and Byzantine heritages, maintaining that ties of blood could overcome such divisions.

After 1910 cultural Yugoslavism became an all absorbing issue for Slovene Yugoslav movements. They debated whether cultural assimilation should be promoted, and, if so, whether it should be begun immediately, or delayed until political union had been completed. In 1913 the journal *Veda*[2] focussed on this very problem, offering a questionnaire to prominent cultural and political leaders in Slovene and other Habsburg lands. At this time Illyrists were demanding deliberate efforts at cultural unification, while Slovene individualists upheld the right of each nation to develop its culture and language independently. Others took a middle position, proposing that each group be permitted to develop its language/dialect and culture at will but maintaining that natural evolution would eventually draw these related units together. Some Slovenes feared that because of their small numbers, they would fall victim to such an evolution; others, like Prijatelj[3] of *Veda*, had faith in the durability of everything Slovene and in effect challenged other Southern Slavs to a healthy competition.

Within the Slovene Social Democratic party a divergence of opinion on the cultural question had emerged at the Tivoli Conference in 1909. All representatives to the conference approved of the Socialist political program, but they were not able to agree on the official cultural program, which called for "*complete national unification of all Yugoslavs.*" The Tivoli resolution aimed at a total cultural union of the four Southern Slav nationalities—Bulgars, Croats, Serbs, and Slovenes. It was held that these four Slavic peoples had originally constituted one nation, which had been divided during its early history. Foreign political powers had penetrated the area, subjugated these Slavs and prevented a common development. During this interval of foreign domination, the Tivoli resolution stated, languages and cultures took divergent roads, and as a consequence the Yugoslavs of the early twentieth century found themselves with different linguistic and cultural heritages. The official position of the Social Democrats was that these differences were not a serious obstacle to either political or cultural unification, both of which, however, were vital to the future of the Southern Slavs. Etbin Kristan, who was in effect author of this Tivoli resolution, felt that cultural and linguistic unity were virtually a prerequisite to political union and that the merging of these four branches of the Southern Slav nation should be effected on the cultural level as soon as possible. The first step would be the acceptance of one common literary language by all four groups. Neither Kristan nor others at the Conference indicated which of the four languages it would be, or if indeed it should be one of these or an artificial language combining them all.

Some at the Tivoli Conference were not in accord with the cultural resolution drafted by the convention. Opinion was divided along the lines which had often before divided the orthodox Social Democrats from the Masarykites. Dermota, Lončar, and also Prepeluh[4] (the latter was essentially a link between the Masarykites and the Social Democrats on many issues) believed in the necessity of a separate *Slovene* national culture. They felt that in order to constitute a strong element in a Yugoslav political unit, it would be imperative for the Slovenes to have a well-developed language and culture of their own. Speaking for the Masarykites on this question, Prepeluh said he opposed the cultural and linguistic unification of the Southern Slavs because it clashed very fundamentally with the basic concept of nationality.

What the Masarykites understood by "nation" and its relationship to culture is clear from the following passage taken from a speech by Prepeluh:

> The nationality of each individual is the framework within which the spiritual development of his soul takes place. We have feelings, ideas, and thoughts pertaining to a certain category of things only within the boundaries of our national consciousness. Nationality is particularly vital in the area of culture. Take the artist, for example. Does he not create his works as a representative of a national whole? A nation demands freedom, liberty, and natural rights . . . it seeks a language so that it can invest its soul with the finesse, the beauty and the harmony, which lies hidden and undeveloped in the depths of the nation's being. A nation which had a joint share in history, a common social history and a yearning for spiritual liberation, searches to find its true self only within the borders of nationality . . . . Each nation yearns to be liberated from foreign subjugation in order to become free to determine its own cultural needs.[5]

According to the Masarykites, the Slovenes as a nation would never reach their goal—would never attain the status of an independent nation—if the cultural clauses of the Tivoli resolution were carried out.

As if anticipating the Tivoli program, Prepeluh in 1907 and again in 1908 had warned against what he felt was a widespread delusion about cultural accommodation. He felt that the major obstacle to the realization of one Yugoslav culture was the fact that the Southern Slavs were divided culturally—some influenced by the West and some by Byzantium. Two distinctly different cultures had shaped the national lives of the Southern Slavs for centuries. In *Hrvatsko Kolo*[6] Prepeluh wrote:

> There were times when fantastic dreams of Yugoslav unification
> were dreamt . . . and there were times when people thought of one
> Yugoslav language, which would save the small Yugoslav nations in the
> future. Childish dreams . . . . It is inconceivable that anyone demand
> that any nation conceal its individuality in the interests of greater cul-
> ~~tural~~ unity. It is impossible if only because of the fact that we Yugo-
> slavs have two basically different cultures, each with its own source.[7]

In the same article Prepeluh went on to say that he envisioned the Yugoslavs of the future as four individual nations each engaged in its own development and thereby contributing to the cultural wealth of all the
others.

After 1909 and the Tivoli Conference this trio—Dermota, Lončar and
Prepeluh—engaged regularly in polemics against proposals for Yugoslav
cultural and linguistic unity. Their vehicle was generally the monthly journal *Naši zapiski*. Dermota as editor formulated policy on matters of cultural development. Yugoslav political unity, for him, could be achieved
only on the basis of equality, each nation having a separate and individual
culture. He refused to have any part of a Yugoslavism requiring that one
national culture be sacrificed for another; he considered all nations, large
or small, of equal worth.[8] Furthermore, he looked upon nationalism as a
powerful motivating force in the world, giving spiritual impetus to underdeveloped peoples to improve their position in society.[9] Depriving the
Slovenes of their national individuality would strip them of this incentive
and the road to socialism for them might be impeded perhaps forever.
Moreover, Dermota felt that national development must precede the internationalism which socialism regarded as one of its ultimate goals.

Lončar and Tuma[10] (a late-comer to the party) contributed regularly
to *Naši zapiski* and attacked proposals for Yugoslav cultural unity on a less
lofty plane. They conceded that perhaps some sacrifices would have to be
made. However, they were adamant that these must not be cultural. Both
refused to cooperate unless others were willing to sacrifice too. Yugoslav
unification, they felt, must be effected on the basis of mutual respect
among Southern Slavs. This required, for example, that Croats stop pres-
suring Slovenes to concede that they were really "mountain Croats." On
these grounds Lončar opposed any Slovene connection with Zagreb University, proposing instead that Slovenes concentrate on the establishment
of their own academy of higher learning in Ljubljana.[11]

In 1913 Prepeluh summed up the position of the *Naši zapiski* group:

> We never put forward the idea of Yugoslavism so that we could some-
> day set aside our own language, our own literature, our own national
> manners and customs in order to become something new overnight,
> that is, that we become a so-called nation, which does not as yet even

exist . . . . We sought out Yugoslavism to find a joint and broad national awareness and a greater defense for our own individual national cultural life . . . . The Yugoslav idea gains nothing . . . if we Slovenes sacrifice for it our national individuality, our hard won culture—our language. On the other hand the idea of Yugoslav unity must necessarily profit a great deal if we fortify our national individuality so as to become sufficiently strong to realize our freedom and our future.[12]

The Clerical attitude revolved around somewhat different issues. To understand the Clerical position, one must keep in mind their political program, which sought to unite Slovenes with Croats in a third basic administrative unit in the Empire. According to Slovene Clericals, trialism based on this Slovene-Croat combination would be founded on a very sturdy Roman Catholic base; furthermore, this Southern Slavic Catholic unit in Austria-Hungary would be the agent which ultimately would convert the Orthodox Yugoslavs outside the Empire to Roman Catholicism and thereby fulfill Austria's civilizing mission in the Balkans. Anxious to work with the Croats because of their common religious affiliation, the Slovene Clericals acknowledged both physical and cultural brotherhood with these Western-oriented Southern Slavs. The same was not true of their feeling for the Orthodox Serbs.

Indeed, the religious factor played a key role in the development of the Clerical attitude. The Clericals would agree with Prepeluh that Western Catholic and Byzantine Orthodox cultural heritages divided the Southern Slavs and prevented close cultural connections. But they were not content to permit these two cultures to develop separately, as Prepeluh and the Masarykites proposed. For the Clericals Roman Catholicism was the rightful orientation of the Slavs, and they were anxious to correct the falterings of their wayward Orthodox brethren. To the Clericals Western culture as determined by Western Christianity was clearly superior; the religion of the Orthodox Slavs, merely one of external observances.[13] On the other hand to the Croats the Clericals attributed deep and genuine religious sentiment as products of a higher Western culture.

For the Clericals language was not the critical determining factor of culture, as it was for the Social Democrats and the Liberals. The Clerical leaders felt that use of Serbo-Croat as the official language of a trialistic Yugoslav unit in the Empire was perhaps a necessity. Toward this end they urged Slovenes to begin learning the Serbo-Croat language, arguing that, "Now we call ourselves Slovenes, sons of a small Slovene nation. Then we would say: we are sons of a great Slav nation (be it called by one name or another.)"[14] The Clericals did not regret the possible extinction of the Slovene language; since in their view the Slovene expressed himself less through language than through his religion. They regarded their task as the preservation of Western culture; they did not consider that assimilating to the Croats linguisitically constituted any betrayal of Slovene culture.

The solution to the cultural problem, according to the Clericals, would come with the triumph of what they called "Christian nationalism."[15] They tended to consider other forms of nationalism (that is, nationalism based on language units) as essentially immoral. For this reason the Slovene Clericals spent a good deal of time trying to convince Austro-German Christian Socialists of the merits of Christian, i.e., Roman Catholic, unity. Since the time of Mahnič in the 1890's Slovene Clericals had been promoting closer Austrian Catholic cooperation. They even favored the strengthening of German-Slav cultural ties on this Catholic basis. This idea of Christian nationalism was to apply to all Austrian Catholics, who were to fulfill Austria's *raison d'être*, which was the maintenance and expansion of civilization in Central Europe.[16] However, propaganda for a great Austrian Catholic community failed to rally the Austro-German Catholics. In fact the Slovene Clericals met with outright resistance from the Austro-German Socialists who in 1910 at Innsbruck held a Catholic Congress to which the Slovene Christian Socialists were not even invited.[17] This forced the Slovene Clericals to concentrate more and more on trialism and on accommodating the Croat Rightists.

Meanwhile the Slovene Liberals had not discarded their Panslav dreams of an All-Slav state sharing a common culture. In 1908, exactly sixty years after the first Slav Congress, there was a general revival of Panslav sentiment in Eastern Europe, which manifested itself in literature and in a profusion of conferences. Renewed enthusiasm for the Great-Slav idea was brought about by what appeared a softening of Russia's policy toward the Poles. Indeed, some believed that the Poles in Russia would be granted autonomy.[18] The Slovene Liberals, who envisioned for the future an All-Slav federation based on equality among Slav nations, had felt that past Polish-Russian antagonisms were a major obstacle to the realization of Panslavic aspirations. But the situation in 1908 was full of promise; the Pole Dmowski, leader of the National Democrats, even agreed to participate in an All-Slav Congress at Prague. The Slovene Liberals rallied to the conference hoping for great things, only to see this spirit of Russo-Polish reconciliation virtually destroyed just one year later when the Tsarist government embarked again upon an anti-Polish policy. Nevertheless Neo-Slavism[19] in 1908 was not quickly extinguished, especially among the Austro-Slavs who subsequently participated in the St. Petersburg and Sofia conferences in 1909 and 1910. Russian autocracy was certainly not compatible with their program, but the Slovene Liberals did not abandon their Panslav reveries; they merely resolved to avoid political questions, and concentrated on fostering cultural and economic cooperation.

All through 1910, the year in which the Sofia conference was held, the Liberal paper *Slovenski narod*[20] enthusiastically promoted Slav unity. The Liberals supported the resolutions of the Sofia conference, encouraging cultural exchanges among Slav nations. Libraries would exchange Slav books and manuscripts; all Slav *belles-lettres* would be translated and published in other Slav languages; copies of books in one Slav language would be sent to libraries in other Slav states free of charge; and an exchange of professors would begin. Such contacts would prepare the Slovenes for a future state in which all Slav cultures and languages would be merged. However, the Slovene Liberals envisioned a very gradual development toward this end, and since Austro-Hungarian relations with Russia had deteriorated seriously since the Bosnian annexation, it appeared that the process would be an even slower one than imagined. For the present the Liberals proposed to concentrate on nurturing Slav unity in areas contiguous to Slovenia. They were anxious to implement this program first with Austria and then extend it to the Balkans. This meant that Austro-Slavs would commence study of one another's languages and cultures; similarly Southern Slavs, whether within or outside the Empire, would become familiar with the cultures and languages of their closest brethren. The Liberals believed that this would bring about the gradual merging of languages, and hence the merging of cultures.

According to the Liberals, the Slovenes would merge first with those Slavs most closely related to them, that is, with the Southern Slavs, and then with the others, until in the end all Slavs would merge with the Russians. Since they felt this would be a very gradual process, the Liberals did not insist upon the immediate adoption of a common language. Indeed, until some sort of Slav political union was effected, the Liberals advocated the maintenance of Slovene culture for the Slovenes, while promoting familiarization with other Slav cultures and tongues. After 1908 a growing emphasis was placed on developing cultural ties in this manner with the Balkan Slavs.

The rank and file of the Slovene Liberal party adhered to this Neo-Slav ideal and pursued a leisurely policy of promoting awareness of other Slav cultures. Hribar formulated this gradualist policy in an era when it was becoming increasingly more urgent to prepare a realistic political program. In fact, the more urgent the situation became, the further it seemed that Liberal leaders retreated into their dreams of Panslavism. As late as 1913, as mentioned earlier, Hribar could experience ecstacies at hearing the Russian language.[21]

The Slovene Liberal Youth of the National Radical Youth (*Narodno radikalno dijastvo*)[22] who espoused the party's ideals of political liberalism and in general its cultural Panslavism, differed from the Liberal party leadership on points of emphasis.[23] They did not dream of union with Russia, as did Hribar; few had contacts with the Eastern Slavs. Their journal *Omladina* (Youth)[24] represented from 1904 to 1914 the new generation whose outlook had been shaped by the turmoil brewing in the Balkans. Magyar oppression of Croats in Transleithia, the Bosnian crisis, the Zagreb treason trials and the Friedjung affair were accepted by them as problems common to all Yugoslavs. Because of this ferment in the South, the Liberal youth became increasingly convinced of the need for Yugoslav solidarity "from Triglav to Salonika and from the Adriatic to the Black Sea,"[25] and they focussed their attention almost exclusively on the Southern Slavs. At a congress in Ljubljana in 1909 the *Omladina* group resolved to devote all their effort to the Yugoslav question, that is, to the cultural aspect of it; and they proposed to invite liberally-oriented Croat and Serb scholars to collaborate with them in working toward Yugoslav cultural solidarity. As a group, however, the Liberal youth were not more effective than their elders; they too believed in a gradual merging of Slav languages and cultures (in this case South Slavic). However, whereas *Omladina* was perceptive enough to realize that concentration on the Yugoslav question should have priority over the broader, less defined Neo-Slavism of the Liberals, most young Liberals were not astute enough to perceive that their concepts of linguistic and cultural evolution were equally vague and indecisive. Like their elders they tended to ignore those political problems, which in 1914 brought the Yugoslav question to a point of crisis.

The battle over whether the Yugoslavs should unite culturally and linguistically was not fought exclusively by political parties, nor were the official party organs the sole media for communicating views on the subject. The real Illyrists were not prominent party people, just as many of the defenders of a separate Slovene culture had no party allegiances. Both were often intellectuals involved in literary activities, and by aligning themselves either for or against Neo-Illyrism, they revived the old controversy of Prešeren and Vraz.

The original Vraz-Prešeren debate[26] raged during the 1830's when Stanko Vraz accepted *štokavian* Croat as the Illyrian (Yugoslav) language and used it in his writings. Vraz and Prešeren both felt the real enemy was Germanization, exacting a heavy toll among Slovene townsmen and intellectuals. Vraz believed (as did the twentieth century Neo-Illyrists) that the Slovenes' only hope for survival was to unite linguistically with other Yugoslavs in order to create a larger cultural unit—one which would be potentially powerful politically. Prešeren disagreed, maintaining that Slovene intellectuals were Germanized because the Slovene language itself was not sufficiently developed to meet the challenge of an urban civilization. Therefore he proposed the language be modernized. To Prešeren the Slovenes were an independent nation in their own right, not merely a branch of a Yugoslav family; adopting a foreign language, no matter how similar to Slovene, would signify surrender and invite annihilation. According to Prešeren, it was a simple matter: the Slovenes without the Slovene language would no longer be Slovenes.

At the beginning of the twentieth century Illyrism revived the Vraz argument for cultural and linguistic amalgamation of all Yugoslavs. The Neo-Illyrists believed that all Southern Slavs really constituted one nation (Illyria), which had become divided and had developed separate cultures through no fault of its own. It was the contention of the Neo-Illyrists that the four branches of this Yugoslav nation (Slovene, Croat, Serb, and Bulgar) should be reunited culturally, and that this would prepare the way for political unification. But political unification was not their major concern. They were primarily interested in linguistic unity, with or without political union.[27]

The most prominent Illyrist was Dr. Fran Ilešič,[28] president of the *Slovenska Matica*,[29] who held that the Slovenes' only chance for survival lay in accepting a common literary language with other Southern Slavs. The language which the Illyrists, including Ilešič, had in mind was the *Štokavian* dialect, which Serbs and some Croats had in common; for the Slovenes not to accept it as their literary language would be unnatural and reactionary Ilešič contended. He maintained that the Slovene literary language was already developing quite naturally in that direction. To speed up the process, as the Illyrists proposed, would not bring about an artificial union of peoples and languages; it would, on the contrary, tend to right the wrong which history had dealt the Southern Slavs by causing the initial separation. Ilešič commended the Slovene Clericals for their cooperation with the Croats on this cultural level, and reprimanded those who might still be learning German for not moving with the spirit of the times.

Perhaps the strongest protest against Neo-Illyrism came from Mihajlo Rostohar,[30] a product of the National Radical Youth (Liberal youth) generation of the turn of the century. Rostohar was one of those who had been educated in Prague, had taught in Prague, and was strongly influenced by Masaryk. He returned believing that the Southern Slavs should be united politically, but he was opposed to achieving this at the price of cultural assimilation. For several years Rostohar was on the editorial staff of *Veda* (Knowledge), a literary journal which preoccupied itself, particularly after the Balkan wars, with the Southern Slav problem. Rostohar broke with *Veda* during a controversy over Austro-Serb relations in 1912 at which time he created a journal of his own entitled *Napredna misel* (Progressive Thought). It lasted until 1914.

Rostohar's chief target in *Napredna misel* was Neo-Illyrism, and he repeatedly warned against expecting miracles from it.

> For Yugoslavism we are prepared to become cultural and political victims. We must calm our youth . . . and make them realize that in addition to Yugoslav nationalism there are also Slovene national interests, which often are not identical with Yugoslav interests.[31]

Rostohar reprimanded the Social Democrats and the Clericals for their promotion of Yugoslav cultural unity, and argued that their ideal of Slovene, Croat, and Serb brotherhood lacked historical foundation. Moreover, he accused them of neglecting to consider the consequences of "Yugoslav unity:" it meant that Slovenes would cease to exist. Rostohar regarded as ridiculous the notion that one could exchange nationality as one would change clothing, for one's nationality was a part of one's psychological make-up.[32] According to Rostohar, the Neo-Illyrists were forcing the Slovenes to choose between Germanization and Croatization or Serbization. The result, he maintained, would be the same, just as a man would be equally dead if a wolf devoured him, or if a tiger tore him to bits, or if another person, for instance his own brother, killed him.[33]

Rostohar commended Slovenes of the Prešeren persuasion as optimistic and truly devoted nationalists determined to preserve Slovene national identity. He accused Vraz and his twentieth century counterparts, the Neo-Illyrists, of national fatalism, pointing out that the Slovenes and Slovene culture had gained nothing from the fact that Vraz became an Illyrist and wrote in Štokavian. "Illyrism for the Slovenes can only mean national suicide."[34] The organization *Preporod*, a radical student group which advocated an independent state for Yugoslavs, and seemed to favor cultural and linguistic conformity,[35] was for Rostohar a sad example of national pessimism. For him *Preporod*'s attitude was particularly depressing, because it indicated that Slovene youth preferred to assimilate culturally rather than undertake the formidable but necessary task of preserving Slovene national identity. Rostohar pleaded with cultural Illyrists of all political temperaments to discard their plans for linguistic assimilation; he pleaded with them to promote Slovene self-awareness, especially in the schools, in preparation for the establishment of Slovene national and cultural autonomy.

In 1911 when *Veda*, the new Slovene literary journal, first appeared its staff included many Masaryk liberals. Some of them had contributed to

Naši zapiski until it was virtually taken over by Social Democrats. *Veda* itself became a haven for politically non-oriented intellectuals, who were primarily concerned with enlightening the Slovenes on various, particularly cultural, facets of the Southern Slav question. Ivan Prijatelj, a cultural historian, and Bogomil Vošnjak, a Slovene linguist connected with the University of Zagreb, were prominent on the editorial board. After Rostohar left *Veda*, Vladimir Knaflič[36] was the most prominent figure on the journal's staff, and carried on a prolonged journalistic duel with Rostohar over Austrian foreign policy. With respect to the Yugoslav cultural question most Vedists believed that the various languages of the Southern Slavs were growing nearer each other and that the differences would eventually be minimal. However, Vedists were not agreed about the pace and direction of the changes. Furthermore they could not agree upon a course of action, or indeed upon whether any action should even be taken.

During 1911 and 1912 Vošnjak, Prijatelj, Knaflič and Rostohar debated the issue. Knaflič and Rostohar held similar views in opposition to Neo-Illyrism. Neither denied that the Southern Slavs were growing closer linguistically, but both rejected suggestions for expediting the process before or after the completion of political union. They feared most of all that the creation of a Yugoslav culture would be attained at the expense of Slovene interests, for Illyrists were encouraging Slovenes to learn Serbo-Croat, to learn the Cyrillic alphabet, and to familiarize themselves in general with other Southern Slav cultures. But Rostohar and Knaflič knew the Serbs and Croats were doing little if anything to promote study of the Slovene language and culture in their respective territories. Most Slovene Masarykites wanted no part of such a one-sided arrangement. Until a program for Yugoslav cultural solidarity was founded on equality and mutual respect, they would have the Slovenes concentrate on Slovene culture.

Prijatelj and Vošnjak had fewer fears on this score, though they both rejected one-sided sacrifices for the Yugoslav cause. Prijatelj began an article on Illyrism (*Naši zapiski*, 1910), with a quotation which the Slovene writer Jurčič had inscribed in a visitor's book in the home (then a museum) of Stanko Vraz. Jurčič wrote: "You are great, Stanko, for you opened the door to the future for us, but if all Slovene writers followed your example, Slovenes would no longer exist."[37] Prijatelj felt that Vraz and the Neo-Illyrists were using the wrong approach in elevating everything Croat. He emphasized the need for reciprocity, and felt that the Slovenes, whom he considered the most moderate of Yugoslavs, should take the lead in promoting this cooperative and reciprocal effort. Never convinced that the adoption of Illyrism required the submergence of Slovene culture, Prijatelj believed, on the contrary, that the Slovene language stood a very good chance of surviving essentially intact in spite of competition from Serbo-Croat. Vošnjak, too, had few misgivings over Illyrism, but for different reasons. He was *Veda*'s most avid campaigner for a Yugoslav cultural merging, and was eager to see linguistic unification implemented as soon as possible. He was anxious to find a "natural" means for bringing the Slovene language closer to Serbo-Croat,[38] but he was less concerned than most over the possible displacement of Slovene culture. Indeed, Vošnjak felt that the new Yugoslav (basically Serbo-Croat) language, of which Slovene would be a part, would more than compensate for the losses, for it would symbolize the reunification of long-separated brethren, and give them the strength needed to pursue a common future.

In 1913 *Veda* opened these Yugoslav cultural debates to the interested public, that is, to prominent Slovene, Southern Slav and other Habsburg Slav politicians and linguists. A lengthy questionnaire was composed for participants; the most critical questions were the following:

> Is it desirable that the Slovene language develop completely independently of the Croat language?
> Is it desirable that the Slovenes completely abandon their language?[39]

If the answer to the latter was "yes," or to the former "no," it was clear that the person favored some form of cultural Illyrism or Yugoslav cultural cooperation. The next question was logically:

> Do you feel that linguistic merging and ultimate linguistic unification should be effected before or after constitutional political changes?[40]

No one advocated total abandonment of the Slovene language apart from several of the Croat and Czech participants, who encouraged the adoption of Serbo-Croat in the interests of unity; they did think, however, that Slovene could be used privately. No Slovene called for the adoption of another language by the Slovenes. However, Ivo Šorli, the writer,[41] maintained that a choice between Slovene and Croat would have to be made by Slovenes, since, as he saw it, Slovene national individuality was not recognized by Croats. Consequently, Šorli went on, the decision which Slovenes had to make was whether or not they wished to become Croats, and this decision would then determine both the political and cultural future of the Slovenes.[42] Other reactions among the thirty-two respondents to the questionnaire were considerably less extreme.

Most who answered the *Veda* questionnaire agreed that the Southern Slavs should first rid their languages of non-Slavic elements. Slovenes, they believed, must therefore remove all Germanisms from their language, since Pan-Germanism for many constituted a mortal threat to Slavdom. Moreover, many felt that an initial purging of non-Slavic elements from South

Slav languages might be followed by the acceptance of common scientific and technical terminology, particularly in areas of technology which had not yet been developed in the Balkans. They believed this type of linguistic programming could easily be implemented.

Ivan Hribar in his reply confirmed the need for a common technical terminology. As mayor of Ljubljana he was aware that the town council had employed a Czech technician since 1882 to supply them with "missing" words for technological innovations (e.g., drainage, electricity).[43] Since the Slovenes had already been using other Slavic words, Hribar saw no reason why Southern Slavs in the future could not all employ the same technological terms. He went on to suggest that in the future Southern Slavs use one language for all technical and scientific writing. He felt that, in particular, the Slovenes as a small nation could not bear the burden of keeping up with all specialized literature, if only because cost of publication and translation would be totally out of proportion with the nation's size and financial capacity. Hribar personally felt that eventually and quite naturally the Slovenes would give up their language for Croat.[44]

Most Slovenes who answered the questionnaire were willing to accept this particular development, at least as far as it applied to Southern Slavs. Most had no objections to the adoption of common technological terminology; however, concurrence of opinion ended here. From this point on there were almost as many proposed plans for Yugoslav cultural cooperation as there were participants in the *Veda* questionnaire. Basically, most approved of programmed elimination of linguistic differences, but they disagreed over the number of areas to be effected by linguistic planning. Some were content to restrict language reform to science and technology; others would have extended it to other areas as well, though even the most far-reaching programs stopped just short of total linguistic assimilation. Final cultural unity would be achieved perhaps sometime after political union had been realized, but they saw no need to blueprint every detail of a plan for Yugoslav cultural cooperation. Natural development would determine much of the process. What was important was that Southern Slavs begin eliminating language and cultural differences immediately; this would facilitate political unification, and once a Yugoslav state existed, cultural developments would seek their own natural level. This was the general concensus of the *Veda* questionnaire.

Illyrists and Slovene Masarykites also participated in the questionnaire. using *Veda* as a vehicle to pursue the old Vraz-Prešeren debate. They both differed from the consensus presented above, but the difference again was only of degree. Illyrists put a premium on linguistic assimilation, but they emphasized achieving it along scientifically determined lines of natural development. The Masarykites stressed the refinement of things Slovene. But they did not totally eliminate the possibility of South Slav cultural union. They would not hasten the process, but would leave it to natural evolution. Illyrists and Masarykites often represented the two extremes of the cultural controversy.

Confronted with the many views on this language question, it is almost impossible to generalize. However, if the political factor is taken into consideration the task becomes much simpler. Ilešič, Vošnjak, others of Illyrist persuasion, and many Croat and Serb participants called for the immediate adoption of a common Croat or Serb language for official purposes, that is, for all communications written or oral among Yugoslavs and for all literature except *belles-lettres* but especially for science and technology. This the Illyrists believed was the first goal, that is, that linguistic unity must *precede* political union.[45] The Masarykites represented the other extreme, placing political union first and relegating cultural cooperation to the realm of the incidental should natural development take that particular course after the Yugoslavs had been brought together in one state. In *Veda* as elsewhere the Masarykites insisted that a common language and culture were not essential for a political unit, much less a prerequisite for political union. Artificial cultural unification, they submitted, might even weaken the political bonds of the state. Those who were neither Illyrists nor Masarykites, as we have seen, felt it beneficial to begin the linguistic work before political union and to complete it afterward. Few could envision a Yugoslav state where no linguistic assimilation took place, and most believed that one day there would exist only one Yugoslav language and one Yugoslav culture.

Reaction to the *Veda* questionnaire was on the whole favorable. The Clericals and the Liberals officially approved the general conclusions of the participants, and pledged support for the goals of cultural unity. The Clerical Ušeničnik,[46] true to Clerical ideals, suggested that linguistic assimilation would be most easily achieved between the Slovenes and the Croats, who already shared a common heritage. Illyrism, wrote Ušeničnik, should therefore initiate its cultural program among Western-oriented Southern Slavs, who would then extend their culture southward. The Liberal party also approved of Yugoslav cultural union, but in a rather conciliatory fashion. They considered the alternatives—Rostohar or Ilešič, Slovene individualsim or Yugoslav solidarity—and concluded that the first was more honorable but that the Slovenes probably did not have the strength to maintain it.[47] The Liberals, moreover, chastised those who opposed political union on the grounds that the elimination of Slovene culture would be too high a price. The Southern Slav language with the most spirit and force would prevail, and if Slovene culture lost out, Slovenes in the long run would be gaining in strength by having accommodated themselves to the stronger force.

All parties, including the Social Democrats, who were already on record (at Tivoli) as standing for a "Yugoslav" culture, promoted a program for the cultural and linguistic union of Southern Slavs. The youth organizations, *Preporod, Omladina*, and the National Catholic Youth sponsored lectures in other Yugoslav tongues; they traveled to the Balkans; they invited Serb, Croat and Bulgar students to Slovenia and provided complimentary housing for them. Yugoslavs exchanged professors; and Slovene students enrolled at Zagreb University (which Illyrists proposed as a center for Slovene-Croat cultural activity). Slovenes studied the Croat and Serb languages and cultures. Some sent volunteers, military and medical, to the Balkan wars to help liberate their Yugoslav brethren from Ottoman oppression. But the movement lacked real organization and direction; and before the world war it had very little time to accomplish anything. Moreover, only a handful of scholars, students, and individual political leaders, who constituted a minute segment of a small and relatively backward nation, participated in this movement for Yugoslav cultural cooperation. They were confronted with inertia among other Southern Slavs, who responded apathetically to Slovene "Yugoslav" ideals unless they involved rejection of the Slovene language; and among Slovenes, too, they met with formidable opposition from the Masarykites, who stood essentially alone, but uncompromisingly, for the preservation of Slovene individualism.[48] Furthermore, where cultural ideals united them, political differences left them at odds.

World War I began before the Slovenes and the Southern Slavs achieved any real accord among themselves as to whether cultural Illyrism was desirable, and if so, how it should be implemented. The war also made obsolete all Slovene political programs to unite South Slavs under Austrian leadership. After 1914 the urgency of the war situation captured Slovene attentions, and the issue of cultural Yugoslavism paled into the background. Yugoslav political unity was achieved as a result of the war, but outside Austria—something few Slovenes would have predicted in 1914. And political unification was accomplished without cultural and linguistic assimilation. Cultural Yugoslavism was not effected before or during the war. The war made it quite clear that Yugoslav political unity was not dependent on cultural unity, for a South Slav state had been created without previous linguistic and cultural assimilation. But many continued to promote Illyrist goals on the grounds that they were natural, practical, and would fortify the state. The issue, in fact, has never really been resolved; the setting is different, but the language debate still continues.

CHAPTER VIII

THE BALKAN WARS, 1912-1913:
THE COMMITMENT TO AUSTRIA QUESTIONED

In 1908 and 1909 Slovene politicians were startled by what appeared to be a deliberate anti-Southern Slav policy on Vienna's part. The shooting in Ljubljana of two young Slovenes in September 1908 made many question the regime's intentions. The annexation crisis and the treason trials seemed further to confirm Vienna's hostility. As Austrian policy unfolded it struck Slovene party leaders that not only the Magyars, but Vienna, too, was the enemy. When, toward the end of 1909, tension subsided somewhat, Slovenes were relieved. Yet a real sense of security was never completely restored. The international crisis passed, Slovene nationalists and politicians retreated to the philosophical realm, to debates involving issues of language and culture, as if to make up for their inadequacies in the world of power politics. But reality was soon upon them again. The Balkan Wars of 1912 and 1913 forced them to come to grips with fundamental issues.

The new crisis in the Balkans, just four years after the Bosnian annexation, was created largely by big power maneuvering. Austro-Russian rivalry for control of Balkan lands was at the heart of it. Indeed the new crisis can be traced to the earlier one, for as soon as the Bosnian affair cooled, Russia began plotting her revenge. To this end the Tsarist government actively urged the Balkan states to form an alliance, specifically to check Austrian advances in South Eastern Europe. But Russia had difficulties implementing such a policy; the Balkan states, particularly Bulgaria, seemed more inclined to cooperate against the Ottoman Empire than against Austria.[1] In the spring of 1912 it appeared briefly that the Russians had been successful in their endeavors. Serbia and Bulgaria concluded a Russian-sponsored defensive alliance in March of 1912; Greece and Bulgaria signed a similar pact in May. In both these agreements the partners pledged support to one another if either were attacked. In the former Serbia and Bulgaria vowed also to defend Balkan territory still under Turkish suzerainty from occupation by any great power, notably Austria.[2] The drafting of a Greek-Bulgarian compact, however, had not been supervised by Russia and was fundamentally anti-Turkish in intent, indicating a basic variance with Russian plans for the area. This anti-Ottoman orientation was strengthened by Montenegro in September and early October, when she concluded agreements with Bulgaria and Serbia. At this time Montenegro pledged to attack the Turks, the Bulgarians agreed to join in before one month of warfare had elapsed, and Serbia presumably assented to a similar arrangement.[3] Clearly the Russians had lost control of the Balkan League which originally had been conceived as anti-Austrian in nature. Subsequently both Austria and Russia became alarmed by the probability of war in the Balkans, and together with France, Germany and Great Britain warned members of the Balkan League that should they acquire any Turkish territory through warfare they would not be permitted to keep it. The warning came too late; that same day, 8 October 1912, Montenegro declared war against the Turks.

The First Balkan War lasted hardly six months; war was declared in October and an armistice was signed in April. The Balkan League comprising Bulgar, Serb, Greek and Montenegrin forces dealt swiftly with the Turk, taking all European Turkish territories except four cities (Constantinople, Adrianople, Yanina, and Scutari) by December of 1912. In April when the truce came the Turks held only Constantinople. By the Treaty of London in the following month the Ottomans barely maintained a foothold on the European continent, retaining only that territory which lay east of the Enez-Midye Line. Other former European Turkish possessions, with the exception of Albanian territory whose fate would be determined by the major powers of Europe, were to be divided between the victors at a Paris conference.[4]

While the various alliances which culminated in the Balkan League were being formed, even after actual hostilities had broken out, Austria-Hungary, it seemed, had no clear policy.[5] Granted for many years Austria had had an interest in the Balkans, but because Magyars and Germans were ever wary of incorporating more Slavs into the Empire, the regime resisted temptations to annex choice segments of the Southern Slav Balkans.[6] Essentially, Austrian Balkan policy in 1912 was preventive. Sensitive to Russian inroads into South Eastern Europe, Austria firmly opposed the strengthening of any Slavic state in the area, lest that state yield to Russian pressures. When the war began Austria believed that it would be a lengthy one, that the Turks would put up a good fight. She was alarmed by the swift victories of the Balkan League and scurried to formulate a decisive policy. In her haste to evaluate and react to Balkan developments, Austrian fears focussed on Serbia. Military victory could only enlarge Serbia, Russia's protegé, thereby fortifying the Russian position in the Balkans. Austria's reaction therefore was to attempt to thwart Serbian expansion. To this end she promoted the enlargement of Bulgaria and became the champion of Albanian independence.

Of the three Slovene political parties only the Socialist denounced the First Balkan War. For that party it was a war provoked by imperialistic interests. The Balkan League itself was regarded by Socialists as a tool of the Tsar—a component of a greater Tsarist Russian plot.[7] Socialists accused Russia of malevolent intent toward the Balkan peoples, not unlike the attitude she had revealed in dealing with the Poles. Slovene Socialists expected the war would divide the Balkan masses in spite of the fact these peoples, united by a common mission, would eventually bring social revolution to the area. Furthermore Socialists suspected Russia's precise wish was to set the peoples of the Balkans against each other.[8]

Though the Slovene Socialists directed the brunt of their attack at Russia, they did not find Austria entirely blameless. Austria had after all made vital inroads into the Balkans and had frequently pressed claims to the Sanjak. That she was not the immediate villain in October 1912 merely meant to Socialists that the Russians had beaten Austria to the punch. Therefore within days of the war's outbreak, the Socialist paper warned Austria to keep her "hands off the Balkan War." "We want peace [as do the people of the Balkans]; leave the Balkans to the Balkan nations."[9] The Slovene Socialists throughout the war continued their admonitions to Russia, but especially to Austria, and appealed to the peoples of the Empire for peace.

Unlike the Socialists, both the Slovene Clericals and the Liberals welcomed the war. Both believed it to be the long-awaited war of liberation. The Clericals hailed it as a battle to free the Christian provinces of Turkey, a struggle for the victory of "European Christian culture."[10] Liberals on the other hand, regarded the war primarily as one for national independence. "Our brothers by birth and language," wrote the Liberal daily, "are going to war against an age-old enemy in order to win for themselves and their long-suffering brethren freedom. . . . Our fraternal sympathy is with these Yugoslav heroes in their battle."[11] Because the victories of the Balkan League were resounding, both Clerical and Liberal journalistic coverage was enthusiastic, depicting the successes of the League as conducive to their own respective objectives.

At the outset of the conflict Slovene Clericals urged Austria to assume leadership of the League. They felt the war afforded Austria a unique opportunity.[12] The war for the Clericals was simply the last in the series of Christian wars against the infidel, wars in which Austria in the past had realized her true purpose and mission as the defender of Western Christianity. This time, they were convinced, the Turk would be driven from Europe for good; and it was fitting that Austria deal the decisive blow. What's more, it was a chance for Austria to be renewed; the war could make Austria great again.[13]

The Clericals were disappointed in Austria's failure to seize the initiative. They observed, moreover, that the Balkan Slavs, for lack of Austrian aid felt compelled to turn to Russia for assistance. For Slovene Clericals this development was the ultimate disaster, for it meant that Orthodoxy would surely triumph by default.[14] As a consequence *Slovenec* the Clerical daily became increasingly critical of Austrian policy.

Liberals criticized Austria, too, but not because Austria declined to lead the battle. On the contrary, Liberals were anxious to keep Austria out of the fray. Slovene Liberals, for whom the ultimate enemy was Germandom,[15] had been feeling uneasy about Vienna, particularly since the Bosnian annexation. Believing that the Empire's policies were imposed by Berlin, that the Triple Alliance was a German conspiracy against Slavdom, the Liberals shuddered at the possibility of Austrian, therefore German, meddling in the Balkans.[16] Slovene Liberals preferred instead that the Balkan peoples liberate themselves. The common effort would instill in them pride and a sense of brotherhood; it would prepare them for federalism when the war ended.

At the same time both Liberals and Clericals urged Austria to extend autonomy to her Southern Slavs, or federalism to the whole Empire.[17] To complement the war of liberation in the South, they believed Austria needed to improve the lot of her own South Slavs. Liberals, for example, feared that if Austria continued to be indifferent toward Yugoslavs of the Empire, these would be drawn toward the Balkans, where after the war peoples would live in federal harmony.[18] Liberals and Clericals[19] hoped Austria would rise to the occasion; even the Social Democrats still regarded an Austrian state essential to Central Europe. Liberals confirmed their loyalty to Austria even during the final moments of that First Balkan War. In mid-April 1913 the National Progressive Party executive committee issued an official statement, assuring the regime that profound longing for Yugoslav cultural and political unity would never cause them to abandon the Empire. They urged Vienna to acknowledge that South Slavs could become the very backbone of Austria. Friendship with the Balkan Slavs was therefore imperative.[20] Clericals formulated much the same Balkan policy but with emphasis on the mission of Western Christendom.[21]

The Albanian issue caused the gravest concern, for Austria, in her shock at the Balkan League's rapid victories, judged that Serbia must because of her ties to Russia be denied any important territorial gain, particularly if it afforded her access to the sea. Consequently Vienna, deaf to her own peoples' appeals for national autonomy, championed Albanian independence, an action ostensibly in accord with the principle of "the Balkans for the Balkan peoples."[22] The regime found considerable support for its anti-Serb policy; some it appears even harkened to the militarism of Austria's chief of staff Conrad von Hötzendorf.[23] But, with little exception, Slovene political parties viewed this development as hypocritical, and they trembled at the probable consequences.

No Slovene party officially approved Austria's Albanian policy. Liberals regarded the development as typically German-inspired and anti-Slavic; indeed they had not expected much more from Vienna.[24] Social Democrats said that they rather approved of independence for Albanians, maintaining cynically that they were rather inclined toward the principle of popular autonomy, especially if it were extended to Austria.[25] But they reprinted articles, written by the Austrian Socialist Otto Bauer, portraying Austria's activity on behalf of Albanian independence as imperialistic meddling. If Albanian independence was designed to crush Serbia—which Socialists believed it was—then it must be opposed, unless Serbia was accorded a corridor to the sea.[26] But Socialists, though they urged that Austria grant the Serbians access to the Adriatic, frankly did not believe that the empire's imperialistic drives could be reversed.

The Slovene Clerical attitude, until then officially most loyal to the regime, was especially interesting. The Slovene Peoples' Party opposed Austrian hostility to Serbia; it feared future relations between the two would be irreparably damaged. The Clericals promoted accord with Serbia, for they knew from diplomatic exchanges in the spring of 1913 that Serbia, in return for a corridor to the Adriatic, was willing to accept Albanian independence. The Czech philosophy professor, Masaryk, by now widely known for his role in the treason trials of 1909,[27] acted as intermediary in pressing Serbia's claims but to no avail.[28] Vienna was adamant. And her attitude created a real crisis in the Clerical camp.

Slovene Clericals, much as they feared a large Orthodox Serbian state which could appear like a Slavic Piedmont to the nationalistic tendencies of some Habsburg South Slavs, opposed a deliberate anti-Serb policy. "A Serbian Adriatic port cannot hurt us," Clericals wrote, "particularly if the monarchy is interested in maintaining friendly relations with Yugoslavs."[29] They feared that without such a corridor, Serbia would carve one through Bosnia, already a part of the Empire and therefore sheltered from Russian Orthodox pressures.[30] That Austria failed to comprehend this, Clericals felt, must surely be evidence of her fierce and irrational attitudes toward Serbia. Clericals themselves favored a Serbian corridor to the sea, and on several occasions they suggested Albanian territory be divided between Greece and Serbia, so that Albanians could benefit from the experiences of states more advanced, economically and culturally, than they.[31] Essentially Clericals could not understand the Empire's support of an independent Albania, too backward to be self-sufficient in any way, while at the same time the more advanced Habsburg Southern Slavs were summarily denied such an option.

It would seem from what has been said, that the Clericals were, like the Liberals and the Socialists, united in opposition to Austria's Balkan policy. *Slovenec*, the Clerical newspaper, certainly conveyed this impression. But *Slovenec* was dominated then by followers of Krek, and Krek had become a great Serbophile by the fall of 1912. Some would argue that Krek's view was so prevalent in *Slovenec* in those months, that accounts of Balkan campaigns read as if they had been written in Belgrade or Sofia.[32] On the other hand the Šušteršič faction of the party tended to back Vienna's foreign policy, though during the early months of the war this was not readily apparent. Krek and Šušteršič ultimately split over the Austrian handling of the Balkan situation, and it would seem, though the evidence is scanty, that the rift was already in the making in the fall of 1912. A factor which complicated matters for the Clericals was that the party had recently (October 1912) effected a merger with the Croat Party of Right.

The union of the Slovene People's Party with the Croat Party of Right had been in the offing for some time. Important contacts between the two had been made already in the last decade of the 19th century when Slovene Clericals accepted a part of the Rightist program.[33] Substantive plans in the direction of merging were initiated late in 1911 and in the early part of 1912. The Croat party had itself expanded in 1911, incorporating related regional Croat parties (Rightist and Christian Socalist); and shortly thereafter the Styrian Clerical leader Anton Korošec announced his support for the Croat Rightists. By mid-summer Slovene and Croat party leaders were meeting frequently, and Catholic youth from the two areas held a joint conference in August.[34] On 9 October 1912 it was concluded that union was advisable. Ninety members of the two parties then met in Ljubljana (20 October) to formalize the merger, creating the Croat-Slovene Party of Right. It was presided over by Mile Starčević and Ivan Šušteršič.[35]

By this merger Slovene Clericals accepted the idea of a "Croat-Slovene" nation.[36] Moreover, the Croat Rightist program became officially the program of Slovene Clericals as well.[37] Essentially, this meant Clericals were committed to a state rights position with respect to the realization of Trialism. An awkward arrangement to say the least, for although Croats had legitimate state rights claims to autonomy, the Slovenes did not.[38] The old Unified Slovenia program based on ethnic demands was offered by the Clericals as their contribution to the common program. Affixing this to the Croat Rightist program was a tricky operation, and it made legalists very uneasy.

Frankists, the most right wing element in the Croat party, were especially dubious and they regularly disrupted the sessions of the October 20 conference. It was largely Frankists who opposed including the name

"Serbs" in the resolution or even stipulating that trialism should be achieved within the monarchy. Their intention was to keep the particulars of the program deliberately vague, presumably so that Croats would not be restricted by any disadvantageous commitments either to the monarchy, to Transleithian Serbs, or, for that matter, to Slovenes.[39] They had weighty reasons for insisting on ambiguity. The Archduke Francis Ferdinand, who had been regularly associated with the idea of trialism, had never specified his intentions. Yet any astute politician could have comprehended that the heir to the throne was not interested in furthering South Slav solidarity in an Empire that would soon be his; he aimed rather at reducing Magyar strength. Removing Transleithian Croats from Magyar domination would further the Archduke's ends; joining Cisleithian Slovenes administratively to Transleithian Croats would not.[40] In general Frankists moreover acted haughtily toward the Serbs of the Empire who were not asked to the Ljubljana meeting, though they had expressed a strong interest in attending. They were not acknowledged as Serbs, for Frankists they were simply Orthodox Croats. Frankists also showed no inclination to regard Slovenes as equals, but rather exuded a marked "Great Croatism" which rubbed off to a certain degree on others in the Croat delegation.

Why then, given the reportedly heated debates and disagreements at the Ljubljana meeting in October, did Slovene Clericals pursue the party merger? It has been suggested that impressive political pressure, originating in the Archduke's circle in Vienna, can explain a great deal about the timing and nature of this party union. According to this interpretation Francis Ferdinand and his advisers sometime in 1910 conceived of building a Catholic rightist coalition to serve as a main support of the Archduke's power.[41] It was projected as anti-Magyar and in terms of foreign policy anti-Serbian—the ultimate purpose being to serve the Great Austrian idea through centralization at home and fortification of the Empire's position in the Balkans. Croat Rightists and Slovene Clericals would constitute logical components of such an alliance. Both were Catholic, conservative, anti-Magyar. Both moreover had broad popular backing among the Empire's Southern Slavs. Slovene Clericals, particularly Ivan Šušteršič, seem to have played a key role in bringing about this Slovene-Croat alignment. It has even been suggested that Šušteršič acted as the Archduke's contact with the Croat Rightists,[42] and that the unpublicized, but real, purpose of the Ljubljana meeting was to achieve a Croat-Slovene Clerical resolution condemning the Balkan League and its activities. If indeed the Archduke's circle had promoted the meeting, it must certainly have been disappointed by the results.[43]

Pro-Serb and pro-League sentiment among many Croat and Slovene Clericals was simply uncontainable. It has already been noted that the

Slovene priest Krek, whose faction determined the journalistic policy of the party organ *Slovenec*, was lyrical about the League's successes. He delighted at the defeat of the Turks and romanticized about an impending Yugoslav union of one people and one land, united by blood and one language. He probably envisioned a federation of both Habsburg and Balkan Southern Slavs, having observed at the time that even all Slovene rivers flowed not toward Vienna, but toward the Balkans.[44] Furthermore Krek tried to convince Austrian German politicians and businessmen that it was in Austria's interests to promote a customs union with Serbia and Bulgaria.[45] "Even for you Germans, there is a shiny future in the Balkans," Krek said to his colleagues in Parliament. "You'll be able to sell your goods everywhere; only you must not carry before you a banner reading German culture."[46] Such pro-Balkan sentiment among Slovenes and Croats was obviously not likely to produce resolutions at Ljubljana denouncing the Balkan League. In fact no specific support for the Empire's Balkan policy was expressed. Although there was a general statement of commitment to the monarchy, the conference made a point to remind Austria of *her* obligation to Southern Slavs.[47]

Participants in the Ljubljana conference were not united in motive. Croats fought each other over commitment to the monarchy, but reached agreement, without Slovene consent, to omit the term "Serbs" from the conference resolution. Among the Slovene Clericals there soon developed a divergence of views as regards the nature of the party program. After the Ljubljana meeting, in a running dialogue during the Balkan wars, this disparity grew, revealing ultimately that some Slovene Clericals were considerably more establishment-oriented than others. Though evidence is not plentiful it seems that the priest Krek, and even Korošec, conceived of trialism in essentially broad, perhaps even democratic, terms. They would have interpreted the particulars of the Ljubljana program very flexibly in order to welcome all who might wish to be included in a Habsburg "Yugoslavia." Krek observed that trialism could, through Croat state rights, be expanded to embrace even the states of Serbia and Montenegro.[48] This, it soon became apparent, was not Šušteršič's plan. His views were more compatible with those of the Croat Rightists—that is, clerical, socially conservative, and somewhat anti-Serb and anti-Orthodox. For him the purpose of trialism was to fortify the Habsburg Catholic power. His approach in other words resembled that of Francis Ferdinand—trialism was a principle to be instituted by the monarchy, not one which might assert itself from below.[49] Šušteršič's commitment to the monarchy—even its anti-Serb foreign policy— was very strong, a fact revealed during the First Balkan War, but particularly in the Second. "It is not *true* [underlining in original] " wrote Šušteršič in

Slovenec in December of 1912, that for Serbia territory on the Albanian coast is a matter of life or death. If because of this Serbia is willing to go to war against Austria, it would be all Serbia's fault . . . ."[50] Such a statement, not unlike those emanating regularly from the Imperial Foreign Office and Conrad's General Staff Headquarters, stands out for its blatant anti-Serbism—this at a time when the Balkan League and the war were very popular among Slovenes, including the Krek wing of Šušteršič's own party. The Second Balkan War widened the breach between Krek and Šušteršič and forced many former colleagues to a parting of the ways. Šušteršič in his support of the monarchy's anti-Serbian policy became a virtual Bulgarophile.[51]

Divisions among Slovene Clericals and disputes between Slovenes and Croats were not conducive to constructive activity. In fact the newly formed party's accomplishments were virtually nil, and the union was terminated in May 1914.[52] The Slovene Clericals, however, could find no alternative course to pursue in the pre-war period. They continued therefore to advocate trialism via the Rightist program adopted at Ljubljana. Throughout 1913 and 1914 they were stressing the logic of Slovene-Croat cooperation. Both people, they maintained, were united by a common historical experience. Most recently that experience was largely one of being the object of German, Magyar, and Serb hostility. In the case of the Germans and Magyars it took the form of regular economic exploitation, with the Slovenes and Croats deprived, for example, of gain from the lucrative tourist, commercial and transport enterprises along the Slavic Adriatic coast. Special reference in such arguments was always made, of course, to the ports of Trieste and Rijeka, which Slovenes and Croats felt belonged rightfully to them.[53] Slovene Clericals also emphasized that they shared with Croats a Western Christian culture; it was infinitely superior to and clearly distinguished from that of the Serbs. Orthodoxy, at the root of Serbian and Eastern civilization, was doctrinally erroneous, replete with Byzantine corruption and politically controlled by hated Russia.[54]

In all this Krek and Šušteršič did not differ substantially. Both urged Slovene-Croat cooperation; both cherished the Western tradition and remained loyal to Austria. But in working toward Slovene political ends Šušteršič put his trust in the regime, believing that the economic and cultural well-being of the Catholic South Slavs would be best nurtured by the monarchy. Krek, on the other hand, seemed to be losing faith in the system.[55] Unlike Šušteršič, he was eager for Austrian-Serbian friendship. He felt that Croat-Slovene cooperation should not aim at excluding Serbs and that trialism itself should serve to broaden rather than restrict the Yugoslav idea.

General European crises had since the mid-19th century made Slovenes anxious. Such periods of uncertainty had precipitated changes in their world view and altered their political allegiances. International disruptions generally evoked the question of Austria's viability as a state and confronted her peoples with the possibility of going their separate ways. That eventuality for Slovenes and other small nations was particularly frightening, given the realities of European politics, for the major states were turning confidently and competively to the pursuit of power and empire. Slovene spokesmen had for at least a century pleaded with Austria to help allay their concerns. Ever more frequently they were disappointed. The period of the Balkan Wars, coming so soon after the Bosnian crisis and revealing so explicitly Vienna's purpose, forced troubled Slovenes to rethink their relationship to Austria.

Slovene intellectuals, journalists, students and some others were abandoning any hope of accommodation with Vienna. Some even actively worked for the Empire's destruction after 1912-13.[56] But even Slovene politicians, who by virtue of their profession were committed in some way to the structure or the system, were given to reconsiderations. When the First Balkan War began it was immediately clear that neither the Slovene Socialists, who opposed the war, nor the Slovene Liberals, who supported it, trusted Vienna's motives. During the course of the debates within the new Croat-Slovene Party of Right, certain Slovene Clericals also came to view Vienna from a new perspective. Many Clerical youth deserted the party and joined the *Preporod* group which vowed destruction of the Empire and proposed an independent Yugoslavia.[57] And, as we have seen, the Krek wing of the party found it increasingly difficult during the First Balkan War to reconcile its loyalty to the regime with its enthusiasm for Serbia. Vienna's continued meddling, which helped bring about a second war in 1913, brought the questioning into still sharper focus.

The Second War, in the summer of 1913, was short; it lasted barely more than a month. It grew out of issues left unresolved by the first war. Because the Great Powers at the London Conference had insisted upon an Albania, cutting the Serbs off from the sea, Serbia, as one of the victors, began demanding compensation elsewhere. In so doing Serbia instantly clashed with Bulgaria, for the compensation the Serbs had in mind was a larger portion of Macedonia. Once the Serbs and Bulgars began to quarrel the Balkan League rapidly disintegrated as an anti-Turkish force. The Greeks soon clashed with the Bulgars over Salonika; and the Romanians, who had not even been members of the original League, demanded a part of Dobruja for having remained neutral in 1912. A new Balkan alliance which was decidedly anti-Bulgarian resulted; at its core was an agreement between the Serbs and the Greeks concluded on 1 June 1913.[58] Before a month had passed Bulgarians had attacked Serb and Greek forces in Macedonia. The latter two then formally declared war on Bulgaria, as did Montenegro, Romania, and even the Turks. Bulgaria was quickly defeated. By the Treaty of Bucharest signed on 10 August 1913[59] she was permitted to retain only a small portion of the Macedonian territory she had claimed after the first war. Serbia received north and central Macedonia; the Greeks got much of its coastal areas; Romania kept most of Dobruja; the Montenegrins extended their boundaries slightly; and the Turks soon thereafter (by the Treaty of Constantinople) regained much of Thrace.

Russia and Austria did much to precipitate the 1913 war. Russia for her part had sought to mediate the differences among League members, hoping thereby to gain their confidence. Austria on the other hand had done all in her power to damage the Serbs. The result was an embittered Bulgaria and the intensification of the rivalry between Austria and Russia.

For Slovene parties the 1913 war was traumatic. It divided former League allies; Serbs and Bulgars, both generally considered brethren by Habsburg South Slavs, had fought on opposite sides. The Šušteršič Clericals supported government policy and therefore chose to back the Bulgars, but others virtually without exception felt closer to and championed the Serbs. The Clerical daily called upon the belligerents to cease the fratricidal fighting;[60] and Slovene Liberals regularly attacked the Bulgarian Tsar Ferdinand in the late summer of 1913, suspecting that he had become an agent of Germandom and of Catholicism.[61] At the time, they proposed, as one might have predicted, a Liberal Neo-Slav alliance to fight official Austrian policy and clericalism as well.[62] But the cause of Neo-Slavism had little prospect of success in 1913; not only did the familiar problem of Poland remain, but now Serbs and Bulgars were at each others' throats. Social Democrats meanwhile for reasons of internationalism objected to this war as they had to the first, but certain individuals in the party, like Tuma and Cankar, became thereafter more nationalistic and more Serbophile.

That Austria encouraged Bulgaria (and Romania) against Serbia in 1913 added a second dimension to the Slovene trauma. Both Social Democrats and Liberals could blame no one but Vienna for the Balkan turmoil.[63] The Socialist Cankar ceased to advocate working within the system and explored the notion of Austria's destruction.[64] Tuma took the same line though more cautiously. The rest of the party, though with growing resistance from the Masarykites due to the language issue, remained committed to Austro-Marxism.[65] As late as June of 1914 the Socialist paper was still damning nationalist causes.[66] The Liberal Hribar seems to have gone through some manner of conversion in that summer of 1913. None of the Clerical elders, however, in spite of division over whom to support in the Balkans, ventured disloyalty. Krek, however, appears to have been very disillusioned with Austria's anti-Serbism; and even Ušeničnik who represented a very stable element in the party could lament that Austria had not taken her cue in 1912 to act as liberator of the Balkan Christians. "The half moon shines from above Hagia Sofia, and in the Balkans Orthdoxy is spreading steadily. Why hasn't Prince Eugene come to the rescue?"[67] Ušeničnik wrote in 1913. And thereafter his writing on the subject of Austria and the Balkans, of Western Christianity and Orthodoxy, took on an increasing urgency and reflected a mood of impending doom. He wrote: "The military conflagration in the Balkans has thrown a strange light on our times. Europe has shown her true colors."[68] For Ušeničnik the Russians were the real villains; nevertheless he could muster little praise for Austria, who instead of pursuing her traditional Christian mission, had embraced the cause of German culture. Ušeničnik charged that crude, materialistic and capitalistic interests were dictating European affairs; he implied, moreover, that Austria had partaken of this moral corruption and that the Austrian idea had been dangerously perverted.[69] When the war began in 1914 Ušeničnik reminded Čas readers of his earlier warnings and premonitions, stating that he hoped ardent nationalists would now be content when they saw what war accomplished: it destroyed civilizations.[70]

CHAPTER IX

STUDENTS AND INDEPENDENTS:
TOWARD A SOLUTION OUTSIDE AUSTRIA*

The Slovene parties remained, then, despite misgivings, committed in one way or another, to "Austria." Few party adherents believed in the possibility of, least of all openly preached, any open break. However, from 1912 onward, outside the established parties and especially among younger people who found official liberal and Socialist doctrines unattractive, there was a growing protest against the ties with Austria. The largest and most active of the anti-Austrian groups was composed of middle school students. They sought to separate themselves from traditional labels and from conventional political forms. They were called Preporodovci after the name of their paper *Preporod* (or Renaissance).[1]

The actual establishment of this revolutionary middle school student organization can be dated precisely. On the 13th of January 1912 at 4 o'clock in the afternoon in a solemn, almost sinister, ceremony, the founding members swore loyalty to the death in the fight for the Yugoslav idea.[2] They took their oaths in a darkened room with a single candle, circled about a table covered with a black cloth on which lay a revolver and the by-laws of the organization.[3] Only eighteen were present at this founding meeting in Ljubljana, and at subsequent meetings in the next few months rarely did more than twenty attend.[4] But the organization, which Vladislav Fabjančič founded and over which he presided, expanded geographically and numerically after events in the Balkans in the fall of 1912 demanded of some young Slovenes that they commit themselves as Yugoslavs. The Ljubljana group played the major role in the radical student movement, but in Idrija, Gorica, Trieste, Maribor, Celje, Ptuj, Novo Mesto, and Kranj revolutionary students also organized. The Ljubljana organization dominated, gave the others direction, integrated the activities, and collected dues from the local units.[5] Fabjančič himself boasted on several occasions that he was the leader of 700 to 1000 determined student radicals.[6]

Within the organization there were three degrees of membership, all relating to the blacksmithing craft. Junior members were referred to as

---

*Much of this chapter appeared in slightly different form in an article entitled "Preporodovci: Slovene Students for an Independent Yugoslavia, 1912-1914," in *Canadian Slavic Studies*, Summer 1971.

"Žeblji" (nails); their leaders were the "kovači" (blacksmiths). The master minds, whose identity was kept secret from the rank and file, were the "kladivarji" or hammersmiths.[7] Consistent with the blacksmithing symbolism (according to a Slovene proverb, "Everyone is his own fortune's smith"), the students proposed to forge their own future. They printed the poem *Kovaška* by Oton Zupančič prominently on the first page of the first issue of *Preporod*,[8] and Zupančič was made an honorary member of the group.

During its short existence this middle school group put forth and fulfilled much of an ambitious program. It organized and expanded at home, then extended its contacts to gymnasium groups in the South, in Croatia, Dalmatia, Bosnia, Herzegovina, and Serbia. It reached out to those university students who sympathized with its Yugoslav program. Ties among these youths were cemented by correspondence, exchange of reading matter, and by travel. Indeed, one of the central activities of the Preporodovci was the promotion of student excursions into South Slav lands, and each year the president of the travel club spent considerable time soliciting free lodging for such students.[9] A membership in the club entitled one to a current listing of gratis housing. The Serbian government further facilitated travel into the Southern Balkans by granting club members reduced rates (one-fourth fare) on the Serbian railroads.[10]

In Slovenia itself the Preporodovci sponsored frequent lectures on "Yugoslav" culture and history. In fact, Preporodovci would maintain that these lectures on South Slav culture were the central function of the group.[11] "Our position was that the schools [offered] too little in the way of information about Yugoslavs. Therefore we wanted to inform ourselves about Yugoslav culture."[12] It was not sufficient, however, to promote Yugoslav studies only for the group, but to educate others, to reach a broader Slovene audience. Therefore the organization participated in a variety of activities, including Sokol gymnastic events (where participants tended to be liberal, anti-clerical, and nationalistic).[13] The Preporodovci also published the journal *Preporod* (first monthly, then bi-monthly) from November of 1912 to June of 1913. Its polemics were frequently censored, and after *Preporod* had been legally forbidden to continue publishing, Avgust Jenko planned his *Glas Juga* (two editions appeared in March and May of 1914) to succeed it.[14] The organization achieved a major triumph in broadening its appeal in March of 1914, when the publication of *Klic od Gospe svete*[15] inspired solidarity among students of all persuasions, giving impetus to five days of student strikes in Ljubljana.[16] The authorities needless to say were very disturbed by these developments, and Ljubljana daily newspapers appealed to out-of-town parents to round up their sons and take them back to school.[17] Thereafter, because police investigators were earnest, though not really successful, in seeking out instigators of the strike, the Preporodovci decided to curb their activities at least temporarily.[18] When the assassination of Francis Ferdinand occurred most students were in the midst of the gymnasium examinations; the post-March strike lull was still in effect.

Immediately after the assassination of Archduke Francis Ferdinand in Sarajevo on June 28, 1914, police authorities in Austria-Hungary began arresting individuals suspected of treasonable activities. Among those detained were twenty-seven Slovene students—the majority were "middle schoolers"[19] in Ljubljana; several were university matriculants in Vienna. Most of the students were apprehended within two or three days of the 28th; the others were arrested within the following month, before the war broke out at the end of July. It was assumed by the Imperial authorities that the assassination stemmed from a Southern Slav conspiracy bred in Serbia with Serbian government complicity but also involving Southern Slavs within Austria-Hungary itself. This included the Slovenes whose loyalty to the Empire had previously not been questioned. Thus Slovene students were drawn into a whirl of investigations, which in their view made them one with developments of momentous international and historic implication. For some, identification with these larger forces produced a real headiness and exhilaration; this was tempered, however, by the anxiety which accompanied arrest, interrogation and trial.

Formal charges against the twenty-seven were made in Ljubljana on 26 September 1914, based on evidence linking them to a secret organization believed by the authorities to have strong pro-Serbian tendencies. However, during the actual trial lasting from the 21st to the 24th of December, all that the prosecution could prove conclusively was that a secret organization of Slovene middle school students had in fact existed for about two and one half years before the Sarajevo assassination. The Yugoslav sentiment of the group was clearly evident from confiscated correspondence, from the organization's by-laws, and from the actual testimony of the accused; but the state could not definitely establish that this Yugoslavism, which the accused maintained was purely cultural, had precise political designs involving collusion with the Kingdom of Serbia. The sentences pronounced by the Ljubljana court on the 24th of December bore out the tenuous nature of this evidence;[20] four were dismissed without punishment; the others, except for two, were to be imprisoned for periods ranging from two weeks to six months, contingent upon the degree of involvement in the organization. The two exceptions, the most serious offenders according to the judgment of the court, were Ivan Endlicher and Janže Novak, because they had actually helped determine policy for this secret society; each, however, was only to be confined for seven months.[21] There were two members of the group who were never arrested: Avgust Jenko and Vladislav Fabjančič, whose Yugoslavism was characterized by the Ljubljana court as more pro-Serb, therefore more dangerous to Austria, and who, in fact, had had suspicious ties with official Serbia. They had fled the Empire directly after the Archduke's death to fight with the Serbs against Austria. Therefore the authorities recorded in the court minutes that in their opinion they had been dealing only with some of the less pivotal members of the group.[22]

During the half year between the assassination and the Ljubljana trial many of the accused students were kept in prison, and since the sentences of the court did not exceed this period of confinement, these students were released on December 24th. In the cases of Endlicher and Novak the state prosecutor refused to accept the court's mild verdict, and nullified the proceeding against the two. The next day they were designated to be retried for treason. They remained in Ljubljana until July 1915, after which they were taken to Graz, where a second trial was to take place on the 6th and 7th of September. Endlicher died in prison on the 4th of that month; Novak, found guilty, was sentenced to from ten to twenty years of hard labor, but this was lightened to five years by the court. Ultimately Novak did not serve his full term; he was among those released in June of 1917 when the Emperor Charles issued a general amnesty.[23]

The precedent for Slovene student participation in affairs which affected the nation's well-being (as this might be defined by Herder and early romantic nationalists) was set by those students active in the 1848 revolution in Vienna, Graz, and Ljubljana.[24] In the most fundamental way the Preporod group of 1912 was a part of this 1848 liberal, nationalist tradition. It was intensely nationalistic, and in its search for some solution to the Slovene predicament espoused a course which envisaged the participation of other South Slavs.[25] The group was also very romantic, though often it was an induced romanticism, stemming from the need for identity; their own reveries placed them in the company of heroes and revolutionaries. Ivan Endlicher, for example, had hung a photograph of Luka Jukić,[26] one such Southern Slav hero-revolutionary, prominently above his desk for proper inspiration, and in a book, *The New Era in Croatia and the Croat Progressive Youth*, found in his room when he had been detained by Sušak police in the fall of 1913, there had been inscribed this revealing notation:

Reread as a nationalist, for I am working for and absorbing the ideas of the nationalist youth who have espoused the program of "Narodno Ujedinjenje" (National Unification).[27]

Endlicher and his Preporod colleagues fancied themselves as legatees of a tradition of genuine opposition to the Imperial regime in Vienna. This regime to them was fundamentally the antithesis of Slovene national liberty, for it prevented free cultural development, and correspondingly stifled individual freedom, which in their eyes was unattainable outside the national context.

But in several ways the Preporodovci were very different from 19th century Slovene students and 19th and even 20th century Slovene nationalists of the older generation. Basically they were unique in that they relied upon extra-legal means to achieve Slovene goals as they construed them; all other differences stemmed from their fundamental aversion to the established order. As a student organization they did not seek even the veil of legality, although since 1869 Slovene university student groups had been meeting with the sanction of the regime.[28] Furthermore, although liberal nationalists themselves, the Preporodovci shunned association with the elder liberals or the National Progressive Party (*Narodna napredna stranka*), an they sought no connection with any other Slovene political organization,[29] precisely because these were legally acceptable. For the Preporodovci legal nationalism involved a contradiction in terms; the desire on the part of the Slovene political leadership to keep its nationalism within legal bounds, had, in effect, rendered it impotent.[30]

The most telling break with the liberal national tradition came when the Preporodovci abandoned their anti-clericalism. Both the organization and the journal *Preporod* had at their founding expressed a strong "anti-clerical spirit," but by March of 1913, *Preporod* had eliminated the word "progressive" from the paper's subtitle, "provincial voice of Yugoslav progressive youth in Slovenia," and the group began actively soliciting cooperation with Slovene clerical students.[31] For the elder liberals, clericalism had been and remained the primary enemy; for the Preporodovci it was the tie to Austrian legality that was most onerous, for it had paralyzed the thought of older Slovene nationalist leaders.[32] The Preporodovci believed the Empire had become obsolete and could not be reformed; and only the young, including the clerical youth, if they acknowledged these points, could be depended upon to save the nation. In 1913 in its campaign to mobilize all students *Preporod* therefore dropped its anti-clericalism, and forbade any associations with legally recognized groups, particularly with Slovene political parties which might be sympathetic to Yugoslavism but nevertheless could not conceive of a Yugoslav political unit outside the framework of an Austrian Empire.

After the turn of the century liberally-oriented Slovene students, both university and middle school, became more bold and radical. In 1902, as has been noted, university students of the Vienna club "Slovenija" set up a new organization called the National Radical Students (*Narodno radikalno dijaštvo*). It published the journal, *Omladina*, from 1904 to 1914,[33] in which a variety of questions, including the national one, were discussed in an increasingly determined and realistic fashion. Meanwhile middle school students in Ljubljana, who were by law forbidden to organize, though literary clubs under faculty supervision were permitted, had formed a secret society known as the National Radical Youth (*Narodna radikalna mladina*).[34] The radicalization of young Slovenes at the university level contributed to a like development among gymnasium students, who were often either their relatives or their friends from the same town or village.[35] For example, Vladislav Fabjančič, who was credited by both the Preporodovci and by the regime with the founding of the Preporod group, received significant help from his brother Fran, then at the university.[36]

A variety of factors contributed to this assumption of a revolutionary attitude by the young. The growth of Austro-Serbian rivalry, punctuated and intensified by a series of events in the Balkans, was an obvious contributory factor. Among these events were the change of dynasty in Serbia in 1903, the 1908 annexation of Bosnia and Herzegovina, the subsequent annexation crisis, the Zagreb treason trials (1909) against fifty-three of the Croat-Serb Coalition, and the Balkan Wars.[37] A growing disillusionment with the Slovene political leadership occurred about the same time, for no matter how anti-Serb (and this appeared anti-Southern Slav) the Austrian regime became, Slovene politicians continued to envisage the future of Slovenes, and of Southern Slavs in general, within an Austrian context. For example, in 1908, because to them including more Slavs in the Empire increased the possibilities of South Slavs being granted autonomy within Austria-Hungary, all Slovene parties welcomed the Bosnian annexation, although this had been a deliberate anti-Serbian act on Austria's part. As tensions in the Balkans grew after 1908, Slovene students sympathized and identified more with the down-trodden Serbs; similarly their hostility to official Austria heightened, at the same time increasing the gap in world view between them and their Slovene elders.

Increased sympathy for Serbia, hostility to Vienna, and disillusionment with official Slovene groups was part of a greater self-consciousness, national awareness and heightened sensitivity among these youth. This increasing subjectivity was characteristic of young Slovenes, who lived in towns, which were dominated by a German-speaking element. Even in Ljubljana, the capital of Carniola, which was overwhelmingly Slovene in population, Germans wielded power disproportionate to their numbers.[38] These youth had from 19th century nationalists inherited a preoccupation with German superiority, for as Slovenes they found their language essentially underdeveloped and inadequate for urban communication, and their social and economic condition too inferior to exert much pressure upon the powers with whom they contended. Germanization for them was the most formidable enemy, and the confrontation of Slovene nationalists with the German element occurred precisely in the towns where both elements came into daily contact.[39] By the early 20th century Slovene inhabitants in these towns had increased their numbers,[40] and many families could claim second, third, and fourth generation townsmen. Among these, where the sense of inferiority to the German element was strong and much resented, nationalism intensified and took on a certain sophistication, arming itself ideologically with Western middle class concepts (sometimes via contacts from Germany or Russia, but, nonetheless, Western and middle class). Of the Preporodovci arrested exactly one half were from major Slovene towns. The others were from villages, but even these were then attending gymnasium classes in Ljubljana and had absorbed the middle class approach and way of speaking with respect to national rights and freedoms. Avgust Jenko, the ideologue of the group, was the son of a well-to-do baker who may have supplied his son with substantial funds to finance the publication of *Glas Juga*;[41] Enlicher's father was a banker,[42] and the mother of Fabjančič, the real founder of the organization who came from the village of Brezovica, was a postmistress. Though many of the Preporodovci were sons of peasants, they were not peasant revolutionaries, as Dedijer maintains the Young Bosnians were.[43] Their mentality was inherently middle class, conditioned by immediate social and economic circumstances, and refined by exposure to Western concepts. They felt inferior in an urban context, and concluded that this was so because they were Slovenes in a German environment.

Adolf Ponikvar, who in March of 1914 authored *Klic od Gospe svete*, an inflammatory pamphlet which contributed to several days of student strikes in Ljubljana, experienced this very sensitivity to the German factor.[44] In the sixth grade of the gymnasium a German, whom Ponikvar described as pedantic, taught him history in German, in terms of a German dynasty, about German power. Though this professor had been in Ljubljana for many years, he spoke no Slovene and ridiculed Slovene students who spoke German poorly. The next year a Slovene lecturer presented history differently to Ponikvar and his schoolmates, emphasizing particularly the French revolution and its ideals.[45] The Slovene professor lectured on the struggle of Frenchmen against monarchical tyranny on behalf of the rights of man; the relevancy of these lectures excited his students. Such an approach to history held the promise of justice for the oppressed; such lecturers, according to both Ponikvar and Lovsin, gave hope and inspiration to the young student nationalists.[46]

Any discussion of the Preporodovci demands further elaboration of their ideology—political, cultural and also social. However, this is a particularly difficult task for a number of reasons. For one, their views, which appeared in the publications *Preporod* and *Glas Juga* were often ambiguously stated, sometimes deliberately to confuse the censor, and sometimes, particularly in the early months of publication, simply because concepts were still vague and in desperate need of definition. Inconsistency of editorial policy also contributed to the lack of real clarity; these two publications counted several editors between them, and policy alternated between militancy and caution, and finally back to militancy again when Jenko produced his *Glas Juga* in the spring of 1914. What the rank and file believed or understood of their leaders' ideas is even more difficult to discern. Evgen Lovšin in his testimony at the Ljubljana trial maintained that many of the middle schoolers did not agree with Vladislav Fabjančič and his general policy in *Preporod*.[47] But then Lovšin may have been lying to the court, as he and others did whenever the prosecutor began probing for evidence of political Yugoslavism.[48] In any case, the total publications of Preporodovci editors were few (fourteen in all), articles were often polemical and vague where real programs were required, and, furthermore, there was little indication as to how the membership reacted to views, either to those advanced in the pages of the two journals, or at local meetings. It is difficult, therefore, to speak of these gymnasium students as having a well-defined collective ideology; yet the court and Lovšin later had some interesting observations on this point.[49] Both suggested that, though concepts may have been incomprehensible to some, and editorials inexplicit, or information (such as the organization's by-laws) unavailable, a feeling, an intuition, drew these students together. Intuition told these youth that the movement was a noble one; that their leaders understood their yearning, that these leaders expressed what they themselves, though their feelings were overwhelming, could not yet articulate. There existed, so to speak, a community of spirit among them.

Post World War I developments, specifically the destruction of the Austro-Hungarian Empire and the succession of several Yugoslav regimes, have also served to blur the portrait of pre-1914 student nationalists. Yugoslav governments since 1919 have characterized such students as heroes, sometimes martyrs, of the Yugoslav nationalist cause; recently socialistic tendencies have also been attributed to them. Such attribution of influence—retrospectively—has colored accounts of pre-war student movements, has sometimes even made it difficult for the students themselves to remember what it was they believed in in their youth, what it was they then understood as the Yugoslav idea.

In spirit what united these students most in the pre-war years, was not so much what they advocated, but rather what they opposed. They were repulsed by German culture, violently so,[50] much more so than the Slovene liberal nationalists who preceded them. They were after all intellectuals who viewed language and culture as instruments of free expression, and they felt their own freedom stifled because German culture was being forced upon them. As they saw it, the agent of this oppression was the Austro-Hungarian regime, and so politically the Preporodovci declared themselves the regime's enemy and vowed to destroy it.[51] Political reform programs, such as trialism or federalism for Austria, were rejected by them as obsolete, unrealistic, utopian.[52] The old empire for them was beyond repair and incompatible with freedom as they conceived it.

For the future these students envisaged an independent Yugoslav state, but what the nature of the government would be was not really determined. They talked in terms of democracy and freedom, Swiss-like federation and possibly a republic, and they romanticized the Kingdom of Serbia;[53] some probably even had connections with officials in the Serbian government.[54]

When the Preporodovci discussed the creation of a Yugoslav culture, it seems, there was and still is even less agreement on what was intended. They avidly learned the Cyrillic alphabet[55] and the languages (or dialects) of other South Slavs; and they often wrote as if they would be willing to abandon Slovene in order to be a part of a greater Yugoslav culture. Contemporaries of the Preporodovci often concluded that they would indeed abandon the Slovene language, and attacked them for being fatalistic nationalists.[56] As a consequence *Preporod* devoted many pages to defending its position, maintaining that Preporodovci were strong advocates of Slovene individualism, but that what was Slovene was after all a component of Yugoslav culture. Many at the time remained to be convinced, and today the debate still continues.

It was regenerated by Vladimir Dedijer in *The Road to Sarajevo*, where he depicted the Preporod group as divided on the cultural issue, maintaining that most were opposed to linguistic assimilation, but that one element among the leadership had favored it.[57] Dedijer's Slovene readers, some of them former Preporodovci, have vigorously denied that any of the students had leaned toward Illyrism, or linguistic assimilation. At best, however, one can say that *Preporod* publications certainly contained articles that were suspiciously Illyristic, stating often, as did Jenko, that natural assimilation was acceptable, though forced assimilation had to be regarded as the worst of evils.[58] Judging from Slovene reaction to the Dedijer book, one can only speculate that, even if sóme of these students had had Illyrist tendencies before 1914, they were not characteristic of the entire group, and very likely affected those who most romanticized the Yugoslav idea, those who felt most alienated and needed to establish a real sense of identity by submerging themselves in Yugoslav culture.

Lack of specific evidence also hampers the discussion of socialism in relation to the Preporodovci. *Preporod* and *Glas Juga* on occasion made reference to the need for social reform, hinting that the establishment of social equality should be the guiding principle of such change. But again the Preporodovci were very inexplicit; at most they lifted lines from evocative poetry by Zupančič, in which laborers of all professions were enumerated and declared to be of equal worth.[59] At the time most Slovenes were equal to other Slovenes at least in this; that they were treated in the same way by their social superiors, who were German. It is in this sense that one can make "socialists" out of the Preporodovci, and it made nationalists of them as well, for it evoked in them a sense of community, of common plight, with all members of the Slovene nation. Clearly what these students minded most was that they were not equal to Germans. So they dreamt of revolution, which would accord them and those like them (all Slovenes) a rightful, respected position in society. That revolution, because of the nature of Austrian society would, by necessity, have to be a national one.

In evaluating this student movement, one must conclude that among Slovenes it made unique ideological and some tangible contributions toward the creation of a Yugoslavia. In Slovene territories before World War I, these students, together with two independent journals and with Ivan Cankar were alone in advocating the formation of a totally independent Yugoslav state. Although each Slovene political party at this time had a Yugoslav program of sorts none was willing to break with Austria; none would risk a revolution. The Preporodovci, however, were fundamentally revolutionaries—at least their leadership was—and it was this turn of mind which distinguished their Yugoslavism from that of all other Slovenes. Later, during the war itself, Preporodovci fought, not for Austria, but for Serbia, either initially, or after a mid-war defection.

In accounting for the emergence and growth of this movement in the pre-war years, it is pertinent to recall that nationalism had been developing among Slovenes for some time. It evolved as Slovene society became more complex, and found its strongest proponents among the Slovene middle class and its intellectuals. Those who might have best represented the rights of the Slovene nation in terms of Western ideals were the liberals (National Progressive Party), but neither they, nor members of the independent Slovene intelligentsia, dared to act, or even think, outside the bounds of "Austrian" legality. The Preporod youth, particularly the leadership, denounced these liberals, their rightful elders, where nationalist ideology was concerned, and accused them of compromising their ideals in return for security and material comfort. So this youth, convinced that the older generation was hypocritical in upholding its values, struck out on its own, intent on revolution, and determined to suit action to the word. In their contempt for such liberals, they concluded not only that revolution and violence[60] were the only means by which they and their nation could achieve equality and respect, but that they, the youth of that nation, had been chosen as its liberators.[61]

The Preporodovci were not, however, the only Slovenes to take a clearly anti-Austrian stand. Such a position had been assumed several years before by the journalist Milan Plut (1881-1925). There is still considerable uncertainty about Plut's background, motives, and affiliations.[62] It is known that he had lived in Serbia during much of the first decade of the century, writing for a number of papers in that country, and he seems to have worked very hard to assure the presence of Slovenes at Peter Karageorgević's coronation in 1904.[63] Some sources connect him with the Serbian *Narodna odbrana* and maintain that Plut's own paper *Jutro*, an independent political daily, which began publication in 1910, was actually financed with money brought illegally into the Habsburg Empire from Belgrade.[64] It was published until 1912, at first in Ljubljana, where it was confiscated regularly, and at the end in Trieste. The literary quality of *Jutro* was not of the highest, but it was distinctly Serbophile in its editorial policy, and it had an unusually wide circulation—7000 subscribers in its first year alone. *Jutro* in its pro-Serbism sought to popularize the idea of Southern Slav political unification among Slovenes. In evoking the notion of a "Slav South" (*Slovanski jug*), however, *Jutro* did not intend to encourage cultural Yugoslavism. In fact, *Jutro* believed linguistic assimilation was both impossible and unnecessary. In its efforts Plut's *Jutro* seems to have been supported most by the young radical wing of the National Progressive Party because the young radicals had broken with Liberals of the older generation over matters of local politics.

Though *Jutro* ceased publication in 1912, Plut's journalistic activities continued. He soon assumed the editorship of another independent daily, *Dan*; it was published in Ljubljana from 1912 to 1914. With Plut as its editor *Dan* quickly took on a Serbophile complexion. This is perhaps most evident from *Dan*'s writing on the Balkan wars. It greeted the first war jubilantly as did even most Slovene politicians, for it promised the final liberation of South Slavs from the Turks. The second war, however, in which Serbs and Bulgarians fought one another in that summer of 1913, caused *Dan* to take a unique stance with respect to the Yugoslav idea. Most Slovenes attributed the fratricidal conflict chiefly to the meddling of major powers; even Preporodovci believed that Serbs and Bulgars would resolve their differences over Macedonia. Then together they would confront the common enemy, Pan-Germanism.[65] But *Dan*, perhaps because Plut was indeed first and foremost a Serbophile, turned abruptly against Serbia's enemy and excluded Bulgars from its "Yugoslav" plans.

Dan during that second Balkan war became increasingly hostile to both Bulgars and Bulgaria, advocating South Slavs adopt a pro-Serbian position on the grounds that of the two Slavic combatants only the Serbs were true Yugoslavs. Bulgars, tainted with Mongol blood, had allowed themselves to become implements of Austria's pro-German, anti-Serbian (and therefore anti-Yugoslav) policy. *Dan* accused the Bulgars of conspiring with Austria in the creation of Albania, the motive being the destruction of Serbia whose remaining territory might then be divided between Austria and Bulgaria.[66] *Dan* granted that the second Balkan War had dealt both Yugoslavism and Pan-Slavism a serious blow, but suggested that in one way the Serb-Bulgar conflict may have been a good thing. It revealed the Bulgars for what they were: selfish and insincere about their Yugoslav commitment.[67] Now that the truth was known, *Dan* wrote, Slovenes, and other South Slavs too must strike Bulgars from their Yugoslav plans. Not even Panslav reveries should be permitted to soften one's attitude toward them.[68]

War in the Balkans had obviously evoked heated debate among Slovenes. *Dan*'s position was only one of several determined stands taken at the time. By the spring of 1913, for example, the cause of Yugoslav independence produced its most outspoken advocate, Ivan Cankar (1876-1918). Son of a tailor, one of twelve children, Cankar as a youth showed intellectual promise. He was sent to Ljubljana with encouragement and a pledge of financial assistance from prominent townspeople of his home town Vrhnika. There he completed the real school (*realka*) and soon after found himself in Vienna, where he commenced engineering studies. He later pursued a curriculum in Slavic and Romance Literatures, though completing neither. He was one of those fragile souls whose constitution would not allow accommodation to institutional discipline. His life style was bohemian; he supported himself by writing, and though he wrote prolifically, somehow it was never enough. His publisher regularly extended advances on a next play or short story, but invariably his funds were depleted before the piece could be finished. So he wrote with greater fever, sustained by drink and cigarettes and coffee. But in this way during his short life he produced some of the best works of Slovene literature. They were imbued with a compassion for the suffering and the victims of social injustice. They also bore strong markings of *fin de siècle* melancholy and the decadence so typical of Viennese literature at the turn of the century. Cankar himself in many ways resembled his own fictional characters and survived only because others looked after him. Kind landladies in Vienna, or later Ljubljana, saw that he had proper nourishment, and friends lent him money or took him into their homes for months at a time.[69]

His economic circumstances drew Cankar to socialism. He eventually joined the Yugoslav Social Democratic Party—one of those he lived with for a time was its head Etbin Kristan—and he even ran for a seat to the Vienna Parliament in 1907 in the first election after universal suffrage had been introduced. He did not win, but he did tally more votes than any Slovene Socialist in Carniola that year.[70] In spite of this foray into politics as a Social Democrat, however, Cankar absented himself from most JSDS activities thereafter and his socialism was not one to be molded to party or ideological prescriptions. It had not resulted from an intellectual investigation of socialist literature, though Cankar did read Karl Marx after his interest had been whetted. Cankar's socialism had been born of a humanitarian impulse, a mark which much of his writing clearly bears. He himself maintained that he had always been a socialist, even from his early days in Vrhnika and his subsequent acquaintance with the the thoughts of Krek; living in a proletarian district of Vienna had simply confirmed that inclination.[71] It remained therefore a socialism broad in its scope, and during the war years, according to some, even tended toward Christian Socialism. Essentially, in his socialism Cankar seemed to be constantly searching, as did Hlapec Jernej, one of his fictional characters, for justice for those who toiled and suffered.

It is not perhaps unusual then that a free spirit such as Cankar's would venture a radical approach to Yugoslavism. In April of 1913, on the 12th of the month precisely, Ivan Cankar, speaking to *Vzajemnost* (Solidarity), a Carniolan workingmen's association, meeting in the Ljubljana town hall,[72] offered his solution to the Yugoslav problem. His talk, entitled "Slovenes and Yugoslavs" (*Slovenci in Jugoslovani*) was very explicit in its preferences. Cankar began by acknowledging the existence of a "Yugoslav" sentiment among Slovenes. The Balkan war had confirmed it:

> Whoever thus far has not been aware of it, now cannot help knowing
> that we are not just Slovenes, much less are we just Austrians, for we
> belong to a great family which extends from the Julian Alps to the

Aegean Sea. When the first shot was sounded in the Balkans its echo was heard in our most remote village. People, who in their entire lives never bothered themselves with politics, watched this great drama with the deepest concern. And in us all there awoke something which is very similar to the yearning of one who is imprisoned. There was reborn in us something else even greater and more precious—that spark of the strength of self-awareness and the force of life, which was released in the south, and also fell upon Slovene soil. He who was weak saw that his brother is strong and he began to have hope and conficence in himself and in his future.[73]

But what was that future to hold? What exactly was the nature of the Yugoslav question in 1913?

For Cankar the Yugoslav problem was not a cultural one. He conceded that it might have been at once time, but that it had been resolved by history when South Slavs had been divided into four nations, each thereafter to pursue a separate cultural existence. Yugoslavs, though brothers by blood, had become in effect only cousins in language.[74] Cankar therefore deplored the resurgence of Illyrism among Slovenes, taking issue with even those of his own party who confined discussions on the Yugoslav question at their 1909 party conference to cultural matters. He especially criticized Etbin Kristan and the Tivoli resolution for urging the cultural and linguistic unification of all Yugoslavs. Cankar believed that Southern Slavs should regard each nation and its respective culture as being of equal worth. The Yugoslav idea could fulfill itself only on such an egalitarian basis. In other words, Cankar was culturally a Slovene.[75]

Politically, however, Cankar had become a Yugoslav. He said, " . . . I regard the Yugoslav problem for that which it is: namely a purely *political* problem" [Cankar's italics],[76] and he urged Slovenes to work for the political unification of all Southern Slavs, including the Bulgarians. Only this, he believed, would allow Southern Slavs to make their mark on the history of mankind. This was after all, unless men had forgotten, the purpose of nations.

His talk understandably got Cankar into difficulty with authorities for he conceived of Yugoslav political unification as taking place *outside* Austria, and he made no attempt to be coy about it. "For official Austria, exponent of German imperialism," he said explicitly, "Yugoslavs are simply *in the way*" [Cankar's italics].[77] Police attending the lecture maintained that Cankar even vulgarly prodded Slovenes "to leave Austria in her own excrement" and follow the example of Mazzini.[78] In any case, Cankar by 1913 had given up on Austria. Her domestic as well as her foreign policy under Berchtold had become increasingly pro-German and anti-Yugoslav; it was therefore hopeless to stay tied to Austria. In a way Austria was repeating stupid mistakes of the mid-19th century, mistakes which had resulted then in the premature creations of Italy and Germany. That Austria had not learned her lesson only meant for Cankar that Yugoslav unification outside Austria was imminent.[79] For that Yugoslav state, Cankar proposed a federative republic. He put the words into the mouth of a simple peasant, who because he would be unaware of the intricacies of European politics, might suggest a practical, uncomplicated resolution to the problem: "If these four nations believe that they are related and that they can live best and most easily if they are united, then let it be as they wish, let there be established in God's name a united Yugoslav republic . . . ."[80]

All of this was too blunt for the authorities. The organization *Vzajemnost* was disbanded by the police within one week of Cankar's talk, while Cankar himself was made to account for his comments before the Ljubljana court. He was sentenced to one week in jail, which he served in September of 1913. His talk sat badly with most Slovenes as well. Clericals in *Slovenec* several days after Cankar's lecture counseled Slovenes, especially the young, to resist irredentist utopias and Great Serb propaganda, for these aimed to destroy Austria.[81] Liberals met on the 18th of April, and partly in response to Cankar's lecture, reaffirmed National Progressive Party loyalty to the Empire. *Zarja* the Socialist daily was the only paper to publish Cankar's speech, but it ventured no editorial comment. Most dwelt on the cultural references in Cankar's talk; these were at the time being widely discussed in *Veda*. They were also a safer topic for public debate. Oddly enough, both *Preporod* and *Dan* which might have otherwise been enthusiastic about Cankar's speech, seemed to be disappointed in his stand on the cultural issue. It was clear, even as Cankar himself said, that he spoke not as a member of a group but as an individual.[82]

Though in 1913 Cankar spoke only for himself, and though *Preporod* and *Dan* spoke for limited audiences, their nationalisms were nevertheless relevant. They were as a matter of fact even in continuity with radical Slovene programs of the previous century, when some Slovenes flirted with extreme solutions whenever European crises gave rise to questions about Austria's viability. Granted, among independent intellectuals in those last years before Sarajevo, not all preferred independence. One Slovene Masarykite journalist at the time, for example, clung more tenaciously to the Austrian idea, even defending official Austria and her project for an independent Albania. That journalist, Vladimir Knaflič, however, applauded Cankar's cultural Slovenism, lamenting what he judged to be a marked fatalism among Preporodovci regarding the cultural issue.[83] Knaflič's thoughts on Yugoslavism, though a unique composite, are, however, evidence of how complex in fact the issues had become by late 1912. Independents in those years had begun to produce radical nationalistic programs of virtually infinite variety. What distinguishes those discussed in this chapter is the fact that their particular political programs gained in relevance with the outbreak of European war. Given that development, there was a real likelihood that Austria would not survive the conflict. It had therefore become possible that the 1914 war would do for Yugoslavs what mid-19th century wars had done for the causes of the Italians and the Germans.

NOTES

CHAPTER I

1. The 1846 Austrian census (1850 in Hungary) revealed these population figures: Slovenes and Serbo-Croats in Carniola 428,000 (92% of population); Slovenes in the following provinces: Styria 363,000 (36%), Carinthia 96,000 (30%), Gorica 128,000 (67%), Trieste 25,000 (31.5%). After 1866 27,000 Slovenes remained in Venetia when it was annexed to Italy and in 1867 45,000 Slovenes were added to Transleithia by the Ausgleich. Figures quoted in F. Zwitter, "The Slovenes and the Austrian Monarchy," *Austrian History Yearbook,* Vol. III, Pt. 2, 1967, p. 159.

2. Trubar's Catechism of 1550 was subtitled, "Catechismus in der Windischenn Sprach;" however by "Windischenn," Trubar meant Slovene." Trubar did use the terms "Slovene" and "Slovenes," but not in the same sense—the popular national one—used in the 19th century.

3. D. Lončar, *Politično življenje Slovencev,* Ljubljana, 1921, p. 10.

4. B. Grafenauer, *Zgodovina slovenskega naroda,* Vol. V, Ljubljana, 1962, p. 126.

5. See below for Slovene association with the pre-Carolingian Duchy of Carinthia.

6. M. Kos, *Zgodovina Slovencev,* Ljubljana, 1933, p. 75.

7. Ibid., p. 42.

8. Ibid., pp. 87-88.

9. Early Slovene history is perhaps most thoroughly examined by M. Kos in *Zgodovina Slovencev,* Ljubljana, 1933. For a brief survey of the same period, see B. Grafenauer, *Zgodovina slovenskega naroda,* Vol. I, pp. 119-175.

10. This ceremony was discontinued in 1414.

11. G. Stökl uses the term in "Der Beginn des Reformationsschrifttums in slowenischer Sprache," *Südost-Forschungen,* Köln, 1954.

12. Trubar never committed himself to any of the new faiths, though he remained constant in his opposition to the Church at Rome. M. Rupel, *Primož Trubar—življenje in delo,* Ljubljana, 1962, is the definitive work on Trubar.

13. Ibid., p. 231.

14. For a short summary of the reigns of Maria Theresa and Joseph II, see C. A. Macartney, *The Habsburg Empire, 1790-1918,* London, 1968, Chapters 1 and 2, pp. 1-118.

15. F. Zwitter, "Illyrisme et Sentiment Yougoslave," *Monde Slave,* Vol. X, no. 4, 1933, p. 42.

16. F. Kidrič, *Zgodovina slovenskega slovstva,* Ljubljana, 1929-38, pp. 160-184.

17. B. Grafenauer, *Zgodovina slovenskega naroda,* Vol. V, Ljubljana, p. 78.

18. Zois, whose mother was Slovene, owned iron founderies in Carniola.

19. B. Grafenauer, *Zgodovina slovenskega naroda,* Vol. V, pp. 82-83.

20. *Županova Micka* and *Ta veseli dan ali Matiček se ženi,* the latter modeled after Beaumarchais' *Marriage of Figaro,* are two of Linhart's better known works.

21. F. Zwitter, "Narodnost in politika pri Slovencih," *Zgodovinski Časopsis*, Vol. I, Ljubljana, 1947, pp. 32-33.

22. Austria acquired these territories in 1797 by the Treaty of Campo-Formio; they had previously been governed by Venice.

23. These military districts had been established by the Austrians in the mid-16th century as the front line of defense against the Turks. They survived well into the 19th century.

24. These territories were ceded to the French by the Treaty of Schönbrunn, 1809.

25. For a more detailed treatment of the Illyrian Provinces, see C. Rogel, "The Illyrian Provinces, 1809-13," Masters Essay, Columbia University, 1961.

26. F. Zwitter, "Illyrisme et sentiment Yougoslave," *Le Monde Slave*, Vol. X, no. 4, April 1933, p. 65.

27. Ibid., Vol. X, no. 6, p. 358.

28. Ibid.

29. Many were written by Vodnik who was school superintendent during the French occupation.

30. French, German and Italian editions were published at various times in its short life-span.

31. The Austrian Emperor retained the title of King of Illyria until 1918.

32. During the 1820's and 1830's an "Alphabet War" was fought between those who wished to retain the Reformation orthography of Bohorič (*bohoričica*) and those who preferred to adopt a new orthography, either that of Metlko or Danjko. All these were rejected in the 1840's in favor of the Czech orthography.

33. Metternich in particular encouraged, even subsidized, such activity with the hope that the developing national consciousness of the age would seek out conservative channels. See A. Haas, "Metternich and the Slavs," *Austrian History Yearbook*, Vol. IV-V, 1968-69, pp. 120-149.

34. F. Zwitter, "Narodnost in politika pri Slovencih," *Zgodovinski Časopis*, Vol. I, Ljubljana, 1947, p. 34.

35. The work was entitled, *Grammatik der Slawischen Sprache in Krain, Kärnten, und Steyermark*.

36. L. Legiša, *Zgodovina slovenskega slovstva*, Vol. II, p. 29. This theory was accepted by reputed Slavic scholars, including Dobrovsky and Safárik at certain points in their careers.

37. Ibid.

38. A. Fischel, *Der Panslawismus bis zum Weltkrieg*, Stuttgart and Berlin, 1919, p. 234.

39. R. Kann attributes to Kopitar authorship of the Great Croat idea, which in the latter 19th and early 20th centuries sought to establish a Catholic South Slav trialist unit in the Habsburg Empire. In such an arrangement Croats, largely because of their numbers, would dominate other Yugoslavs who might be included in this unit. F. Zwitter contends that Kopitar could not have contributed much to the Great Croat idea since he did not even recognize the existence of a separate Croat nation. In his linguistic studies he had concluded that there were only three basic South Slav language groupings—the Bulgarian, and the štokavian and kajkavian. (Štokavians are basically Serbs and those Croats who use the word što to signify "what"; the kajkavians are Slovenes and those Croats who use kaj to mean "what.") The Croats would

fall into both the štokavian (Serb) and the kajkavian (Slovene) categories. Consequently, Zwitter points out Croats were either Slovenes or Serbs as far as Kopitar was concerned. For the arguments of Kann and Zwitter see R. Kann, *The Multinational Empire*, Vol. I, New York, 1950, pp. 250-53, and F. Zwitter, "The Slovenes and the Habsburg Monarchy," *The Austrian History Yearbook*, Vol. III, Pt. 2, 1967, pp. 164-65, respectively.

40. L. Legiša, *Zgodovina slovenskega slovstva*, Vol. II, p. 23.

41. F. Zwitter, "Narodnost in politika pri Slovencih," *Zgodovinski Časopis*, Vol. I, Ljubljana, 1947, p. 37.

42. A. Slodnjak, *Prešernovo življenje*, Ljubljana, 1964, p. 139.

43. B. Grafenauer, *Zgodovina slovenskega naroda*, Vol. V, p. 140.

44. A. Slodnjak, *Prešervovo življenje*, p. 140.

45. Ibid, p. 44.

46. H. Kohn, *Panslavism*, New York, 1960, p. 11.

47. Originally Gaj was interested in developing a Croat language, using the kajkavian dialect for this purpose; however, in 1835 he reconsidered, adopted the štokavian and transformed his movement into an Illyrian one aimed at uniting all Southern Slavs, even non-Habsburg ones, in language and culture. The fact that štokavian was used by the majority of South Slavs influenced his decision. F. Petré, *Poiskus Ilirizma pri Slovencih*, Ljubljana, 1939, p. 110.

48. Count Janko Drašković would have included most Slovene territories in his plan. See Fran Zwitter, "Problem narodnega preroda pri južnih slovanih v Avstriji: Legitimizem in narodnostno načelo," *Zgodovinski Časopis*, Vol. IX, 1955, p. 165.

49. B. Grafenauer, *Zgodovina slovenskega naroda*, Vol. V, p. 200. There were a few Illyrists in Carinthia and Carniola. In Ljubljana Illyrists were generally clerics. See F. Petrè, *Poizkus Ilirizma pri Slovencih*, Ljubljana, 1939, p. 220.

50. See F. Petrè, *Poizkus Ilirizma pri Slovencih* for a detailed study of Vraz and Illyrism among the Slovenes between 1835 and 1849.

51. L. Legiša, *Zgodovina slovenskega slovstva*, Vol. II, Ljubljana, 1959, p. 32.

52. F. Zwitter, "Problem narodnega preroda pri južnih slovanih v Avstriji: Legitimizem in narodnostno načelo," *Zgodovinski Časopis*, Vol. IX, 1955, p. 164.

CHAPTER II

1. J. Apih, *Slovenci in 1848*, Ljubljana, 1888, p. 49.

2. F. Petrè, *Poizkus ilirizma pri Slovencih*, Ljubljana, 1939, p. 308.

3. J. Apih, *Slovenci in 1848*, p. 76.

4. I. Prijatelj, *Slovenska kulturnopolitična in slovstvena zgodovina, 1848-1895*, Ljubljana, 1955, Vol. I, p. 38.

5. Fran Zwitter agrees that the Unified Slovenia program was first presented officially in written form in 1848, but contends that it lived in the minds and spoken words of Slovenes since the days of the Illyrian Provinces. See F. Zwitter, "Slovenski politični prerod XIX stoletja v okviru evropske nacionalne probelmatike," *Zgodovinski Časopis*, XVIII, 1965, p. 110.

6. J. Apih, *Slovenci in 1848*, p. 87.

7. Ibid, pp. 144-45.

8. F. Zwitter, "Narodnost in politika pri Slovencih," *Zgodovinski Časopis*, Vol. I, 1947, p. 40.

9. D. Lončar, *Politično življenje Slovencev*, Ljubljana, 1921, p. 19. Lončar discussed the 1848 political programs in terms of two categories: the minimum program which called for a United Slovenia, and the maximum program which tended toward Yugoslav political cooperation.

10. Quoted in I. Prijatelj, *Slovenska kulturnopolitična in slovstvena zgodovinia*, Vol. I, p. 41.

11. J. Apih, *Slovenci in 1848*, p. 85, ("Ne pozabite na vse oživljajočo vzajemnost s svojimi brati okrog Veltave, Visle in Tatre.").

12. Ibid., p. 130.

13. D. Lončar, *Bleiweis in njegova doba*, Ljubljana, 1910, p. 20.

14. J. Apih, *Slovenci in 1848*, p. 107.

15. Pleterski credits Majar with originating the Unified Slovenia program. See Janko Pleterski, *Narodna in politična zavest na Koroskem*, Ljubljana, 1965, p. 32.

16. I. Prijatelj, *Slovenska kulturnopolitična in slovstvena zgodovina*, Vol. I, p. 42.

17. D. Lončar, *Bleiweis in njegova doba*, Ljubljana, 1910, p. 18.

18. I. Prijatelj, *Slovenska kulturnopolitična in slovstvena zgodovina*, Vol. I, p. 108.

19. Lončar, p. 18. Also see B. Grafenauer, "Slovenski kmet v letu 1848, *Zgodovinski Časopis*, Vol. II-III, pp. 7-68.

20. Apih, *Slovenci in 1848*, p. 97.

21. Ibid., p. 74.

22. Prijatelj, *Slovenska kulturnopolitična in slovstvena zgodovina*, Vol. I, p. 108. Also see Vasilij Melik, "Frankfurtske volitve 1848 na Slovenskem," *Zgodovinski Časopis*, Vol. II-III, pp. 69-134.

23. F. Zwitter, "Narodnost in politika pri Slovencih," *Zgodovinski Časopis*, Vol. I, p. 39.

24. I. Prijatelj, *Slovenska kulturnopolitična in slovstvena zgodovina*, Vol. I, pp. 40-41.

25. R. Kann, *The Multinational Empire*, Vol. II, New York, 1950, p. 26.

26. Slomšek was even appalled by the Kremsier constitution because of its secular approaches. It would have established legal equality for all churches and introduced secular education. See F. Zwitter, "Narodnost in politika pri Slovencih," *Zgodovinski Časopis*, Vol. I, 1947, p. 38.

27. Marušič gives the 1869 figure for reading rooms as 56: Carniola 16, Gorica 16, Styria 13, Trieste 9, Carinthia 2. In the 1860's these reading rooms also centered political meetings. See Branko Marušič, "Razvoj političnega življena Goriških Slovencev od uvedbe ustavnega življenja do prvega političnega razkola," *Zgodovinski Časopis*, Vol. XXIII, 1969, pp. 1-30, p. 16.

One of those who contributed financially to Slovene reading rooms was the Croat Bishop Strossmayer, who figures prominently in the Croat movement for Southern Slav unity in the latter 19th century. See I. Prijatelj, *Slovenska kulturnopolitična in slovstvena zgodovina*, Ljubljana, 1955-61, Vol. II, p. 146.

28. See C. A. Macartney, *The Habsburg Empire, 1790-1918*, Chapter 11, pp. 495-568, for details.

29. See V. Melik, *Volitve na Slovenskem*, pp. 203-11, for election figures of 1861.

30. V. Melik, "O nekaterih vprašanjih slovenske politike v začetku sestdesetih let 19 stoletja," *Zgodovinski Časopis*, Vol. XVIII, 1965, pp. 151-70, p. 169.

31. T. Zorn, "Andrej Einspieler in slovensko politično gibanje na koroškem v 60. letih 19. stoletja," *Zgodovinski Časopis*, Vol. XXIII, 1969, pp. 31-51, pp. 33-34.

32. Ibid., pp. 31-51.

33. Non-Slovenes who might be included in such a unit would be represented proportionate to their numbers by a curial system.

34. Matija Majar would have modified the plan to include only the Slovene parts of Southern Styria in "Inner Austria" or "Illyria." This would have presented legal problems, however, since Southern Styria had never been a part of Illyria, and there was no other valid historical basis for dividing the crownland.

35. This periodization of Slovene history is that of Ivan Prijatelj in his monumental 5 volume study, entitled *Slovenska kulturnopolitična in slovstvena zgodovina*, Ljubljana, second edition 1955-61. The first edition was entitled *Kulturna in politična zgodovina Slovencev 1848-1895* and was published between 1938 and 1940. Prijatelj broke down the conservative and liberal periods more precisely, but for our purposes the general divisions are sufficient.

36. Lončar believed that Slovene political history of the second half of the 19th century could better be divided in the following manner: 1848-51 the presentation of minimum and maximum political programs; 1852-59 Bach absolutism; 1860-67 the promotion of language rights and national equality; 1868-1907 formation of political spirits); 1908 on, struggle for national liberty. See D. Lončar, "K Prijateljevi kulturni in politični zgodovinci Slovencev, 1848-1895," *Zgodovinski Časopis*, Vol. IV, 1950, pp. 183-94, p. 184.

37. F. Zwitter, "Slovenski politični prerod XIX stoletja v okviru evropske nacionalne problematike," *Zgodovinski Časopis*, Vol. XVIII, 1965, pp. 75-153, p. 105.

For a provocative essay on Slovene politics in the early years of Austro-Hungarian dualism, see V. Melik, "Slovenska politika ob začetku dualizma," *Zgodovinski Časopis*, Vol. XXII, 1968, pp. 25-59.

38. In the Carniolan diet Slovenes received 25 of 36 seats, and won all the seats alloted the "peasant" curia in Styria, increasing their number from two to eight. See Vasilij Melik, "Sprememba programa slovenskega političnega tabora v letu 1867," *Zgodovinski Časopis*, XVIII, 1965, pp. 309-17, p. 311. Also see V. Melik, "O nekaterih uprašanjih slovenske politike v začetku šestdesetih let 19 stoletja," *Zgodovinski Časopis*, XVIII, 1965, pp. 155-70.

39. Melik, *Zgodovinski Časopis*, XVIII, 1965, p. 316.

40. V. Melik, "Slovensko narodno gibanje za časa taborov," *Zgodovinski Časopis*, XXIII, 1969, pp. 75-88, pp. 83-85. Both conservatives and liberals judged the national issue had priority, and throughout most of the sixties the liberals even maintained that the Church had done much good for the nation. But as the Catholic and anti-Catholic factions grew elsewhere in Austria, Slovene leaders were required to take sides.

41. F. Zwitter, "The Slovenes and the Habsburg Monarchy," *Austrian History Yearbook*, III, Pt. 2, p. 157.

42. D. Lončar, *Bleiweis in njegova doba*, Ljubljana, 1910, p. 41.

43. After the Hohenwart government ended in 1871, the diet reverted to historic claims as did the Slovene conservatives. See V. Melik, "Nekaj značilnosti razvoja na kranjskem 1867-1871," *Zgodovinski Časopis*, XXIII, 1969, p. 72; also see Melik, "Slovensko narodno gibanje za čase taborov," *Zgodovinski Časopis* XXIII, 1969,

p. 77; Fran Zwitter, "Nekej problemov okrog jugoslovanskega kongresa v Ljubljani leta 1870," *Zgodovinski Časopis*, XIV, 1962, p. 162.

44. V. Melik, Ibid, (taborov), p. 75.

45. Ibid., p. 80.

46. I. Prijatelj, Vol. III, pp. 164-66.

47. F. Zwitter, "Nekaj problemov okrog jugoslovanskega kongresa v Ljubljani leta 1870, *Zgodovinski Časopis*, XVI, 1960, p. 148.

48. V. Melik, Ibid., p. 79.

49. K. Milutinović, "Problematika Ljubljanskog Jugoslovenskog programa 1870 kod Srba i Hrvata," *Zgodovinski Časopis*, X-XI (1956-57), p. 159.

50. Ibid., p. 160. Kermavner contends that Bleiweis was also invited, but did not go. See D. Kermavner, "Nakaj kritičnih pripomb k razpravljanju dr. Koste Milutinovića v tem časopisu," *Zgodovinski Časopis*, XIV, 1960, p. 206.

51. Milutinović writes that originally Zagreb had been selected for this meeting, but fear of Croatia's governor Rauch caused the Sisak conferees to reconsider that location. Milutinović, Ibid., p. 162. Kermavner, however, disputes this contention, maintaining there is no evidence to substantiate that a Zagreb meeting had been planned. On the other hand, because Slovene liberals were very likely unhappy about the Sisak discussions (regarding confederation within Hungary) there was every reason to appease the Slovenes by holding a second session in Ljubljana, their capital. See D. Kermavner, "Nekaj kritičnih primomb k razpravljanju Dr. Koste Milutivovića v tem časopisu," *Zgodovinski Časopis*, XIV, 1960, p. 206.

52. See I. Prijatelj, Vol. III, Ch. 3; Milutinović, "Problematika Ljubljanskog Jugoslovenskog programa 1870 kod Srba i Hrvata," *Zgodovinski Časopis*, X-XI (1956-57), pp. 154-182; D. Kermavner, "Nekaj kritičnih pripomb k razpravljanju Dr. Koste Milutinovića v tem časopisu," *Zgodovinski Časopis*, XIV, (1960), pp. 203-17; D. Kermavner, "Hegemonistična prekonstrukcija jugoslovanskega programa v Ljubljani leta 1870," *Zgodovinski Časopis*, XVI, (1962), pp. 81-144; D. Kermavner, "Še nekaj gradiva o ljubljanskem kongresu leta 1870," *Zgodovinski Časopis*, XVII, (1963), pp. 155-170; D. Kermavner, "Se iz pred zgodovine jugoslovanskega kongresa v Ljubljani decembra 1870," *Zgodovinski Časopis*, 1965-66, pp. 319-54; F. Zwitter, "Nekaj problemov okrog jugoslovanskega kongresa v Ljubljani leta 1870," *Zgodovinski Časopis*, XVI, 1962, pp. 145-70.

53. F. Zwitter, "Nekaj problemov okrog jugoslovanskega kongresa v Ljubljani leta 1870," *Zgodovinski Časopis*, XVI, 1962, pp. 167-68.

54. There is considerable disagreement as to whether Miletić was a revolutionary regarding this or not. Zwitter maintains that Miletić was certainly anti-Austrian and that already after the 1866 war, when he participated in a Magyar-Croat-Serb plot against Austria in favor of joining Serbia. The plot had been encouraged by the Serbian Prince Michael (assassinated in 1868) as a step toward his plan for a Balkan-Danubian federation. F. Zwitter, Ibid., pp. 150-151.

55. *Slovenski Narod* in April of 1869, considering the possible collapse of the Austrian Empire, stated that Slovenes would in that case prefer to become Russians rather than Prussians. See Lončar, *Bleiweis in njegova doba*, p. 77.

56. Zwitter, Ibid., pp. 166-68.

57. Zwitter, Ibid., p. 145, pp. 166-67; Miletić, Ibid., p. 164, 180.

58. Until about 1897 when the German Christian Socialists began adopting a very nationalistic program, one which would leave non-Germans stranded.

59. I. Prijatelj, Vol. III, pp. 370-371.

60. I. Prijatelj, Vol. IV, p. 485.

61. Those liberals who cooperated actively with the Taaffe government were often referred to as "the elastics" or "opportunists." Some liberals, however, criticized these strongly, preferring themselves to promote a more radical national program than was possible from within the governing coalition. Zwitter, "The Slovenes and the Habsburg Monarchy," *Austrian History Yearbook*, Vol. III, part 2, p. 173.

62. In 1895 the Windischgrätz ministry fell when German liberals withdrew their support. These liberals were objecting to the establishment of a Slovene gymnasium in Cilli (Celje) in Styria.

63. A term used by Taaffe's opponents to describe the nature of his rule.

CHAPTER III

1. On 1905 the party extended itself beyond the boundaries of Carniola, where Slovenes constituted 94% of the population, in order to work with Slovene politicians in other provinces of Cisleithian Austria, where Slovenes were less numerous. The party picked up members and support in Carinthia (21% Slovene), and in Stryia (29%) Slovene). (Percentages based on 1910 census figures; see J. Pleterski, "Položaj Slovencev pred prvo svetovno vojno," *Jugoslovenski narodi pred prvi svetski rat*, p. 786). The latter province contributed significantly in the person of Anton Korošec, the cleric, who was in 1918 largely responsible for bringing Slovene statesmen into the new Yugoslav state; subsequently, he became the leading Slovene statesman in interwar Yugoslavia. In any case, the new 1905 title was designed to make the point that the party's activities would no longer be restricted to Carniola. See F. Erjavec, *Zgodovina katoliškega gibanja na slovenskem*, Ljubljana, 1938, p. 116.

Brumen in his new biography of J. Ev. Krek, one of the party's key figures, maintains that Krek devised the new name in order to facilitate elimination of philosophical divisions among parties within Carniola itself, hoping to encourage an eventual merger into one united Slovene party. Ivan Šušteršič, who was then president (after 1902) of the party, was less bent on achieving inter-party unity; he held firmly to the concept of Catholic party solidarity and his preference prevailed. See Vinko Brumen, *Srce v sredini*, Buenos Aires, 1968, pp. 115-16.

2. Appending "all" to the party name was meant to indicate that Slovene politicians of similar philosophies had merged with the 1905 group.

3. See below, Ch. VIII.

4. Rendering *Slovenska ljudska stranka* into English is a problem the author has struggled with for some time. *Ljudstvo* may be translated as "nation" or "people." I have chosen to use the term "people." "National" concures up images of European liberal intelligentsia, while the term "people" is more in keeping with the "populist" bent of this party.

5. For those who might object to the term "Clericals" on the ground that it implies derogation, due to its initially being used by political opponents, let me say that I will attempt to be consistent in the use of popular designations. In succeeding chapters I will discuss the activities of the Slovene Progressive Party (*Slovenska napredna stranka*) and the Yugoslav Social Democratic Party (*Jugoslovenska socialna*

demokratska stranka), where these will be referred to as "Liberals" and "Socialists respectively. I trust that this nomenclature will not only tend to simplify things for the reader, but that it will be deemed equitable. In any case, distinguished historians have employed these terms. See, for example, C. A. Macartney, *The Habsburg Empire, 1790-1918*, London, 1968, p. 645, and F. Zwitter, "The Slovenes and the Habsburg Monarchy," *Austrian History Yearbook*, Vol. III, Pt. 2, 1967, pp. 159-188.

6. Vošnjak, *Ob stoletnici rojstva Mihe Vošnjaka*, Belgrade, 1937, p. 21.

7. Zwitter labels these Liberals "opportunists." See "Narodnost in politika pri Slovencih," *Zgodovinski Časopis*, Vol. I, Ljubljana, 1947, p. 50.

8. See W. A. Jenks, *Austria Under the Iron Ring*, Charlottesville, 1963, for a study of the Taaffe regime.

9. A. Mahnič, "Nekaj več o našem programu," *Rimski Katolik*, Vol. III, 1891, pp. 1-6.

10. "Vse za vero, dom, cesarja," in Slovene. A. Mahnič, "Politični oddelek," *Rimski Katolik*, Vol. III, pp. 73-85, 342-46. See pp. 82-85. The author was very harsh with *Slovenec* for backing certain liberals during elections in 1891; "if the Slovene nation needed to be saved, and no one managed to do it, God would, and he certainly didn't need the help of Tavčar and Hribar" (Liberal types approved by *Slovenec* for 1891 elections), see p. 84.

11. The author maintained that the liberal leader, Ivan Tavčar, was equally opportunistic vis-à-vis the Taaffe regime. Moreover, he wrote, the two daily papers *Slovenec* and *Slovenski Narod* served to propagate the policies of Klun and Tavčar respectively. Therefore, the papers, too deserved to be reprimanded.

12. Ibid., p. 81. Also see "Čehi z ozirom na Slovence," *Rimski Katolik*, Vol. III, 1891, pp. 401-69, for a portrayal of Young Czechs as anti-religious liberals.

13. A. Mahnič, "Nekaj več o nasem programu," *Rimski Katolik*, Vol. III, 1891, pp. 1-6, p. 1.

14. See "Katoliški Liberalizem," *Rimski Katolik*, Vol. I, 1889, pp. 26-34, 138-140, 380-92, 477-91. For *Rimski Katolik* this designation constituted a contradiction in terms. One simply could not be a "liberal" and a "Catholic" at the same time; the terms were philosophically antithetical. Pp. 138-39.

15. Ibid., p. 29. Of the Popes of the second half of the 19th century, Mahnič distinctly preferred Pius IX, whose 1870 pronouncement on Papal infallibility suited Mahnič's approach. In 1889 Mahnič termed Pius' anti-liberal Syllabus of 1864 the most outstanding Papal document of the 19th century. Also see A. Mahnič, "Nekaj več o našem programu," *Rimski Katolik*, Vol. III, 1891, pp. 1-6, p. 3.

16. "Katoliški liberalizem," *Rimski Katolik*, Vol. I, 1889, pp. 26-34, 138-40, 380-392, 477-91, p. 31. Mahnič denounced Josephinism in Austria and praised that Austrian regime which had concluded a Concordat with the Church in 1855.

17. A. Mahnič, "Nekaj več o našem program," *Rimski Katolik*, Vol. III, 1891, pp. 1-6, p. 3.

18. A. Mahnič, "Politični oddelek," *Rimski Katolik*, Vol. III, 1891, pp. 73-85, 342-346, p. 345. The author used the example of the Italian national revolution vis-à-vis the Papacy to illustrate his point.

19. See *Poročilo pripravljalnega odbora o I slovenskem katolškem shodu*, Ljubljana, 1893, for proceedings of this congress.

20. Mahnič believed that Roman Catholicism had helped preserve the Slovene nation, allowing, in general, for a more natural and freer development for Slav nations

than had the Orthodox Church. He attacked both Byzantines and Russians alike for their mistreatment of Slavs. See A. Mahnič, "Narodnost," *Rimski Katolik*, Vol. IV, 1892, pp. 24-32, 170-76, 240-43.

21. Mahnič, in urging a determined Catholic program, stressed that " . . . life, especially political life, was war, that Jesus Christ had brought to the world fire and the sword (for the purpose of executing this war)." See A. Mahnič, "Politične svatbe. Koalicija-Katoliski centrum," *Rimski Katolik*, Vol. VI, 1894, pp. 1-24, p. 20.

22. *Katoliski Obzornik* was published by Leonova Družba, a society founded in 1894 to concern itself with philosophical and cultural questions.
1893, pp. 269-70.

23. See *Poročilo prepravljalnega odbora o I slovenskem katoliškem shodu*, Ljubljana, 1893, pp. 269-70. (Here Sustersic expresses his loyalty to both the Church and Austria.)

24. See R. Jurčec, *I. E. Krek*, Ljubljana, 1935, p. 115, for circumstances leading up to the founding of this society.

25. In 1904 the state threatened to dismiss Krek from his professorial post (chair of Thomist philosophy at the Ljubljana theological seminary) because of these activities. Bishop Jeglič of Ljubljana defended him at that time, but in 1916, with the war and political tensions mounting, Jeglič, too, agreed that Krek must go. See V. Brumen, *Srce v sredini*, Buenos Aires, 1968, pp. 37-38.

26.I. Šušteršič, *Moj Odgovor*, 1922, p. 182.

27. Krek was a representative to the Vienna Parliament from 1897 to 1900, and again from 1907 to 1917; from 1902 to 1917 he sat in the Carniolan provincial diet. Šušteršič served in the Vienna Parliament between 1896-98 and 1900-1918; from 1901 on he also sat in the Carniolan diet. See V. Melik, *Volitve na Slovenskem*, pp. 360-63.

The Slovene People's Party because it needed to work in Vienna with parties, most of them very conservative, even feudalistic, could not become as liberal or modern as Krek would have wished. Poles, Czechs, etc.,were often defending very traditional positions and were antipathetic to Christian Socialism. Because Šušteršič, the key Slovene man in Vienna, dealt with these, his politics were correspondingly more conservative. See R. Jurcec, *I. E. Krek*, Ljubljana, 1935, pp. 88, 112-13.

28. Krek, making up Clerical election lists in 1907, restricted the number of clerical candidates to two. V. Brumen, *Srce v sredini*, Buenos Aires, 1968, p. 110.

29. Ibid., p. 119. Brumen maintains also that since Krek was responsible for drawing up election lists, actually seeking those who would speak for the Slovene People's Party, he, Krek, was the most powerful figure among party members. Brumen does concede that Šušteršič, by his very presence in Vienna (he was a Parliamentary representative and also president of the party), was able to dominate Slovene Catholic representatives there.

30. Krek had considerable success with members of other parties. He managed to help snatch Fran Šuklje away from the Slovene liberal party; and after 1908 Krek was on very cordial terms with the Socialist Albin Prepeluh. Ibid., p. 117. Also see A. Ušeničnik, "Dr. Jan. Ev. Krek sociolog," *Čas* XX, 1925/26, pp. 97-121, p. 106. F. Šuklje, "Jan. Ev. Krek v parlamentu," *Čas* XX 1925/26, pp. 121-37, p. 128.

31. He was a student of Vogelsang in his Christian Socialism and also in his belief that Austria would exist only so long as she was Catholic. See R. Jurčec, *I. E. Krek*, Ljubljana, 1935, p. 114.

32. Krek extended his worker cooperatives to Croats in Istria and Dalmatia as well. Ibid., p. 75.

33. The first edition was quickly sold out; a second edition appeared in 1925 as Vol. III of Krek's *Izbrani Spisi* (Selected Works).

34. Krek in discussing Rousseau was very understanding, saying that Rousseau was essentially reacting (properly so) to the inhumanity of the time, to the capitalist corruption of society. Unfortunately, wrote Krek, Rousseau's prescription for these ills was fundamentally materialistic. Rousseau erred in that he did not acknowledge the power of God in the universal makeup of things. For Krek it was necessary to build socialism upon this latter premise.

35. Krek maintained that Austria, too, had fallen victim to liberalism. Autonomous institutions no longer functioned properly, and though Austria had a constitution and a Parliament, centralism and bureaucracy prevailed. A. Ušeničnik, "Dr. Jan. Ev. Krek, sociolog," *Čas* XX, 1925/26, pp. 102-06. Of the European peasant situation Krek wrote that liberal capitalism and a money economy were destroying the security and freedom provided by traditional institutions. He especially lamented the crushing of peasant communes among the Slavic peoples. See J. Sovran (Krek pseudonym), "Iz črnih bukev kmečkega stanu," *Slovenec*, No. 162-236, included in J. E. Krek, *Izbrani Spisi*, Vol. II, no. 2, pp. 255-315.

36. J. E. Krek, *Socializem*, Ljubljana, 1926, p. 588. Krek approved of the British Constitution; its natural development and ministerial responsibility appealed to him.

37. Krek felt that all men were equal before God, but in society, because rights and responsibilities varied, men fell into class groupings, each of which was ultimately responsible to and dependent upon God.

38. J. E. Krek. *Socializem*, p. 142. The state's task was to protect the natural rights of its people; this, according to Krek, also required provision for social and economic well-being. Also see A. Ušeničnik, "Dr. Jan. Ev. Krek sociolog," *Čas* XX, 1925/26, pp. 100-01; R. Jurčec, *I. E. Krek*, Ljubljana, 1935, pp. 101-158 for an excellent presentation of Krek's economic and social philosophy.

39. J. E. Krek, *Socializem*, p. 180.

40. Ibid., p. 113.

41. Krek and other Clericals were certain that the results of the 1907 elections bore out this contention. Socialists were winnning (both Christian Socialists and Social Democrats); therefore, liberalism was on its way out.

42. Already in 1894 Krek advocated the adoption of universal, equal, and direct vote (the only Austrian clergyman then to do so). V. Brumen, *Srce v sredini*, Buenos Aires, 1968, p. 141. In this he included women, arguing that if women lived in a society that compelled them to work in factories along with men, then that society was duty bound to accord them voting rights, along with men. Later, the party itself supported universal suffrage for the Imperial Parliament as well as for the Carniolan Diet. Šušteršič, writing from exile in 1922, maintained he initiated and worked hardest for universal suffrage in the local body; he claims that equal suffrage because of the vested interests of German nobles in Carniola was, however, not attainable. I. Šušteršič, *Moj Odgovor*, 1922, p. 181.

43. J. E. Krek, *Socializem*, p. 134-35.

44. "National sentiment is a part of social feeling" (Tudi narodnostno čustvo je del socialnega čustva), Krek wrote. See Liga +2 (Krek pseudonum) "Kje Manjka?" *Slovenec* No. 218, included in J. E. Krek, *Izbrani Spisi*, Vol. II, p. 197.

45. Ude would contend that the Trieste issue was a central one to Slovene nationalism. L. Ude, "Slovenci in jugoslovanska ideja," *Jugoslovenski narodi pred prvi svetski rat*, Belgrade, 1967, p. 889.

Krek felt that only a strong Austria should have Trieste. See Dolenc, "Razvoj jugoslovanske misli pri Kreku," *Čas* XX, 1925/26, p. 147.

46. Ibid., p. 144.

47. Krek's Ukrainian colleagues, in an expression of fondness, even made him an honorary hetman of the Ukrainian organization "Sič," Ibid., p. 144.

48. F. Grivec, "Vzhodno cerkveno vprašanje v luči moderne historiografije," *Čas* I, 1907, pp. 18-25.

49. L. Leonard, "Nekaj slovanskih vprašanj," *Čas* III, 1909, pp. 136-39. F. Stelè expresses this same contention to Catholic youth in a student journal. See F. Stelè, "Dve slovanski svetišči," *Mentor* Vol. II, 1909/10, pp. 56-60.

50. F. Grivec, "Vzhodno cerkveno vprašanje v luči moderne historiografije," *Čas* I, 1907, p. 143.

51. J. E. Krek, *Izbrani Spisi*, Vol. I, p. 142.

52. Krek therefore disputed the contention of Soloviev that the natural spiritual orientation of Slavs was Orthodoxy. Others rather took up the argument of Russians like Chaadayev, who openly preferred a Western orientation for Russia. See F. Grivec, "Vzhodno cerkveno vprašanje v luči moderne historiografije," *Čas* Vol. I, 1907, p. 24.

53. Krek's views on Bismarck, Protestantism, and on German and Magyar anti-Catholicism can be found in reports he wrote from Westphalia in 1899, when he traveled there to minister to Slovene and Czech workers, who requested a native priest for Easter duties. See *Izbrani Spisi*, Vo.l. IV, especially pp. 147-151.

54. J. E. Krek, "Protestantizem in Slovenstvo," *Slovenec*, No. 5, 1898 (unsigned), *Izbrani Spisi*, Vol. IV, pp. 10-11.

55. Slovene Clericals maintained that German Liberals both within and outside Austria had made common cause against Catholicism; it was no accident, they felt, that the battle against the 1855 Austrian Concordat with the Church began in 1871, the same year that the German Empire was created. See J. E. Krek, "Ob rojstvu naše ustave," *Katoliški Obzornik*, VI, 1902, p. 241.

56. Ibid., p. 237.

57. A. Ušeničnik, "Pomen krščanske sociologije," *Čas* I, 1907, pp. 402-412. Ušeničnik was of the same opinion as Krek. Liberalism is egoism gone berserk, he maintained; it destroys all that is natural, and everyone—the whole family—ends up in a factory for the good of the capitalist.

58. J. E. Krek, *Socializem*, pp. 137-39. Here Krek views the liberal national states (Germany, Italy) as centralized, all powerful, acting as tools of capitalists.

59. Slovene Clericals also counseled Austria to beware of Italian designs on Trieste. J. Gruden, "Balkanski problemi," *Čas*, Vol. I, 1907, pp. 31-33. Also see R. Jurčec, *I. E. Krek*, Ljubljana, 1935, p. 77.

60. J. Krek, "Iz razprave: Katolištvo—naša edina rešitev," *Katoliški Obzornik*, IV, 1900, included in Krek, *Izbrani Spisi*, IV, pp. 212-27. Here Krek discusses at length the dangers of Pan Germanism vis-à-vis Slovenes, Austria, and the Church.

61. *Slovenec* No. 232, 9 October 1912. Also see I. Dolenc, "Razvoj jugoslovanske misli pri Kreku," *Čas* XX, 1925/26, p. 156.

62. "... državna ideja Avstrije je bila že iz prvega početka ta, da varuje evropski narode turškega nasilstva." (Author's italics) J. Gruden, "Zgodovinski poklic Avstrije

na Balkanu," *Katoliški Obzornik* VIII, 1904, pp. 175-76.

63. At each of the Slovene Catholic congresses this sentiment was expressed and the intention to maintain it reconfirmed. For example, see *Poročilo pripravljalnega odbora o I slovenskem katoliškem shodu*, pp. 143-44; *Slovensko-Hrvatski katoliški shod v Ljubljani*, 1913, pp. 34-41.

64. Gruden, p. 173.

65. Krek, for one, strongly believed that for geographic and historic reasons it was Austria's duty to liberate the Balkans. I. Dolenc, "Razvoj jugoslovanske misli pri Kreku," *Čas* XX, 1925/26, pp. 137-39.

66. See below, Ch. VI.

67. *Slovenec*, No. 232, 9 October, 1912.

68. There was some hint among Slovene Catholic writers that converting Balkan Slavs to Catholicism was yet part of a larger mission to convert all Slavs, even the Russians.

69. At the Slovene Catholic Congress of 1892 certain elements strongly supported an alliance with the Croats; others such as Mahnič preferred to concentrate on combat with Liberals. The issue remained unsolved in the congress' final resolution. See *Poročilo pripravljalnega odbora o I slovenśkem katoliškem shodu*, p. 142. Also see "Poročilo o Krekovem govoru na zborovanje Hrvatske stranke prava na Sušaku, dne 12 Oktobra 1898," *Slovenec*, No. 236, 1898, included in J. E. Krek, *Izbrani Spisi* IV, pp. 116-17.

70. The Croats by the Compromise of 1867 legally fell under Magyar domination in the Transleithian half of the dual monarchy. For an introduction to Croat problems resulting from this arrangement see R. W. Seton-Watson, *The Southern Slav Question and the Habsburg Monarchy*, London, 1911.

71. "Poročilo o Krekovem govoru na zborovanju Hrvatske stranke prava na Sušaku dne 12 Oktobra 1898," *Slovenec*, No. 236, 1898, included in J. E. Krek, *Izbrani Spisi*, IV, pp. 116-17.

72. Political developments involving Slovene parties from 1908 to 1914 will be examined in later chapters.

73. Seton-Watson, *The Southern Slav Question and the Habsburg Monarchy*, pp. 107-08.

74. The Croat Pragmatic Sanction of 1712 linked Croat lands with the Slovene provinces of Carinthia, Carniola dn Styria. See R. W. Seton-Watson, *The Southern Slav Question and the Habsburg Monarchy*, Appendix III, pp. 349-50.

75. Pleterski feels that certain aspects of Slovene trialism (essentially Krek's approach) were fundamentally democratic and compatible with—if not a first step toward—a democratic federalism for the Empire. Such trialism or Yugoslavism from below, Pleterski maintains, was unmistakably distasteful to the Archduke. J. Pleterski, "Trializem pri Slovencih in Jugoslavanske zedinjenje," *Zgodovinski Časopis*, XXII, 1968, p. 172.

76. Ibid., p. 169. Pleterski further contents that Slovene trialism by 1912, as conceived by Krek, expressed a genuine popular sentiment, one which revealed itself quite clearly in the war years, when Šušteršič and those like him—whose trialism was more clerical and dynastic, closer to that of the Archduke—were defeated.

77. S. Kranjec, "Korošćevo predavanje o postanku Jugoslavije," *Zgodovinski Časopis*, XVI, 1962, p. 220.

78. Pleterski, too, depicts Clerical trialism before the First World War as one characterized by an illusion of the Archduke's program. J. Pleterski, "Trializem pri Slovencih in Jugoslovanske zedinjenje," *Zgodovinski Časopis*, XXII, 1968, p. 173.

79. I. Dolenc, "Razvoj jugoslovanske misli pri Kreku," *Čas* XX, 1925/26, p. 156.

80. An incidental speaker at the First Slovene Catholic Congress in 1892 publicly agreed with the speaker of the Linz Catholic Congress of that year, who were confident that "Austria is in our camp." See *Poročilo pripravljalnega odbora o I slovenskem katoliškem shodu* Ljubljana, 1893, p. 269. Subsequent congresses expressed the same sentiment.

CHAPTER IV

1. Sometimes also called "Progressives" or "Nationalists" after the paper Slovene Nation (*Slovenski narod*) in which they expressed their views.

2. See Chapter II.

3. See Chapter II.

4. This trend seemed to culminate logically in the Whitsun Program in 1899 when all Austrian German parties, except the Catholic People's Party, formed a German Front (Deutsche Gemeinbürgschaft) against the nationalistic pressures of non-German peoples in Austria).

5. C. A. Macartney, *The Habsburg Empire, 1790-1918*, London, 1968, pp. 658-659. Fran Šuklje, *Iz mojih spominov*, Ljubljana, 1929, Vol. II, pp. 164-66.

6. V. Melik, *Volitve na Slovenskem*, Ljubljana, 1965, p. 263. Ivan Tavčar, later one of the party's key figures, attempted in vain, for example, to challenge the party list in 1883.

7. Ivan Hribar, leading Liberal and mayor of Ljubljana from 1896 to 1910, in his autobiography is extremely critical of Šuklje, whom he charges with having been largely responsible for Slovene political quarrels in the 1880's which culminated in the final Clerical-Liberal split in 1890. Ivan Hribar, *Moji Spomini*, Vol. I, Ljubljana, 1928, p. 150.

8. Melik, p. 265; pp. 275-76.

9. This was most true for Carniola where Slovenes constituted 94% of the population. Elsewhere, where Slovenes had a larger German element to contend with, Slovene politicians tended to act cooperatively.

10. The first Slovene mayor of Ljubljana, Peter Grasselli, who held that post from 1882 to 1895, was also of a Liberal bent. See *Slovenski biografski leksikon*, Vol. I, no. 2. Ljubljana, 1926, pp. 244-45.

11. Hribar, Vol. I, p. 368.

12. Hribar discusses these town improvement projects at length in his memoirs. See Hribar, Vol. I, pp. 275-326.

13. Hribar, Vol. I, pp. 328-333.

14. Hribar, Vol. I, p. 421.

15. Both Hribar and Tavčar opposed broadening the franchise for elections to the Carniolan diet where Liberal representation was strong; but reform was nevertheless instituted, resulting in a Clerical victory in the next provincial election, much as the

Liberals had feared. Hribar, Vol. I, p. 405. Hribar maintains, however, that as regards the Imperial Parliament, he favored the introduction of universal suffrage (achieved in 1907), feeling it would strengthen Slavic representation vis-à-vis the Germans; Tavčar and the party, perhaps more in keeping with typically anti-democratic European liberalism, fought to the end the introduction of universal suffrage. Hribar, Vol. I, pp. 461-62.

16. *Slovenski narod* began publishing in Maribor as a weekly; in 1872 it moved to Ljubljana. In the following year it became the first Slovene daily.

17. Hribar, Vol. I, p. 58.

18. Hribar, Vol. I, pp. 256-63.

19. Hribar, Vol. I, pp. 266-74.

20. Hribar maintained that he believed in "Liberty, equality, and brotherhood."

21. Hribar, Vol. I, p. 391.

22. As early as 1898 Hribar proposed a Slovene university for Ljubljana, and because the regime showed little inclination in this direction, he wrote John D. Rockefeller about subsidizing his project. Hribar does not indicate whether Rockefeller ever responded to his letter. Hribar, Vol. I, pp. 304-10.

23. Slovene Clericals espoused, but only to a degree, the notion of an Austrian—not German—civilizing mission in South Eastern Europe. But certain Slovene Liberals (Young Slovenes), like Füster and Dežman, chose to abandon Slovene liberalism in favor of what they judged to be a more advanced German liberalism. See Fran Zwitter, "Narodnost in politika pri Slovencih," *Zgodovinski časopis*, I, 1947, pp. 31-69, 45-47.

24. Hribar, Vol. I, pp. 275-76.

25. Hribar's opponents accused him, despite his protests, of not trying hard enough for Slovene markers. See, Ivan Hribar, Vol. I, p. 267; Vol. III, Ljubljana, 1932, pp. 44-83.

26. See below, Chapter VI.

27. Anton Aškerc (1856-1912), an advocate of brotherhood among Slavic nations, wrote largely in the 1880's and 90's about Slovene peasant society.

Simon Gregorčič (1844-1905), born in the Gorica area, wrote poetry in its dialect. As a priest his writing was attacked by radical churchmen (e.g., Mahnič) for its irreligiousness.

28. Hribar, Vol. I, p. 113. The Papacy of Leo XIII was favorably regarded by Slovene Liberals. Hribar even wrote Leo urging the use of Slovene in religious services in ethnically Slovene areas. Hribar, Vol. I, p. 250.

29. Anton Bonaventura Jeglič 1850-1937.

30. Hribar, Vol. I, pp. 361-65.

31. Hribar's feud with Fran Šuklje, for one, continued heatedly through the early 1930's. See especially Hribar, Vol. IV, subtitled "Odgovor Franu Erjavecu in Franu Sukljetu," Ljubljana, 1933.

32. Hribar contends that he was not party to the initiation of the policy, yet Hribar was himself exceptionally determined to destroy certain Clerical politicians even to the point of gloating self-righteously at their misfortunes, e.g., at an early death for Šušteršič, at death by arsenic poisoning for Lampe, etc. Hribar, Vol. I, p. 409.

33. Hribar in his memoirs defends the coalition with the Germans, saying that Slovenes derived immediate cultural benefits from it, for Germans agreed to vote for a Slovene language school in Postojna and to help support a Slovene national theater (opposed by the Clerical Šušteršič). Hribar credits Count Badeni with suggesting cooperation with the Germans; the latter as a Pole knew well that cooperation often produced positive results for non-Germans in the Empire. In any case, states Hribar, if the Liberals had not made their pact with the Germans, the Clericals would have, for they did in 1910 as soon as the opportunity arose. Hribar, Vol. III, pp. 20-35.

Slovene Clericals on the other hand maintain that the coalition made Slovene Liberals soft on certain national issues particularly where a forceful stand against Germans was required. The relative indifference of Slovene Liberals to the issue of a Slovene parallel gymnasium in Celje (Styria) is often cited by Slovene Clericals as an example of Liberals permitting the German coalition to compromise their principles. See Fran Erjavec, *Zgodovina katoliskega gibanja na Slovenskem*, pp. 79-88.

The battle for the Celje school, which because of growing German nationalism brought the ruin of the Windischgrätz regime in 1895, was in fact fought largely by Styrian Slovene Clericals. See Berthold Sutter, *Die Badenischen Sprachenverordnungen von 1897*, 2 Vol., Graz-Köln, 1960 and 1965, Vol. I, Ch. IV, pp. 107-127.

34. Even on the eve of World War I *Slovenski narod* was calling for such a federated Austrian state. See for example, *Slovenski narod*, no. 91, April 23, 1914.

35. See Chapter VI for details. Also see Hribar, Vol. I, pp. 339-54 for his account of the affair.

36. See Hribar, Vol. I, Introduction, p. 4. Hribar strongly implies that his faith in Austria had been shattered by the Emperor's snub, that thereafter his loyalties had decidedly shifted.

37. *Slovenski narod*, no. 81, April 10, 1912.

38. See Chapter VIII.

39. Hribar, Vol. II, pp. 43-44.

40. *Slovenski narod*, no. 264, November 16, 1912.

41. Hribar, for example, often was reminded of Prešeren's works, "Največ sveta otrokom sliši Slave." Hribar, Vol. I, p. 230.

42. Hribar, Vol. I, p. 190.

43. Hribar made a number of trips to Russia and encouraged others to do the same. Hribar, Vol. I, p. 172. One who did was the poet-priest Anton Aškerc, who wrote about it subsequently in *Ljubljanski Zvon*. Anton Aškerc, "Dva izleta na Rusko," *Ljubljanski Zvon*, 1903.

44. By the 1880's Czechs and Slovenes were exchanging regular visits; in 1886 the one-thousandth anniversary of St. Methodius' death and in 1889 the twenty-fifth anniversary of the founding of the Czech Sokol occasioned several excursions. Hribar, Vol. I, p. 194, p. 241.

Ivan Hribar also traveled to Prague in 1897 to participate in laying the cornerstone for a Palacky monument. Hribar, Vol. I, p. 196.

45. D. Kermavner, *Slovenska publicistika in prva ruska revolucija*, Ljubljana, 1960, p. 20, p. 8.

46. The term was intended to distinguish the movement from earlier Panslavism which had not repudiated Russian Imperialism. Neoslavism championed instead equality, freedom, and brotherhood for all Slavic peoples. Hugo Hantsch maintains, however,

that there was much that was old style Panslavism in Neoslavism in 1908; he prefers therefore to call it Neo-Panslavism. Hugo Hantsch, "Pan-slavism, Austro-Slavism, Neo-Slavism." *The Austrian History Yearbook*, Vol. I, 1965, pp. 23-37, p. 31.

47. Hans Kohn, *Panslavism*, New York, 1960, pp. 246-47.

48. Hribar, Vol. I, pp. 233-34.

49. *Slovenski narod*, no. 91, April 23, 1914.

50. Hribar, Vol. I, p. 237.

51. Hribar, Vol. II, p. 80.

52. Hribar, Vol. II, p. 22.

53. Hribar, Vol. I, p. 226.

54. Strossmayer engaged in active correspondence with William E. Gladstone, English Liberal leader, in the mid-1870's, an acquaintanceship initiated by Lord Acton, who had met the Croat bishop in Rome in 1870. Strossmayer distinguished himself by casting one of the three lone votes against the doctrine of Papal Infallibility. A segment of that correspondence is contained in the Appendices of R. W. Seton-Watson, *The Southern Slav Question and the Hapsburg Monarchy*, reprinted 1969, first published in 1911, pp. 416-44.

55. Strossmayer generously patronized numerous Slavic cultural projects and was instrumental in founding both the Yugoslav (Croat) Academy of Arts and Sciences in 1867 and the University of Zagreb in 1874.

56. Hribar, Vol. I, p. 107.

57. Hribar, Vol. I, p. 111.

58. Hribar, Vol. I, p. 226.

59. Hribar, Vol. I, pp. 213-26.

60. R. W. Seton-Watson, *The Southern Slav Question and the Hapsburg Monarchy*, pp. 146-54.

61. Hribar, Vol. I, pp. 237-38.

62. Slovene Liberals hailed the inclusion of more South Slavs into the Empire but deplored the effect on Austro-Serb and Austro-Russian relations. See Chapter VI.

63. *Slovenski narod*, No. 264, 16 November 1912.

64. Hribar, Vol. II, pp. 47-54.

65. Young Liberals deserted the party in great numbers in the last half decade before the war, largely because of the party's support of Vienna. See below, Ch. IX.

66. Hribar's only reward for his efforts was a meeting with Serbia's Prime Minister Pašić—one of the most sacred "najsvetejsi") experiences of his lifetime. The two men in 1913 enthusiastically discussed Serbia's prospects as a Southern Slav Piedmont, parting with an especially firm handshake and tear-filled eyes. See Hribar, Vol. II, p. 58.

For Hribar's account of his arrest and imprisonment, see, Hribar, Vol. II, pp. 118-174.

Hribar saw the creation of the South Slav state after World War I, becoming its diplomatic representative to Prague in 1919 and a Senator in Belgrade in 1931. On 18 April, 1941, dejected by the recent collapse of Yugoslavia to the Nazis, Hribar, nearly 90, drowned himself in the Ljubljanica.

CHAPTER V

1. The first workers' society was organized in Ljubljana that year. It had a German as well as a Slovene membership. Dušan Kermavner, *Začetki Slovenske Socialne Demokracije v desetletju, 1884-1894*, Ljubljana, 1963, pp. 56-57.

2. By the turn of the century there were approximately 50,000 workers in Slovene parts of the Empire.

3. Rudolf Golouh, *Pol stoletja spominov*, Ljubljana, 1966, p. 52.

4. See Kermavner for a survey of Slovene worker activities in the decade 1884-1894.

5. Kermavner, p. 371.

6. Železnikar (1843-1903) himself was arrested in 1884 and sentenced to a ten year prison term. In that decade, due largely to continued police surveillance, radical workingmen's activities were severely curtailed. Kermavner, pp. 27-28.

7. Kermavner, pp. 89-90.

8. Hans Mommsen, *Die Sozialdemokratie und die Nationalitätenfrage in Habsburgischen Vielvölkerstaat*, Vol. I, Vienna, 1963, p. 151. Also see, Kermavner, p. 100.

9. No Slovene from either Ljubljana or Trieste attended the Third Congress of the Austrian Social Democratic Party in 1892. See Kermavner, p. 3.

10. Robert Kann, *The Multinational Empire*, New York, 1950, Vol. I, p. 104.

11. James Joll, *The Second International 1889-1914*, New York, 1966, Chapter I.

12. These were: *Delavec* (1893-98) and *Svoboda* (1896-98)—Lončar says these were virtually the same paper, which moved from place to place; *Delavec-Rdeči prapor* (1898-1905); *Rdeči prapor* (1905-1911); *Zarja* (1911-1914); *Naprej* (1903-1911); *Delavski List* (1908-1909). Dragotin Lončar, *Politično življenje Slovencev*, Ljubljana, 1921, pp. 135-37.

13. When Ludvik Zadnik, a tailor, was assigned the task of founding a Slovene language Socialist paper with the money Victor Adler had given Slovene Socialists for that purpose in 1889, he was widely criticized for not having proper educational qualifications, that he did not have enough school instruction ("zadostne šolske izobrazbe.") Kermavner, p. 151.

14. Kristan was probably directed by the Austrian party to found a separate Slovene organization. See Henrik Tuma, *Iz mojega življenja*, Ljubljana, 1937, p. 312.

15. Golouh, p. 24.

16. *Naši zapiski* (1902/03-1907) was published in Ljubljana and from 1909 to 1914 in Gorica; after 1920 it was published again in Ljubljana. Henrik Tuma maintains this review appealed only to the most radical intellectuals and never had more than three hundred subscribers. Tuma, p. 327.

17. Dušan Kermavner's comments on Albin Prepeluh, *Pripombe k naši prevratni dobi*, Ljubljana, 1938, p. 328.

18. *Slovenski biografski leksikon*, Vol. 4, Ljubljana, 1932, pp. 572-73.

19. The first Socialist from Slovene territories was elected to the Vienna Parliament in 1897; in 1907 there were seven and in 1911 three elected from Slovene and mixed national areas. Vasilij Melik, *Volitve na Slovenskem*, Ljubljana, 1965, p. 306.

20. See Kermavner on Prepeluh, pp. 307-332.

21. See Tuma on Anton Kristan's philosophy, pp. 321-24.

22. Such Masarykites were: Anton Dermota (1876-1914), who rejected the materialist world view, contending that "spiritual" regeneration was the means to economic betterment; Dragotin Lončar (1876-1954) the historian, who in rejecting Marxist materialism, advocated voluntary transfer of private property to public hands; and Anton Kristan (1881-1930), who became very active in cooperative organizations.

23. All Socialists did not regard Masarykites in a positive way. Karel Linhart (1882-1918) had contempt for their conversion to Socialism, regarding it the ultimate hypocrisy, the last compromising stages of a dying bourgeois liberalism. See Kermavner on Prepeluh, p. 336.

24. Czech Social Democrats in 1910 argued before the Copenhagen meeting of the International on behalf of national trade union organizations. When this was rejected a good number of Czechs broke away from the Austrian party. They had from the beginning of their association with German-Austrian Socialists had "nationalistic" quarrels with them.

25. Tuma, p. 313.

26. That conference had condemned private ownership of productive property, class privilege, and a standing army; it proclaimed working class solidarity, irrespective of national origin. It declared the immediate goals of the party to be the winning of universal suffrage, complete secularization of public education, broadening of worker welfare legislation, and introduction of an eight hour working day. A. J. May, *The Habsburg Monarchy*, Harvard, 1965, p. 158.

27. Tuma, pp. 312-24.

28. Prepeluh, p. 32.

29. Kermavner on Prepeluh, pp. 312-13, 338.

30. See Tuma, Chapter X, pp. 290-306.

31. Ibid, p. 259.

32. See Dušan Kermavner's comments on Tuma in Tuma, *Iz mojega življenja*, pp. 436-437.

33. See Kermavner on Prepeluh, pp. 365-367.

34. Abditus (Albin Prepeluh), *Socialni problemi*, Ljubljana, 1912, pp. 147-152.

35. Kermavner on Prepeluh, pp. 404-406.

36. Ibid., p. 402.

37. Dušan Kermavner, *Začetki Slovenski socialne demokracije v desetletju 1884-1894*, Ljubljana, 1963, pp. 25-28.

38. Hans Mommsen, *Die Sozialdemokratie und die Nationalitätenfrage im Habsburgischen Vielvölkerstaat*, Vol. I, Vienna, 1963, p. 153.

39. Arthur Kogan, "The Social Democrats and the Conflict of Nationalities in the Habsburg Monarchy," *Journal of Modern History*, Vol. 21 (1949), p. 210.

40. See Kogan, pp. 204-17 for a discussion of the meaning of the Brno program. Both Kogan and R. A. Kann, *The Multinational Empire*, Vol. I, Columbia University Press, New York, 1950, p. 105, regard the Brno program to be within that federalist tradition established at Kremsier in 1848.

41. The idea seems to have antedated Brno by at least one year. Renner under the pseudonym Synopticus wrote about it in *Staat und Nation* in 1899, but before the congress Etbin Kristan presented it in the journal *Akademie* in 1898 in an article entitled "Nationalismus und Sozialdemokratie." Renner seems to have hit upon the

"principle of personality" from the vantage point of a legalist searching for a compromise, while Kristan approached it as one representing a "non-historic" nation, one which needed to offer proposals alternate to state rights arguments. Each may have come upon the concept independently, but Mommsen suggests that Renner may have learned about it from Kristan. Renner and Friedrich Austerlitz at the time were on the editorial board of *Arbeiter Zeitung*, and Austerlitz also wrote for *Akademie*, the journal in which Kristan first suggested this solution. Mommsen, pp. 325-331.

Also see *Zgodovinski arhiv komunistične partije Jugoslavije*, Vol. V, (Socialistično gibanje v Sloveniji 1869-1920), Belgrade, 1951, pp. 62-67.

42. According to Henrik Tuma, it was he who convinced the party it was inappropriate for Socialists to draft such a statement. See Tuma, p. 331.

43. See below, Chapter IX.

44. It had been generally assumed that Slovene Socialists had used the term to attract Cisleithanian Southern Slavs, i.e., those from Dalmatia and Istria. However, in an interview with Etbin Kristan, Fran Zwitter learned that Slovene Socialists were rather particularly anxious to draw Hungarian or Zagreb "Yugoslavs" into their organization. See F. Zwitter, "Vprašanje koroške kandidature Ivana Cankarja leta 1907, *Koledar slovenske Koroske*, Klagenfurt, 1958, p. 5.

45. Abditus, "Jugoslovanstvo," *Naši zapiski* (October 1907), pp. 145-148.

46. Much of what appeared in this booklet (1000 copies were printed) had previously been published in article form in the Croat journal *Svoboda*. Tuma, p. 330.

47. Tuma, p. 329.

48. He felt especially strongly about keeping Trieste away from Italy.

49. Tuma, p. 300.

50. See Kermavner on Tuma, p. 439.

51. Ibid., taken from Tuma in *Naši List*, no. 11, March 17, 1906.

52. Tuma believed such a federation would also end European wars, which in the 19th century had, for the most part, resulted from Balkan tensions. Kermavner on Tuma, p. 439.

53. In 1915 the German, Friedrich Naumann, in a book entitled *Mitteleuropa* proposed the economic integration of Germany and Austria-Hungary.

54. Kermavner on Tuma, p. 428, quoted from *Naši List*, no. 11, March 17, 1906.

55. See Chapter VI for details.

56. *Zgodovinski arhiv komunistične partije Jugoslavije*, Vol. V, p. 171.

57. *Rdeči prapor*, no 128, 25 November 1909. Also see *Zgodovinski arhiv komunistične partije Jugoslavije*, Vol. V for provisions of Tivoli Resolution, pp. 201-03, and pp. 142-45 for Etbin Kristan's views on Yugoslavism.

58. See Chapter VII.

59. *Naši zapiski*, VI, 1909, p. 57.

60. The Slovenes were sometimes referred to as "mountain Croats" and some called for Croat-Slovene union on the grounds that there was no national difference between them.

61. *Rdeči prapor*, no. 81, 10 October 1908.

62. *Zarja*, no. 405, 10 October 1912.

63. *Zarja*, no. 426, 5 November 1912; no. 464, 19 December 1912.

64. See below, Chapter IX.

65. *Zgodovinski arhiv komunistične partije Jugoslavije*, Vol. V, pp. 280-12.

CHAPTER VI

1. From 1867 to 1877 Slovenes were in the majority in the Carniolan diet, but from 1877 to 1883 Germans captured control. After 1883, however, Slovenes never lost their majority in that body. See V. Melik, *Volitve na Slovenskem*, p. 297.

2. Much sympathy for the Croats was expressed by Slovenes in April of 1903 when Croat demonstrators were shot at (one was killed) by the police. Both the army and the police were required to put down ensuing demonstrations throughout Croatia. Slovenes protested in their daily papers, in Parliament, and at a protest gathering in Ljubljana. When Khuen Hedervary, hated Hungarian governor of Croatia for twenty years, was dismissed a few weeks after these demonstrations, Slovenes felt that their protests had had some effect. See L. Ude, "Slovenci in Jugoslovanska ideja," *Jugoslovenski narod pred prvi svetski rat*, p. 891.

3. Ivan Hribar, describing these events, designates as Germanophile, those Slovenes who voted for German candidates in the elections of the previous year. See Ivan Hribar, *Moji Spomini*, Vol. I, p. 340.

4. The soldiers belonged to the 27th infantry regiment from Graz.

5. *Slovenec*, No. 219, 24 September 1908.

6. Hribar's open support of the anti-German activity in the autumn of 1908 ultimately cost him his mayoral post. When he was reelected in 1910, the Emperor refused to confirm his election. See I. Hribar, *Moji Spomini*, Vol. I, p. 339. Hribar considered this Imperial snub a major turning point in his life. See Hribar's introduction to his memoirs, Vol. I.

7. See *Slovenec* and *Slovenski narod* issues for October 1 through October 6, 1908 for a sense that the annexation was imminent.

8. *Slovenec* No. 232, 9 October, 1908.

9. *Slovenec* No. 233, 10 October, 1908.

10. Erjavec, *Zgodovina katoliškega gibanja na slovenskem*, p. 171.

11. *Slovenec* No. 248, 28 October, 1908. (Italics in original.) Šušteršič used this phrase in a speech to a plenary session of the Austrian delegation to Parliament on October 27.

12. See B. Schmidt's *The Annexation of Bosnia*, p. 76.

13. Erjavec, *op. cit.*, p. 171.

14. *Slovenec* No. 291, 18 December, 1908.

15. *Slovenec* No. 247, October 27, 1908.

16. *Obravnave deželnega zbora kranjskega* (Minutes of the Carniolan diet.) January 19, 1909, Vol. 47, p. 271.

17. *Slovenski narod* No. 249, 24 October, 1908.

18. *Obravnave deželnega zbora kranjskega*, January 16, 1909, Vol. 47, p. 273.

19. *Slovenski narod* No. 296, 19 December 1908.

20. *Naši zapiski*, VI, 1909, p. 57.

21. *Rdeči prapor* No. 81, 10 October 1908.

22. H. Tuma in 1908 did warn, however, that if such developments did not take place, if Austria continued to mistreat her South Slavs, the Yugoslav question could precipitate a general European war. See Tuma in *Rdeči prapor* No. 96, 2 December 1908 and No. 97, 5 December 1908.

23. *Rdeči prapor* No. 93, 21 November 1908.

24. "Poraz?" *Naši zapiski*, VI, 1909, p. 51.

25. A. J. May, *The Habsburg Monarchy, 1867-1914*, p. 420.

26. For a detailed treatment of this trial and the Friedjung trial which followed see R. W. Seton-Watson, *The Southern Slav Question and the Habsburg Monarchy*. Seton-Watson as a journalist covered the trials and helped to publicize them widely.

27. C. A. Macartney, *The Habsburg Empire, 1790-1918*, p. 786.

28. *Naši zapiski*, VII, 1910, pp. 63-64.

29. *Rdeči prapor*, No. 93, 21 November 1908.

30. *Slovenec*, No. 162, 20 July 1909.

31. I. Šušteršič, *Moj Odgovor*, p. 63.

32. See Chapter V.

33. *Rdeči prapor* wrote on the eve of the conference that a fundamental decision would have to be made by the delegates as to whether their Marxist ideology precluded involvement with Yugoslavism. *Rdeči prapor*, No. 216, 20 November 1909.

34. Etbin Kristan, Juraj Demetrović, and Henrik Tuma were responsible for the final document. A. Prepeluh, *Pripombe k naši prevratni dobi*, Ljubljana, 1938, p. 71.

35. *Zgodovinski arhiv komunistične partije Jugoslavije*, Vol. V, Belgrade, 1951, pp. 201-03.

36. Prepeluh in his memoirs made this point, registering amazement at the fact that neither the regime nor local Germans seemed disturbed by the Tivoli program. Prepeluh therefore concluded that the entire document was too utopian for anyone to take seriously. See A. Prepeluh, *Pripombe k naši prevratni dobi*, Ljubljana, 1938, p. 71.

37. *Rdeči prapor*, No. 128, 25 November 1909.

38. D. Lončar, *Politično življenje Slovencev*, Ljubljana, 1921, p. 82.

39. Shortly after the conference *Rdeči prapor* published the following explanation of Yugoslavism:

"As we see it, Yugoslavism is a new idea with new economic foundations. It means creating one nation of the Croats, Serbs, Slovenes, and Bulgars, uniting them nationally and culturally, inspiring them with one political goal and thus making one political nation of them, however, not according to the idea of a nation state as the bourgeois parties see it. To create of the Yugoslavs one nation, means giving them one unified national thought, and giving them a political base; with respect to economic aspects of the problem, we as Social Democrats stand for Socialist proletarian cooperation." The political implications seem to stand out clearly. See *Rdeči prapor*, No. 134, 2 December 1909.

40. *Zgodovinski arhiv komunistične partije Jugoslavije*, Vol. V, Belgrade, 1951, pp. 204-05.

See Chapter VII for treatment of cultural nationalism among the Slovenes.

41. H. Tuma, *Iz mojega življenja*, Ljubljana, 1937, p. 330.

42. *Rdeči prapor*, No. 5, 13 January 1910; No. 7, 18 January 1910.

43. *Rdeči prapor*, No. 5, 13 January 1910.

CHAPTER VII

1. This chapter appeared in slightly different form in *Canadian Slavic Studies*, Vol. II, no. 1 (Spring, 1968), pp. 46-67. ("The Slovenes and Cultural Yugoslavism on the Eve of World War I").

2. *Veda* (Knowledge) was a Slovene literary journal published from 1911 to 1914. Most views on the merits of cultural Yugoslavism were expressed in its four volumes at one time or another.

3. Ivan Prijatelj (1875-1937) is best known for his *Slovenska kulturno-politična in Slovstvena zgodovina, 1848-1895* (Slovene cultural-political and literary history, 1848-1895), a five volume definitive work, published between 1938 and 1940. In the pre-World War I days, however, he was an editor of *Veda*, where he along with others debated the issue of cultural Yugoslavism.

4. Anton Dermota (1876-1914), Dragotin Lončar (1876-1954), and Albin Prepeluh (1881-1937) were all Masarykites, who joined the Social Democrats, but differed with the party on the issue of cultural Yugoslavism.

5. *Naši zapiski*, IX (1912), p. 48.

6. *Hrvatsko Kolo* (The Croat Circle) was published in Zagreb after 1904.

7. *Op. cit.*, IV (1908), pp. 380-81.

8. *Naši zapiski*, IX (1912), pp. 289-92.

9. Ibid., pp. 179-85. Prepeluh used the word "underdeveloped" to mean Slovenes as well.

10. Henrik Tuma (1858-1935) edited *Naši zapiski* after 1912. He was a member of the Yugoslav Social Democratic Party, and after 1908, with regard to the Yugoslav question, promoted Austrian expansion into the Balkans.

11. *Naši zapiski*, VII (1910), pp. 257-60.

12. *Op. cit.*, X (1913), pp. 137-40.

13. I. Mazovec, *Čas* (1912), pp. 25-40, 123-42.

14. Ibid., pp. 487-88.

15. F. Terseglav, *Čas* (1914), pp. 249-52.

16. Ibid.

17. *Slovenec*, No. 197, 31 August 1910.

18. H. Kohn, *Panslavism* (New York, 1960), pp. 245-46.

19. Ibid., p. 247. The Pan-Slavs in 1908 coined this term to distinguish their brand of Pan-Slavism from a Pan-Slavism associated with Russian imperialism, autocracy and Orthodoxy.

20. *Slovenski narod* (The Slovene Nation) was the official Liberal paper, published in Ljubljana from 1868 to 1945.

21. I. Hribar, *Moji spomini* (Ljubljana, 1928-33), II, p. 22.

22. *Narodno radikalno dijaštvo* came into existence aș an auxiliary of the Liberal party (National Progressive Party) in 1904.

23. The Liberal youth criticized the Liberal party for its social conservatism, and accepted the Masaryk position with regard to social reform. They did not join the Social Democrats as did the older generation of Masarykites, but remained within the National Progressive Party (Liberal) framework.

24. *Omladina* was published in Ljubljana from 1904 to 1912, but transferred to Prague for the period between 1912 and 1914.

25. *Omladina* (1909/1910), p. 160.

26. See Chapter II.

27. Neo-Illyrist views can be found in the *Veda* "Ankete." See *Veda*, III (1913). No specific study has been made of this Neo-Illyrist movement.

28. Fran Ilešič (1871-1942) was president of the *Slovenska Matica* from 1907 to 1914.

29. *Slovenska Matica* was established in 1864 as a publishing house and distributor of national literature.

30. Mihajlo Rostohar (1878-1966).

31. *Napredna misel* (1912), p. 112.

32. Ibid., p. 113.

33. Ibid., p. 118.

34. Ibid., p. 181.

35. *Preporod* organized officially in 1912. See below, Chapter IX.

36. Vladimir Knaflič (1888-   ) like Rostohar and many of the Slovene Masarykites, strongly held that the Slovene language must be preserved. His feeling was that political unity must not depend, nor could it be fortified with, language concessions.

37. *Naši zapiski*, VII (1910), p. 235.

38. *Veda*, II (1912), pp. 209-14.

39. Ibid., III (1913), p. 97.

40. Ibid.

41. Ivo Šorli (1877-1957).

42. *Veda*, III (1913), pp. 98-99.

43. Ibid., pp. 508-16.

44. Ibid.

45. Ibid., pp. 105, 311-15. No group among the Slovenes, with the exception of the student organization *Preporod*, advocated political independence from Austria. In *Veda* when the Slovenes discussed a Yugoslav political unit, they meant one inside Austria, one made up of Austro-Southern Slavs, who in the future might be joined voluntarily by other Balkan Slavs.

46. Aleš Ušeničnik (1868-1952) was a prominent Catholic theologian and clerical ideologue. He wrote for the journals *Rimski katolik, Katoliški obzornik,* and *Čas.*

47. *Slovenski narod*, No. 122, 31 May 1913.

48. Ivan Cankar, a prolific writer and a member of the Social Democratic Party, viewed the Yugoslav problem much as did the Masarykites. He was firmly opposed to cultural and linguistic assimilation and made a speech to that effect in the spring of 1913. His impact on the Slovene youth was particularly strong. See Chapter IX for detailed treatment of Cankar's impact on Slovene Yugoslavism.

CHAPTER VIII

1. E. C. Helmreich, *The Diplomacy of the Balkan War, 1912-1913*, Harvard, 1938, p. 58.

2. The issue which had divided Serbia and Bulgaria until this time was Macedonia to which both laid claim. In the March treaty the two parties agreed to seize Macedonia, technically still Turkish territory, and divided the bulk of it between them, leaving a small contested area in central Macedonia for the Tsar of Russia to allocate to the claimants. Ibid., p. 55.

3. The Serbian agreement with Montenegro has never been published. Ibid., p. 88.

4. Ibid., p. 328.

5. Ibid., p. 165.

6. In 1912 Austria even minimized her interest in the Sanjak of Novi Bazar through which she had previously intended to build a railway to Salonika; this would have connected Austria with the Aegean.

7. *Zarja*, No. 405, 10 October 1912.

8. Ibid.

9. *Zarja*, No. 408, 14 October 1912; also see *Zarja*, No. 426, 5 November 1912 and *Zarja*, No. 476, 7 January 1913.

10. *Slovenec*, No. 232, 9 October 1912.

11. *Slovenski narod*, 233, 10 October 1912.

12. *Slovenec*, No. 232, 9 October 1912.

13. *Slovenec*, No. 227, 3 October 1912 and No. 232, 9 October 1912.

14. *Slovenec*, No. 232, 9 October 1912.

15. *Slovenski narod* shortly after the war began expressed the Liberal view very explicitly: "We Slovenes have a universal historical role to fulfill, to prevent Germandom from reaching the Adriatic and the Balkans." *Slovenski narod*, No. 264, 16 November 1912.

16. *Slovenski narod*, No. 258, 9 November 1912; No. 81, 10 April 1913. Clericals were also concerned that anti-Slavic elements dominated the Triple Alliance. In this they included the Magyars. See *Slovenec*, No. 249, 29 October 1912; No. 284, 10 December 1912.

17. The Social Democrats and the Liberals were advocates of federalism, and the Krek element among the Clericals by 1912 or 1913 probably was in favor of it as well. See J. Pleterski, "Trializem pri Slovencih in Jugoslovansko zedinjenje," *Zgodovinski Časopis*, Vol. XXII, 1968, pp. 169-184.

18. *Slovenski narod*, No. 264, 16 November 1912.

19. *Slovenec*, No. 227, 3 October 1912.

20. The statement was issued on 18 April, 1913. See D. Lončar, *Politično življenje Slovencev*, Ljubljana, 1921, p. 85.

21. *Slovenec*, No. 79, 8 April 1913.

22. E. C. Helmreich, *The Diplomacy of the Balkan Wars, 1912-1913*, p. 209.

23. A. J. May, *The Habsburg Monarchy, 1867-1914*, Harvard, 1951, p. 463.

24. *Slovenski narod*, No. 81, 10 April 1913.

25. *Zarja*, No. 476, 7 January 1913.

26. *Zarja*, No. 464, 19 December 1912.

27. See Chapter VI.

28. E. C. Helmreich, *The Diplomacy of the Balkan Wars, 1912-1913*, p. 209.

29. *Slovenec*, No. 260, 12 November 1912.

30. D. Biber, "Jugoslovanska ideja in slovensko narodno vprašanje v slovenski publicistiki med balkanskimi vojnami v letih 1912-13," *Istorija XX Veka*, Belgrade, 1959, p. 288. Also see, *Slovenec*, No. 285, 11 December 1912.

31. *Slovenec*, No. 260, 12 November 1912.

32. I. Dolenc, "Razvoj jugoslovanske misli pri Kreku," *Čas*, Vol. XX, 1925/26, p. 163.

33. See above, Chapter III.

34. *Slovenec*, No. 174, 1 August 1912.

35. Fran Erjavec, *Zgodovina katoliškega gibanja na Slovenskem*, Ljubljana, 1928, pp. 202-3.

36. *Slovenec*, No. 242, 20 October 1912.

37. Slovene Clericals accepted in entirety the Rightist 1894 program at this time. See Dragotin Lončar, *Politično življenje Slovenev*, p. 84.

38. The Croat leader Starčević speaking at the Ljubljana meeting evoked the Croat Pragmatic Sanction of 1712 to justify the union. See *Slovenec*, No. 242, 20 October 1912. The 1712 document stipulated that in default of Habsburg male heirs, Croatia would accept princesses of that family who also ruled in the duchies of Austria, Styria and Carniola (Slovenes lived in the latter two.)

39. Silvo Kranjec, "Koroščevo predavanje o postanku Jugoslavije," *Zgodovinski Časopis*, Vol. XVI, 1962, p. 221. The term "Serb" was omitted; trialism within the monarchy, however, was stipulated.

40. See above, Chapter III.

41. The death of Karl Lueger in 1910 had left Austrian-German Catholics without dynamic leadership.

42. Jaroslav Šidak, Mirjana Gross, et. al., *Povijest hrvatskog naroda 1860-1914*, Zagreb, 1968, pp. 273-76.

43. Ibid., pp. 287-88.

44. Ivan Dolenc, "Razvoj jugoslovankse misli pri Kreku," in *Čas*, XX, 1925/26, pp. 160-62.

45. Ibid., p. 163.

46. Quoted in Ibid., p. 175.

47. Jaroslav Šidak, Mirjana Gross, et. al., *Povijest hrvatskog naroda 1860-1914*, Zagreb, 1968, p. 287.

48. Brumen, V., *Srce v sredini*, Buenos Aires, 1968, p. 139.

49. Janko Pleterski, "Trializem pri Slovencih in Jugoslovansko zedinjenje," *Zgodovinski Časopis* XXII, 1968, pp. 169-184, for an excellent discussion of these two approaches to trialism.

50. *Slovenec*, 7 December 1912. Quoted in Dolenc, "Beseda k časopisni kritiki Krekove številke," in *Čas* XX 1925/26, p. 271.

51. Brumen, V., *Srce v sredini*, Buenos Aires, 1908, p. 138.

52. Fran Erjavec, *Zgodovina Katoliškega gibanja*, Ljubljana, 1928, p. 208.

53. Ivan Mazovec, "Vzajemnost med Slovenci in Hrvati," *Čas*, VI, 1912, pp. 25-40, pp. 123-42.

54. A. Ušeničnik, "Nacionalizem in Jugoslovani," *Čas*, VI, 1914, pp. 289-311. Franc Terseglav, "Življenjski problem Avstrije," *Čas*, VII, 1914, pp. 249-52.

55. Krek continued to maintain Austria was a European necessity even in June 1914. See Ivan Dolenc, "Razvoj jugoslovanske misli pri Kreku," *Čas* XX, 1925/1926, p. 175. But Krek also stated quite explicitly in Parliament the previous year: "We don't want a German-Magyar Austria-Hungary, we want our state to grant equal rights to everyone, that it become a sort of large-scale Switzerland." Quoted in *Slovenec* No. 116, 24 May 1913.

56. See Chapter IX.

57. See Chapter IX. Also see Fran Erjavec, *Zgodovina katoliškega gibanja na Slovenskem*, Ljubljana, 1928, p. 219.

58. E. C. Helmreich, *The Diplomacy of the Balkan Wars, 1912-1913*, p. 349.

59. Ibid., p. 396.

60. *Slovenec* No 149, 2 July 1913.

61. *Slovenski narod* No. 186, 14 August 1913; No. 246, 25 October 1913.

62. Ibid., No. 10, 13 January 1912; No. 91, 23 April 1914; No. 93, 25 April 1914. The Liberals as in the past promoted federalism for the Empire based on cultural (and religious) and political equality for all nations. And they sought unrealistically to encourage a rapprochement between official Austria and Russia in order to diminish Germany's influence over Vienna.

63. Ibid., No. 168, 24 July 1913; *Zarja* No. 622, 3 July 1913.

64. See Chapter IX.

65. Most Masarykites broke with the party during World War I and promoted an independent Yugoslavia.

66. *Rdeči prapor-Zarja* No. 843, 6 June 1914; No. 846, 17 June, 1914.

67. A. Ušeničnik, "Verstvo in kultura. Kam plovemo?" *Čas* VII, 1913, pp. 223-p. 229.

68. A. Ušeničnik, "Balkanski problem in krščanska načela," *Čas* VII, 1913, pp. 55-63, p. 55.

69. Ibid., pp. 57-58.

70. A. Ušeničnik, "Svetovna vojska," *Čas* VIII, 1914, pp. 396-97.

CHAPTER IX

1. In 1930 Ivan Kolar wrote a useful study of these students and their movement, entitled *Preporodovci, 1912-14*. Kolar's book is relatively short and is based largely upon his own experiences as a member of the group, on conversations with its leaders, and on his use of the Ljubljana court records. Kolar also lived with some of the founders of the organization, and was therefore privy to much of the policy-making. Interview with Ivan Kolar, 25 June 1968.

Kolar did not, however, have access to the proceedings of the Graz court where two Preporodovci were tried in 1915. These materials, recently uncovered in Graz, have been transferred to Ljubljana, where in the summer of 1968 they were being processed and catalogued by the Institute for the History of the Workers' Movement. Vladimir Dedijer, preparing *The Road to Sarajevo* (Simon and Schuster, New York, 1966) came upon the Graz documents and was able with the aid of the above institute (Institut za zgodovino delovskega gibanja) to have them transferred to Ljubljana. See *Naši Razgledi*, 9 September 1967, p. 472. The Slovene Academy of Arts and Sciences has microfilm copy of all these materials and kindly made it available to the author.

Since Kolar's study little has been written on the Preporodovci. Indeed until the mid-60's these students remained relatively forgotten by historians. A formidable study of Slovene volunteers (*Dobrovoljci*) to the Serbian front, many of whom were Preporodovci or sympathized with them, was published in 1936,; but here the emphasis was on the war period. See *Dobrovoljci kladivarji Jugoslavije 1912-1918*, Ljubljana, 1936.

Several articles on the Preporodovci have appeared recently, inspired by anniversaries of either the founding of the movement or of the outbreak of the First World War. See especially Ernest Turk, "Značilnost preporodovskega gibanja na Slovenskem v zadnjih dveh letih pred prvo svetovno vojno," in *Razprave Slovenske akademije znanosti in umetnosti razred za agodovinske in družbene vede*, Vol. V, Ljubljana, 1966, pp. 389-418.

The availability of the Graz materials has again revived interest in the group. Moreover, the movement itself is being reevaluated in terms of post-World War II developments in Yugoslavia, an approach which views the Preporodovci, not only as champions of Yugoslav nationalism, but as precursors of a people's liberation movement as well. In effect, they are being credited with laying a cornerstone, so to speak, for Yugoslav socialism. The Slovene republic has recently awarded those Preporodovci-Dobrovoljci still living public recognition and a monetary token in the form of a pension supplement for those with meager retirements. Historians are just beginning to explore the new evidence on the movement before 1914, and it is very likely that, in time, still further relevant material will be uncovered. See Franc Rozman, "Prepoved Izdanjanja 'Preporoda' " in *Zgodovinski Časopis* XXII, 1968, pp. 105-06. Rozman discusses a government document, discovered in the Slovene Archives, prohibiting the publication of the student paper *Preporod*. He suggests that other valuable information may still be contained in the Slovene Archives, especially in sections relating to the Austrian Ministry of Interior.

Also see, *Preporodovci proti Avstriji*, Ljubljana, 1970, for survivors' accounts of the movement.

2. Kolar, p. 26.

3. The by-laws and minutes of some of the meetings were confiscated at the Fabjančič home in Brezovica on 11 July 1914, and provided the prosecution with valuable evidence as to the purpose of the organization. See Kolar, p. 27. It is pertinent to add here, however, that the by-laws were not widely circulated, if at all; it is doubtful, in fact, that many other than Fabjančič even read them, a point confirmed by Kolar, Lovšin, and Ponikvar in interviews on 25 and 26 June 1968. For the Ljubljana court the fact that the by-laws had not been made available even to the initiated disposed the court to leniency toward those put on trial in late 1914. The court even suggested that Fabjančič had deliberately tried to deceive the membership, that very likely many of the members really did not know precisely what the organization was all about. The court record had it that Fabjančič was an "evil spirit" (*zli duh*) who forced (*usilil*) the National Radical Youth to accept his program. Vr 643/14 412.

4. See testimony of Evgen Lovšin at the Ljubljana trial. Vr 643/14 412.

5. Ibid.

6. Fabjančič told Michael Čop that he was the leader of 700 youth. (Čop met Fabjančič in Belgrade in October 1913, where the latter offered Čop as much as 2000K to help him with the revolutionary organization.) See Čop testimony at the Ljubljana trial, Vr 643/14 412. Somewhat later, in a letter Fabjančič wrote to Dr. Božo Marković on the history of the revolutionary movement among Slovene students, he estimated his following at 1000. The letter was dated Winter 1914-15 and written in Niš. (Letter courtesy of Ivan Kolar.)

7. Kolar, p. 45.

8. We who are blacksmiths, we all will do some forging,
Forging of our hearts and, forging our nature,
And we'll listen for the ringing, ringing of our souls,
Why?
Because, perhaps the hammer will one day produce one whose heart is
    truest bronze,
One that will ring, and draw one to it like a bell.
And we will find ourselves around it gathered.

That is why we smiths shall continue forging,
Earnestly forging, closely listening,
That we'll not fail to recognize when
The hour has come,
The day has dawned,
When a truly mighty hammersmith has risen among us.

(Mi, kar nas je kovačev, mi bomo vsi kovali,
kovali svoja srca, kovali svoj značaj,
kako zvene nam duše, bomo poslušali—
kakaj:
Morda pa pod kladivi se nam oglasi kedaj
srce, ki v njem bo pravi bron,
da pelo bo, vabilo kot zvon,
da bomo krog njega se zbrali . . .

Zato bomo mi kovači kovali,
trdo kovali, tenko polušali,
da ne bo med nami nespoznan,
ko pride čas,
ko sine dan,
da vstane, plane kladivar silni iz nas!)

Above is the version printed in *Preporod*, no. 1, 1 November 1912; in subsequent editions of Zupančič's poetry some minor changes, usually in punctuation, have appeared.

9. Some Slovene students traveled in the Balkans already in summers of 1912 and 1913. In 1914 extended excursions were to begin after a congress of university students in Vienna dispersed on 29 June 1914 (the Ljubljana middle schoolers sent Vladislav Fabjančič as an official representative); however, the Archduke's assassination abruptly terminated these travel plans.

10. Kolar, p. 93.

11. Lovšin and others in making such statements at the trial were attempting to detract from the political nature of the organization by stressing the group's cultural projects. This, in order to thwart the prosecution in its charges of treason. However, it is very likely that these lectures were extremely important to members of the group themselves, who needed to sharpen their sense of identity with a Yugoslav cultural community.

12. "Mi smo šli iz stališča, da nudi šola premalo izobrazbe glede Jugoslovanov. Zato smo se hoteli izobraževati o jugoslovanski kulturi . . ." Lovšin testimony at Ljubljana trial. Vr. 642/14 410.

13. Janže Novak, who took the aims of the organization very seriously, even became an exemplary gymnast when the organization sent him on a proselytizing mission to Gorica in 1912-13, hoping thereby to gain the confidence and the minds of the Sokolers. (He won first place in an important tournament there.) See police interrogation report on Rakuščék. Vr. 643/14 405.

14. Publication figures for *Glas Juga* are not available. It is estimated, however, that *Preporod* was coming out in numbers of 2,500 by the spring of 1913. See F. Rozman, "Prepoved Izdajanja 'Preporoda,' " *Zgodovinski Časopis*, XXII, 1968, pp. 105-106.

15. Written by Adolf Ponikar on the occasion of the 500th anniversary of the last enthronement of an independent Slovene ruler (the Duke of Carinthia), 18 March 1414. Authorities never learned who the author had been.

16. About 400 participated in the Ljubljana strike on the 18th, 600 on the 20th. See Turk, pp. 412-13. Original figures appear in *Slovenec*, no. 63, p. 5 and no. 64, p. 3.

17. Kolar, pp. 122-129.

18. Most of the students judged that finishing the school year, passing exams, should be given prime attention. (Moreover, the authorities had threatened strikers with one year suspensions from the gymnasium. See Kolar, p. 125). According to the testimony of several at the Ljubljana trial, many of the records of the organization were destroyed after this March strike. Vr 643/14 412.

19. These were *srednošolci* in the fifth to eighth grades of the gymnasium. Most were seventeen to nineteen years old. Actually thirty-two students were charged, but five, who were by then in the Austrian army, were to be dealt with by military authorities. Of the thirty-two, twenty-six were middle school students, six were at the university. See I. Kolar, *Preporodovci, 1912-14*, Kamnik, 1930, p. 154.

20. Not only was the evidence inconclusive, but the six member court was divided. The three Slovene judges felt that the students' activities did not amount to treason, while the three Germans thought that the students were guilty of the charges. The president of the court was Slovene and tended towards leniency where the accused were concerned, so the charge of treason did not hold.

21. Of the twenty-seven most were legally under age, and the older who were university students, were treated less harshly, since they only corresponded by mail with the secret organization in question. These university students themselves had a "Yugoslav" club, but it was legally registered with the regime and was therefore more acceptable.

22. See statement of the judicial senate at the Ljubljana trial. Vr 643/14 413.

23. See Kolar, pp. 162-63.

24. Because Ljubljana had no university until the post-World War I period, Slovene students wishing to attend university lectures went to Vienna and Graz. Later in the 19th century some traveled even to Prague, while in the early years of the 20th century Zagreb University attracted some students with Illyrist or Yugoslav cultural affinities.

25. In 1848 Slovenes became politically active for the first time. Their program for the most part aimed at unifying all Slovenes, then scattered among several Austrian provinces, in one administrative unity. Already in 1848 some Slovenes sought the help of other South Slavs to further their aims. See above, Chapter II.

26. Jukić had attempted to assassinate the Governor and Royal Commissioner of Croatia Count Cuvaj on 8 June 1912. Jukić was sentenced to death for this act and thereafter became a great hero for South Slav revolutionary youth. See V. Dedijer, *The Road to Sarajevo*, New York, 1966, Ch. XII, pp. 261-84.

27. See report of inquest in Sušak, 6 October 1913 sent to Graz inquest in 1915, where the prosecution was preparing the second proceeding against Endlicher.

"Narodno Ujedinjenje" was the name of a revolutionary organization in Belgrade. Vr III 1076/15 499.

28. One university student club (Zora) in Vienna still met with government approval on the very weekend of the assassination, with the express purpose of organizing a broader movement for the Yugoslav cause. There is every indication that the Yugoslavism of this group was a greater threat to Austria than was that of the Ljubljana middle school organization, but Vienna tolerated it because its proceedings were open.

29. In the 1890's three distinct political parties emerged among the Slovenes. Beside the National Progressive Party, there was the Slovene People's Party (*Slovenska ljudska stranka*) and the Yugoslav Social Democratic Party (*Jugoslovanska socialna demokraticna stranka*). All three until 1914 were implicitly loyal to Austria.

30. To confine oneself to Parliamentary methods is utopian, wrote *Preporod* in June 1913; Slovene representatives, *Preporod* felt, went to Parliament only to fill their stomachs. *Preporod*, no. 11, 1 June 1913.

31. Even Lovšin at the Ljubljana trial discussed at length the debates which culminated in the *Preporod* decision to abandon its anti-clericalism. Vr 643/14 412.

32. For a more detailed treatment of Slovene Yugoslavism see "The Slovenes and Political Yugoslavism on the Eve of World War I," *East European Quarterly*, Vol. IV, no. 4, pp. 408-418. Also see Loze Ude, "Slovenci in Jugoslovanska ideja v letih 1903-1914," in *Jugoslovenski narod pred prvi svetski rat*, Belgrade, 1967, pp. 887-934.

33. *Omladina* was published in Ljubljana from 1904-1912; from 1912-1914 it was published in Prague.

34. Kolar, p. 23.

35. These two middle school groups united in October of 1912, after the Balkan War convinced the more moderate types that radicalism was indeed in order.

36. Kolar, p. 24.

37. For a detailed treatment of the Zagreb trials as well as an account of the Friedjung affair of the same year, which confirmed the corruption of the regime with respect to the Southern Slav question, see R. W. Seton-Watson, *The Southern Slav Question and the Habsburg Monarchy*, London, 1911.

38. Slovenes were particularly underrepresented in the provincial diets, which had not been affected by the Austrian electoral reform of 1907, instituting universal suffrage in the Vienna Parliament. In these local diets Slovenes received only 52 mandates out of 382. If these had been allotted according to population Slovenes should have had 131. J. Pleterski, "Položaj Slovencev pred prvo svetovno vojno," in *Jugoslovenski narod pred prvi svetski rat*, pp. 785-86. For a complete study on voting in the Slovene areas, see V. Melik, *Volitve na Slovenskem, 1861-1918*, Ljubljana, 1965.

39. See Fran Zwitter, *Les problèmes nationaux dans la monarchie des Habsbourg*, Belgrade, 1960. Zwitter sees the nationality problems of the Habsburg monarchy as basically social conflicts between the dominant ruling element (German in Cisleithania) and the lesser, largely peasant nationality elements, who in the 19th century had begun migrating to towns in fairly substantial numbers. The result was a growth of nationalism among the socially inferior groups as their numbers in the towns increased.

40. See Pleterski for statistics on class and occupation, pp. 786-87.

41. Juš Kozak testified at the Ljubljana trial that the elder Jenko had telegraphed 850 K to his son Avgust in Vienna, which was then used to finance the publication of *Glas Juga* (more below). The state prosecutor, however, was of the opinion that the money had come from Serbia.

42. E. Turk, "Značilnost Preporodovskega gibanja na Slovenskem v zadnjih letih pred prvo svetovno vojno,", in *Razprave Slovenske akademije znanosti in umetnosti, razred za zgodovinske in družbene vede*, Vol. V, Ljubljana, 1966, p. 407.

43. In *The Road to Sarajevo* Dedijer characterizes the Young Bosnians as primitive or people's revolutionaries, who were nourished by a heritage of brigandage and centuries of opposition to Turkish oppression. Their leadership in the early 20th century, Dedijer maintains, emerged directly from a peasant milieu.

44. Interview with Adolf Ponikvar and Evgen Lovšin, 26 June 1968.

45. Lovšin agreed that he, too, had been impressed with lectures on the French Revolution; other Preporodovci seemed similarly moved, given their idealizing of the 1793 French Constitution, see *Preporod*, no. 3, 1 January 1913.

46. Interview with Ponikvar and Lovšin, 26 June 1968.

47. See Lovšin testimony at the Ljubljana trial. Vr 643/14 412.

48. All Preporodovci at the Ljubljana trial repeatedly denied any connection between the middle school organization and the journal *Preporod*, since the latter had been designated subversive and made to cease publication.

49. The court concluded in its case against Novak in Graz, that his associations with other leaders of the movement were sufficient to convict him. It was not necessary to prove that Novak had been aware of or understood in depth the philosophy of Endlicher or others; that he kept up his contacts with them was proof enough that he approved of what they were up to; whether or not he knew precisely what this was the court deemed irrelevant. G. Z. Vr III 1076/15 522.

Lovšin in an interview (26 June 1968) stated that details of programs and philosophy were rarely debated, that this was somehow unnecessary. He had sensed at the time, as had others, he said, that there was agreement on principle which bound these students together.

50. For examples, see *Preporod*, no. 2, 1 December 1912, "Zakaj hočemo biti Jugoslovani?"*Preporod*, no. 3, 1 January 1913, "Naša smrt in naše vstajenje."

51. See *Preporod*, no. 5, 1 March 1913, "Še jedna priča."

52. See *Preporod*, no. 7, 1 April 1913, "Kaj hočemo s trializmom in federalizmom?"

53. See *Preporod*, no. 6, 15 March 1913, "Beograd brez maske."

54. Vladislav Fabjančič in Belgrade had a good deal of money at his disposal, and he offered some to Michael Čop in return for help with the revolution. Ostensibly he came by his money holding a clerical job in Belgrade, but in a letter to his mother, he boasted that he really did little work for his pay. See testimony of Michael Čop at the Ljubljana trial. Vr IX 643/14 312.

55. Viktor Zalar, when he edited *Glas Juga*, further urged the study of Cyrillic in an article entitled "Učimo se cirilice!"

56. See Mihajlo Rostohar's *Napredna misel*, I, no. 4, 1912, pp. 189-92; *Preporod* replied in no. 1, 1 November 1912; no. 4, February 1913; and no. 5, 1 March 1913.

57. Dedijer based his conclusion on private information from Juš Kozak, the writer, who is since deceased and cannot be called upon to clarify matters. See Dedijer, pp. 220-21.

For the views of surviving Preporodovci on the cultural issue, see *Preporodovci proti Avstriji*, Ljubljana, 1970, especially pp. 131-32.

58. See Nare Sanov (Jenko pseudonym), "Misli o našem narodnem problemu," *Preporod*, no. 5, 1 March 1913.

59. When questioned about *Preporod*'s socialistic tendencies in June 1968, Lovšin read the author excerpts from Zupančič, and himself characterized the socialism of the Preporodovci as essentially romantic. Interview with Lovšin and Poinikvar, 26 June 1968.

60. Fran Fabjančič authored the most emotional and militant of *Preporod*'s articles, many of which demanded violence and bloodshed. He contended that only blood-letting, a blood baptism could create a real Yugoslav nation. See "Zakaj hočemo biti Jugoslavani?" in *Preporod*, no. 1, 1 November 1912.

61. "The nation is waiting for its youth, its Slovene youth." (Narod čaka na svojo mladino, na slovensko mladino), *Preporod*, no. 1, 1 November 1912.

62. Lojze Ude, "Slovenci in jugoslovanska ideja," *Jugoslovenski narod pred prvi svetski rat*, Belgrade, 1967, pp. 910-11. Ude is skeptical about the information on Plut in the *Slovenski biografski leksikon* (see Footnote 63), but can offer no alternative.

63. *Slovenski biografski leksikon*, Vol. 7, Ljubljana, 1949, pp. 388-89.

64. Ibid. Also see Fran Erjavec, *Zgovodovina katoliškega gibanja na Slovenskem*, Ljubljana, 1928, pp. 183-84.

65. *Preporod*, no. 12, 25 June 1913.

66, *Dan*, no. 550, 7 July 1913.

67. *Dan*, no. 566, 22 July 1913.

68. *Dan*, no. 567, 23 July 1913.

69. For a biographical survey on Cankar, see *Slovenski biografski leksikon*, Vol. I, Ljubljana, 1925, pp. 67-72. Also see Lino Legiša, *Zgodovina Slovenskega slovstva*, Vol. V, Ljubljana, 1964, pp. 61-147 for a brief biography and survey of his work.

70. Vasilij Melik, *Volitve na Slovenskem*, Ljubljana, 1965, pp. 363-66.

71. Ivan Cankar, "Kako sem postal socialist," *Izbrana dela*, Vol. X, Ljubljana, 1959, pp. 403-412. This piece was originally published in 1918.

72. About 250 attended the lecture according to police records. See "Cankar pred sodnijo," *Cankarjev zbornik*, Ljubljana, 1921, p. 149.

73. Ivan Cankar, "Slovenci in Jugoslovani," in *Izbrani dela*, pp. 392-93.

74. Ibid., pp. 398-99.

75. Ibid., p. 400.

76. Ibid., p. 398.

77. Ibid., p. 396.

78. "Cankar pred sodnijo," pp. 150-51. This does not appear in the published version of Cankar's speech, though it was undoubtedly included in the oral presentation. Cankar spent considerable time explaining away his indelicate statement before the court one month later.

79. Ivan Cankar, "Slovenci in Jugoslovani," *Izbrani dela*, pp. 394-95.

80. Ibid., pp. 393-94.

81. *Slovenec*, no. 86, 16 April 1913.

82. Ivan Cankar, "Slovenci in Jugoslovani," *Izbrani dela*, p. 391.

83. Knaflič's major publication on Yugoslav nationalism was *Jugoslovansko vprašanje* (The Yugoslav Question), Ljubljana, 1912. He advocated political federalism for Austria, but cultural autonomy for each of her national groups. He believed that such principles should also be extended to areas formerly a part of European Turkey, which should be joined to Austria in a political and customs union.

BIBLIOGRAPHY

I. Primary Materials

Bibliographies and Official Publications

Obravnave deželnega zbora kranjskega. Ljubljana, 1903, 1908-1914.
Slovenski biografski leksikon. Ljubljana, Volumes I through X, 1925-1967.
Zgodovinski arhiv komunistične partije Jugoslavije, Belgrade, Volume V, 1951.

Contemporary Publications

Abditus (Albin Prepeluh). *Problemi malega naroda.* Ljubljana, 1918.
──────*Socialni problemi.* Ljubljana, 1912.
Ilešič, Fran. *Kultura in politika.* Zagreb, 1908.
Knaflič, Vladimir. *Jugoslovansko vprašanje.* Ljubljana, 1912.
Kristan, Etbin. *Narodno vprašanje in Slovenci.* Ljubljana, 1908.
Šušteršič, Ivan. *Moj odgovor.* 1922.
Tuma, Henrik. *Jugoslovanska ideja in Slovenci.* Gorica, 1907.
Vošnjak, Bogomil. *Ob stoletnici rojstva Mihe Vošnjaka.* Belgrade, 1937.

Interviews

Kolar, Ivan. June 25, 1968.
Lovšin, Evgen. June 26, 1968.
Ponikvar, Adolf. June 26, 1968.

Memoirs and Collected Works

Hribar, Ivan. *Moji spomini.* Volumes I-IV, Ljubljana, 1928-1933.
Krek, Janez Ev. *Izbrani spisi.* Volumes I-IV, Ljubljana, 1923-1933. Volume III, entitled *Socializem*, printed originally in 1901, was reissued as a part of Krek's collected works in 1925.
Prepeluh, Albin. *Pripombe k naši prevratni dobi.* Ljubljana, 1938.
Šuklje, Franjo. *Iz mojih spominov.* Volumes I-III, Ljubljana, 1926-1929.
Tuma, Henrik. *Iz mojega življenja.* Ljubljana, 1937.

Newspapers and Periodicals

Čas. Ljubljana, 1907-1942.
Dan. Ljubljana, 1912-1914.
Delavec-Rdeči prapor.
    Trieste, 1903-1905.
    Ljubljana, 1905-1911 (title shortened to *Rdeči prapor*).
    Ljubljana, 1911-1914 (title changed to *Zarja*).
  For other socialist papers not consulted, see Chapter V, footnote 12.
Glas Juga. Ljubljana, March-May 1914.
Hrvatsko Kolo. Zagreb, 1904-1914.

Jutro. Trieste and Ljubljana, 1910-1912.
Katoliški Obzornik. Ljubljana, 1897-1906.
Ljubljanski Zvon, Ljubljana, 1881-19
Mentor, Ljubljana. 1908/09-1922/23.
Napredna misel. Krsko, 1912; Prague, 1913-1914.
Naši zapiski. Ljubljana, 1902/03-1907; Gorica, 1909-1914; Ljubljana, 1920-1922.
Omladina. Ljubljana, 1904-1912; Prague, 1912-1914.
Preporod. Ljubljana, 1912-1913.
Rimski Katolik. Gorica, 1889-1896.
Slovenec. Ljubljana, 1873-1945.
Slovenski narod. Ljubljana, 1869-1945.
Veda. Gorica, 1911-1915.

II. Secondary Materials

Books

Apih, Josip. *Slovenci in leto 1848*. Ljubljana, 1888.
Arnez, John. *Slovenia in European Affairs*. New York and Washington, 1958.
Brumen, Vinko. *Srce v sredini*. Buenos Aires, 1968.
Dedijer, Vladimir. *The Road to Sarajevo*. New York, 1966.
Erjavec, Fran. *Zgodovina katoliškega gibanja na Slovenskem*. Ljubljana, 1928.
Farkaš, Andrej. *Dr. Anton Korošec*. Ljubljana, 1941.
Fischel, A. *Der Panslawismus bis zum Weltkrieg*. Stuttgart and Berlin, 1919.
Gestrin, Ferdo, and Melik, Vasilij. *Slovenska zgodovina, 1813-1914*. Ljubljana, 1950.
Glonar, J. (ed.) *Cankarjev zbornik*, Ljubljana, 1921.
Golouh, Rudolf. *Pol stoletja spominov*. Ljubljana, 1966.
Grafenauer, Bogo. *Zgodovina slovenska naroda*. Volumes I-V, Ljubljana, 1954-1962.
Haumant, Émile. *La Formation de la Yougoslavie*. Paris, 1930.
Helmreich, E. C. *The Diplomacy of the Balkan Wars, 1912-1913*. Harvard, 1938.
Jagodič, Jože. *Nadškof Jeglič*. Celovec, 1952.
Jászi, Oscar. *The Dissolution of the Habsburg Monarchy*. Chicago, 1961.
Jenks, William. *Austria under the Iron Ring*. Charlottesville, 1963.
Joll, James. *The Second International, 1889-1914*. New York, 1966.
Jurčec, Ruda. *I. E. Krek*. Ljubljana, 1935.
Kann, Robert. *The Multinational Empire*. Volumes I and II, New York, 1950.
Kermavner, Dušan. *Slovenska publicistika in prva ruska revolucija*. Ljubljana, 1960.
———— *Začeti slovenske socialne demokracije v desetletju 1884-1894*. Ljubljana, 1963.
Kidrič, France. *Zgodovina slovenskega slovstva*. Ljubljana, 1929-1938.
Kohn, Hans. *Panslavism*. New York, 1960.
Kolar, Ivan. *Preporodovci, 1912-1914*. Kamnik, 1930.
Kos, Milko. *Zgodovina Slovencev*. Ljubljana, 1933.
Kranjec, Silvo. *Kako smo se zedinili?* Celje, 1928.
Lah, Ivan. *Vodniki in preroki*. Ljubljana, 1927.
Lampe, Evgen. *III slovenski katoliški shod v Ljubljani*. Ljubljana, 1907.
Legiša, Lino (ed.) *Zgodovina slovenskega slovstva*. Volume II, Romantika in Realizem I. Ljubljana, 1959.
Lončar, Dragotin. *Janez Bleiweis in njegova doba*. Ljubljana, 1910.
———— *Politično življenje Slovencev*. Ljubljana, 1921.

Macartney, C. A. *The Habsburg Empire, 1790-1918*. London. 1968.

May, A. J. *The Hapsburg Monarchy, 1867-1914*. Harvard, 1951.

Melik, Vasilij. *Volitve na Slovenskem*. Ljubljana, 1965.

Merhar, B. (ed.) *Ivan Cankar—Izbrana dela*. Ljubljana, 1951.

Milčinović, A., and Krek, J. E. *Kroaten und Slowene*. Jena, 1916.

Mommsen, Hans. *Die Sozialdemokratie und die Nationalitätenfrage im Habsburgischen Vielvölkerstaat*. Volume I. Wien, 1963.

Paulová, Milada. *Jugoslovenski Odbor*. Zagreb, 1924.

Petrè, F. *Poizkus ilirizma pri Slovencih, 1835-1849*. Ljubljana, 1939.

Pleterski, Janko. *Narodna in politična zavest na Koroškem*. Ljubljana, 1965.

Poročilo pripravljalnega odbora o I slovenskem katoliškem shodu. Ljubljana, 1893.

Preporodovci proti Avstriji. (edited by Adolf Ponikvar) Ljubljana, 1970.

Prijatelj, Ivan. *Janko Kersnik—njego delo in doba*. Ljubljana, 1910.

——————— *Slovenska kulturnopolitična in slovstvena zgodovina, 1848-1895*.
    Volumes I-V, Ljubljana, 1955-1961.

Rupel, Mirko. *Primož Trubar—Življenje in delo*. Ljubljana, 1962.

Schmitt, Bernadotte. *The Annexation of Bosnia, 1908-1909*. Cambridge, 1937.

Seton-Watson, R. W. *The Southern Slav Question and the Habsburg Monarchy*.
    London, 1911.

Slodnjak, Anton. *Prešernovo življenje*. Ljubljana, 1913.

Slovensko-Hrvatski katoliški shod v Ljubljani. Ljubljana, 1913.

Sperans. (Edvard Kardelj). *Razvoj slovenskega narodnega vprašanje*. Ljubljana, 1957.
    (first edition, 1939).

Stavrianos, L. S. *Balkan Federation*. Smith College Studies in History, Volume XXVII.
    Northampton, Massachusetts, October, 1941-July, 1942.

——————— *The Balkans Since 1453*. New York, 1961.

Sutter, Berthold. *Die Badenischen Sprachenverordnungen von 1897*. Volumes I and
    II. Graz-Köln, 1960 and 1965.

Šidak, Jaroslav, Gross, Mirjana, et al. *Povijest hrvatskog naroda, 1860-1914*. Zagreb,
    1968.

Ude, Lojze. *Slovenci in Jugoslovanska Skupnost*. Maribor, 1972.

Wendel, Hermann. *Der Kampf der Südslawen um Freiheit und Einheit*. Frankfurt/Main,
    1925.

——————— *Die Habsburger und die Südslawen Frage*. Belgrade and Leipzig, 1924.

Zeman, Z. A. B. *The Break-Up of the Habsburg Empire, 1914-1918*. London, 1961.

Zwitter, Fran. *Les problemes nationaux dans la monarchie des Habsbourg*. Belgrade,
    1960.

——————— *Nacionalci problemi v habsburški monarhiji*. Ljubljana, 1962.

Articles

Biber, Dušan. "Jugoslovanska ideja in slovensko narodno vprašanje v slovenski publicistiki med balkanskimi vojnami v letih 1912-1913," *Istorija XX Veka*, Vol. I, Belgrade, 1959, pp. 285-326.

Dolenc, Ivan. "Razvoj jugoslovanske misli pri Kreku," *Čas*, XX, 1925/26, pp. 137-179.

Grafenauer, Bogo. "Slovenski kmet v letu 1848," *Zgodovinski časopis*, Vol. II-III, Ljubljana, 1948-49, pp. 7-68.

Haas, Arthur. "Metternich and the Slavs," *Austrian History Yearbook*, Vol. IV-V, Rice University, 1968-69, pp. 120-49.

Hantsch, Hugo. "Pan-Slavism, Austro-Slavism, Neo-Slavism: The All-Slav Congresses and the Nationality Problems of Austria-Hungary," *Austrian History Yearbook*, Vol. I, Rice University, 1965, pp. 23-32.

Kermavner, Dušan. "Hegemonistična prekonstrukcija jugoslovanskega programa v Ljubljani leta 1870," *Zgodovinski časopis*, Vol. XVI, Ljubljana, 1962, pp. 81-144.

————— "Nekaj kritičnih pripomb k razpravljanju dr. Koste Milutinovića v tem časopisu," *Zgodovinski časopis*, Vol. XIV, Ljubljana, 1960, pp. 207-17.

————— "Slovenske stranke v volivnoreformni situaciji in narodnostna politika slovenske socialne demokracije, 1905-1907," *Novi svet*. No. 7, 1952.

————— "Še iz pred zgodovine jugoslovanskega kongresa v Ljubljani decembra 1870," *Zgodovinski časopis*, Vol. XIX-XX, Ljubljana, 1965-66, pp. 319-54.

————— "Še nekaj gradive o Ljubljanskem kongresu leta 1870," *Zgodovinski časopis*, Vol. XVII, Ljubljana, 1963, pp. 155-170.

Klopčič, France. "Mali narodi in socialism," *Zgodovinski časopis*, Vol. XXVI, Ljubljana, 1972, pp. 383-85.

————— "Protivojno stališče slovenske socialnodemokratske stranke leta 1914 in 1915," *Zgodovinski časopis*, Vol. XXIV, Ljubljana, 1970, pp. 53-75.

Kogan, Arthur, "The Social Democrats and the Conflict of Nationalities in the Habsburg Monarchy," *Journal of Modern History*, Vol. 21, 1949, pp. 204-17.

Kranjec, Silvo, "Korošćevo predavanje o postanku Jugoslavije," *Zgodovinski časopis*, Vol. XVI, Ljubljana, 1962, pp. 218-229.

————— "Slovenci na poti v Jugoslavijo," *Spominski Zbornik*, Ljubljana, 1939, p. 32.

Lončar, Dragotin. "K Prijateljevi kulturni in politični zgodovini Slovencev, 1848-1895," *Zgodovinski časopis*, Vol. IV, Ljubljana, 1950, pp. 183-94.

Marušič, Branko. "Razvoj političnega življenja Goriških Slovencev od uvedbe ustavnega življenja do prvega političnega razkola," *Zgodovinski časopis*, Vol. XXIII, Ljubljana, 1969, pp. 1-30.

Melik, Vasilij. "Frankfurtske volitve 1848 na Slovenskem," *Zgodovinski časopis*, Vol. II-III, Ljubljana, 1948-1949, pp. 69-134.

————— "Nekaj značilnost razvoja na kranjskem 1867-1871," *Zgodovinski časopis*, Vol. XXIII, Ljubljana, 1969, pp. 65-74.

————— "O nekaterih vprašanjih slovenske politike v začetku šestdesetih let 19 stoletja," *Zgodovinski časopis*, Vol. XVIII, Ljubljana, 1965, pp. 155-70.

————— "O razvoju slovenske nacionalno-politične zavesti 1861-1918," *Zgodovinski časopis*, Vol. XXIV, Ljubljana, 1970, pp. 39-51.

————— "Razcep med staroslovenci in mladoslovenci," *Zgodovinski časopis*, Vol. XXVI, Ljubljana, 1972, pp. 85-98.

————— " Slovensko narodno gibanje za časa taborov," *Zgodovinski časopis*, XXIII, Ljubljana, 1969, pp. 75-88.

————— "Slovenska politika ob začetku dualizma," *Zgodovinski časopis*, Vol. XXII, Ljubljana, 1968, pp. 25-59.

————— "Sprememba programa slovenskega političnega tabora v letu 1867," *Zgodovinski časopis*, Vol. XVIII, Ljubljana, 1965, pp. 309-17.

————— "Volitve v Trstu 1907-1913," *Zgodovinski časopis*, Vol. I, Ljubljana, 1947, pp. 70-122.

Milutinović, Kosta, "Problematika Ljubljanskog Jugoslovenskog programa 1870 kod Srba i Hrvata," *Zgodovinski časopis*, Vol. X-XI, Ljubljana, 1956-57, pp. 154-82.

Pleterski, Janko, "Položaj Slovencev pred prvo svetovno vojno," *Jugoslovenski narod pred prvi svetski rat*, Belgrade, 1967, pp. 761-788.

Pleterski, Janko, "Trializem pri Slovencih in Jugoslovanske zedinjenje," *Zgodovinski časopis*, Vol. XXII, Ljubljana, 1968, pp. 169-184.

Rogel, Carole, "Preporodovci: Slovene Students for an Independent Yugoslavia, 1912-1914, *Canadian Slavic Studies*, Vol. V, no. 2, 1971, pp. 196-212.

——————— "The Slovenes and Cultural Yugoslavism on the Eve of World War I," *Canadian Slavic Studies*, Vol. II, no. 1, 1968, pp. 46-67.

——————— "The Slovenes and Political Yugoslavism on the Eve of World War I," *East European Quarterly*, Vol. IV, no. 4, pp. 408-18.

Stökl, Gunther. "Der Beginn des Reformationsscrifttums in slowenischer Sprache," *Südost-Forschungen*, Köln, 1954.

Šlebinger, J. "Slovenski časniki in časopisi," *Razstava slovenskega novinarstva*, Ljubljana, 1917.

Šuklje, Fran, "Jan. Ev. Krek v parlamentu," *Čas*, XX, Ljubljana, 1925-26, pp. 121-37.

Turk, Ernest. "Značilnost Preporodovskega gibanja na Slovenskem v zadnih letih pred prvo svetovno vojno," *Razprave slovenske akademije znanosti in umetnosti, razred za zgodovinske in družbene vede*, Vol. V, Ljubljana, 1966, pp. 389-418.

Ude, Lojze. "Slovenci in jugoslovanska ideja v letih 1903-1914," *Jugoslovenski narod pred prvi svetski rat*, Belgrade, 1967, pp. 887-941.

Ušeničnik, Ales. "Dr. Jan. Ev. Krek sociolog," *Čas*, XX, Ljubljana, 1925-26, pp. 97-121.

Wendel, Herman, "Marxism and the Southern Slav Question," *Slavonic Review*, December, 1923, pp. 263-88.

Zorn, Tone. "Andrej Einspieler in slovensko politično gibanje na Koroškem v 60 letih XIX stoletja," *Zgodovinski časopis*, Vol. XXIII, Ljubljana, 1969, pp. 31-51.

Zwitter, Fran. "Illirisme et Sentiment Yougoslave," *Le Monde Slave*, Vol. X, 1933, pp. 39-71, 161-85, 358-75.

——————— "Narodost in politika pri Slovencih," *Zgodovinski časopis*, Vol. I, Ljubljana, 1947, pp. 31-69.

——————— "Nekaj problemov okrog jugoslovanskega kongresa v Ljubljani leta 1870" *Zgodovinski časopis*, Vol. XVI, Ljubljana, 1962, ρp. 145-70.

——————— "Problem narodnega preroda pri južnih slovanih v Avstriji: Legitimizem in narodnostno načelo," *Zgodovinski časopis*, Vol. IX, Ljubljana, 1955, pp. 162-69.

——————— "Slovenski politični prerod XIX stoletja v okviru evropske nacionalne problematike," *Zgodovinski časopis*, XVIII, Ljubljana, 1964, pp. 75-153.

——————— "The Slovenes and the Habsburg Monarchy," *Austrian History Yearbook*, Vol. III, Pt. 2, Rice University, 1967, pp. 159-188.

——————— "Vprašanje koroške kandidature Ivana Cankarja leta 1907," *Koledar slovenske Koroske*, 1958.

——————— "Vzroki in posledice Avstrijsko-ogrskega sporazuma," *Zgodovinski časopis*, Vol. XXII, Ljubljana, 1968, pp. 1-24.

Unpublished Works

Rogel, Carole, "The Illyrian Provinces, 1809-13," Master's Essay, Coumbia University, 1961.

——————— "The Slovenes and the Southern Slav Question, 1889-1914," doctoral dissertation, Columbia University, 1966.

Abditus (See Prepeluh, Albin)

Adler, Victor, 52,57

Adriatic Sea, v,46,48,59

Albania, 91,93,94,98,99

All Slovene People's Party (Vse-slovenska ljudska stranka) (See Clericals)

Arbeiter Zeitung, 52

Archduke John, 15

Auersperg-Lasser government, 20,43

Austria (Also see Vienna),v,6,7, 14,21,39,115-116; and Slovene cultural nationalism, 10; 1848, 14,15,18; foreign involvements in 1860's, 19; constitutional experiments of 1860's, 19-22; and Russo-Turkish War, 26; Western Christian mission, 26, 30, 33-34, 92,93; raison d'être, 36-37, 79-80; "German" mission, 37; Slovene Liberals and, 40,45; anti-Slavic, 45; workers and workers' organizations, 51-52; an economic unit, 59-60; Slovene Socialists and, 61-62; Slovene parties and, 63,66; Balkan policy, 90-91,95,101; Austro-Russian rivalry, 90; and Balkan Wars, 90-91,92,100; and Albania, 93-94; Preporod and, 106-112 passim

Austrian Social Democratic Party (Sozialdemokratische Partei Oesterreiches—SPÖ), 51-52, 57-58

Austromarxism, 57-58,60,61,62, 69

Austroslavism, vi,17,72; and Slovene Liberals, 45-47

Bach, Alexander, 18

Balkans, 26,34,39,46,81; Socialists and, 59

Balkan League, 91-92,96,99

Balkan Wars (1912-1913), 61-62, 84,107,113,114; Slovene volunteers, 89; Slovenes and, 90-101

Bauer, Otto, 58,94

Belcredi, Richard, 20,22

Belgrade, 72,95; Social Democratic Conference (1910), 62,74

Bernstein, Eduard, 53-54

Bismarck, Otto von, 25; Kulturkampf, 34-35

Bleiweis, Janez, 13,14,15,17

Bohorič, Adam, 5

Bosnia and Herzegovina, 38,49,60,61; annexation of, 39, 45,60,61,81,82,99,107; Slovene parties and annexation, 63-74

Bosnians,36; Young Bosnians,108

Brno (Brünn), 54,61; Program of, 57-58

Bulgaria, 46,47,65,73,76,99-200; Balkan Wars and, 62,90-91,113

Cankar, Ivan, 58,62,100,113-116

Carinthia, 3; Slovene migration to, 4; dukedom, 4; ducal enthronement, 4; incorporated into Austria, 4; language of, 6; "Carinthia" synonomous with "Slovene", 4; workers, 51

Carniola, 3,14,45,50,107; language of, 3,6; to France (1809), 7; diet of, 22,41,63,67; Slovene-German conflict (1908), 64-65

Čas (Time), 30,34,101

Catholic National Party(Katoliška narodna stranka) (See Clericals)

Catholic Political Society (*Katoliško politično društvo*), 28
Christian Socialism, 31-33,39,56; and nationalism, 80
Cisleithia (Austrian part of Habsburg Empire after 1867) (See Austria)
Clericals (Slovene People's Party/ *Slovenska ljudska stranka*), iv, 40,41,44,52,56,65,74,75,116; conservatives before 1890, 21, 25,26,27; party founding and ideology, 28-39; leaders and ideologues, 30-32; Catholic national program, 33-35,36; cooperatives, 31-32,42; and Bosnian annexation, 65-68; treason trials (1909), 72; and Illyrism, 79-80,84,88-89; and Balkan Wars, 92-95 passim, 99-100; merger with Croat Party of Right, 95-98
Clergy, German and Italian, 4; and Prešeren, 11; alienates peasantry (1848), 16
Compromise of 1867, 22
Congress of Berlin (1878), 26,65, 66
Conrad von Hötzendorf, 93
Čop, Matija, work with Preseren, 11
Croat-Slovene Part of Right (*Hrvatsja-slovenska stranka prava*), 28,95-98,99
Croats, iv,8,28,35,48,63,73,76, 82,83-84,86,98; Rightists, 49,50,80; national identity, 9; in 1848, 15; and Slovene Yugoslavism (1860's), 23-25; National Party, 23,25; Slovene Clericals and, 37-38; trialism, 38;

Declaration of Rijeka, 49; Croato-Serb Coalition, 49,50, 70-72, 107; and Slovene Socialists, 58; at Tivoli Conference, 73; Croat Party of Right, 95-98
Croatia, v; to France (1890), 7; and Slavonia and Dalmatia, 16; state rights program, 37
Czechs, 16,17,23,35; 19th century political alignments, 21; Catholics, 29; Young Czechs, 40; and Slovene Liberals, 46-47; Socialists, 54; and trialism, 68
Dalmatin, Jurij, translation of Bible, 5
Dan, 112,113,116
Declarations of Zadar and Rijeka, (1905), 49
Delavec-Rdeči prapor (The Worker-Red Banner), 72,74 (Also see *Zarja*)
Dermota, Anton, 53,71,77,78
Drašković, Janko, 12
Družba sv. Mohorja, 19
Dualism, 25,61; Slovene Socialists oppose, 57; crisis (1908-1909), 68

Einspieler, Andrej, 20
Endlicher, Ivan, 104-06, 108
Enlightenment, 6,7; influences on Slovene writers, 7; influences on Liberals, 43
Fabjančič, Fran, 102,107,108
Fabjančič, Vladislav, 105,107,108
February Patent (1861), 19-20
Ferdinand (Bulgarian Tsar), 50,100
Fiume, to France (1809), 7; Declaration of Rijeka, 49

France, French Revolution, 7,43, 108; rule in Illyrian Provinces, 8; war with Prussia, 24,25; and Balkan Wars, 91
Francis I (Emperor of Austria), 9
Francis Ferdinand (Archduke of Austria), 37-38,72,96,97,104, 105
Francis Joseph (Emperor of Austria-King of Hungary), 25, 26; and Hribar's election, 45; fast eater, 55
Franco-Prussian War (1870), 24
Frankists, 95-96
Franks, 4
Frankfurt Parliament (1848-49), 14,15; Graz Slovenes oppose, 16-17
Friedjung, Heinrich, 70-71

Gaj, Ljudevit, 11,12,13; and 1848 Revolution, 16
Germans (Austro-), iii,4,9,15,16, 17,75; nobility,3; nationalism, iii,40; imperialism, vi,35; language, 11; Germanization of Slovenes, 11,12,16,42,63,107-108; German Liberals, 14,17, 20,26,28,35,43; German Confederation, 14,24; Great Germany, 14,17; Conservatives, 27; Catholics, 34; Pan-Germanism, 34,46,86,113; Slovene anti-Germanism, 64; and Bosnian annexation, 68
Germany, 33,69; Austro-Prussian War, 19,22; Franco-Prussian War, 24,25; bastion of Protestantism, 33-34; and Slovene Liberals, 45; and Balkan Wars, 91

Glas Juga (The Voice of the South), 103,108,109,111
Gorica, 3; to France (1809), 7; election to diet, 41; 400 years of Habsburg rule, 55
Gosposvetski polje, 4, 103
Graz, 14,16; trials of Preporodovci, 105
Greece, 90-91, 94,99-100

Hainfeld, 52; program, 54-57
Habsburg Empire (See Austria), vi,3,16; Carinthia incorporated, 4; war with France, 7
Herder, Johann Gottfried, 6
Hohenwart Club, 27
Hribar, Ivan, 65,100; Liberal leader and Ljubljana mayor, 41-42; Ljubljana earthquake relief, 42; and Slovene language, 44; and Panslavism, 47-50 passim, 81,82,87; "Slavic" banking, 47-48; and Strossmayer, 48-49; and Serbia, 49-50
Hrvatska-slovenska stranka prava (See Croat-Slovene Party of Right)
Hrvatsko Kolo (The Croatian Circle), 77
Hungarians (See Magyars)
Hungary, iii (See Magyars)

Ilešič, Fran, 83,88
Illyria, 8; Illyrians, 8; "Illyrian" language, 9; Kingdom of, 9,20
Illyrian Provinces (1809-1813), 3,7,8,9; French rule, 8
Illyrism (cultural Yugoslavism), vi,9,74; pre-March 1848, 13; in 1848, 15,16,17; Tivoli Program, 60-61,73-74; and Neo-Illyrism

Illyrism *(cont.)* 75-89 passim, and Preporod, 110-111; and Cankar, 115

Innerösterreich, 20; *Stimmen aus*, 20

Istria, 3; to France (1809), 7

Italy, Austrian war with Sardinia, 1922

Izvolsky, Alexander, 48

Jeglič, Anton Bonaventura, 44

Jelačić, Josip, 15

Jenko. Avgust, 103,105,107,111

Jugoslovanska socialnodemokratična stranka (Yugoslav Social Democratic Party) (See Socialists)

Joseph II (Habsburg Emperor), 6 9

Jukić, Luka, 105

Jurčič, Josip, 85

Jutro, 112

Kajkavian, 12

Karadžić, Vuk, 10

Katoliška narodna stranka (Catholic National Party) (See Clericals)

Katoliški obzornik (Catholic Review), 30

Kautsky, Karl, 56

Kavčič, Matija, 17

Kingdom of Serbs, Croats, and Slovenes (Also see Yugoslavia), iii

Klic od Gospe svete (The Call from Gospa sveta), 103,108

Klun, Karel, 28,29,30,31

Kmetijske in rokodelske novice (Peasant and Craftsman News), 13

Knaflič, Vladimir, 85,116

Kollár, Jan, 11-12

Kopitar, Jernej, 3,10,11,13,120-121; work with Vuk Karadžić, 10; state censor, 10; Illyrism, 12

Kordelič, Karl, 51

Korošec, Anton, 38,95,97

Kovaška, 103

Kramař, Karl, 47

Kranjska Čbelica (The Carniolan Bee), 13

Kranjska špraha (See Slovene language), 3

Krek, Janez Evangelist, 30,31,39, 52,56; Christian Socialist, 31-33; *Socializem*, 32; social and political thought of, 32-36; and Bosnian annexation, 66-67; and Balkan Wars, 95,97,98,99,101

Krelj, Sebastijan, 5

Kremsier Parliment, 17,18; Kremsier Constitution, 18

Kristan, Anton, 53,54

Kristan, Etbin, 52-53,58,114; "Slovene Bebel", 53; Vienna training, 54; "principle of personality," 58; Tivoli Program, 61-62,74,76-77

Leo XIII (Pope), 32

Leopold II (Habsburg Emperor), 9

Liberals (National Progressive Party/*Narodna napredna stranka*), 79,102,112,116; liberals before 1890, 17,21,23,25,26,27,28,35, 105; party founding and ideology, 40-50; leaders, 41-43; writers and journalists, 42; anticlericalism, 44-45; and German

Liberals (cont.) landowners, 45; anti-German,45-46; national federalism for Austria, 45-46, 50,93: Panslavism, 46-48; Sokols, 47,103; and Bosnian trials (1909), 71-72; and Illyrism, 80-82; and Balkan Wars, 92-95, 99-100; and Preporod, 106,111

Linhart, Anton, 7

Linhart, Karl, 52

Ljubljana, 78,82,97,102,107, 112,113; in 1848,14,15; site of Yugoslav Conference (1870), 24; Liberal mayors of, 41,63; growth and economic development, 41; earthquake (1895), 42-43; 1908 shooting of two youths, 45,64-65,71,90; workers in, 51; Conference (1912), 95-98; student strikes (1914), 103-104; Ljubljana trial of Preporodovci, 104-105

Ljubljana Credit Bank (Ljubljanska kreditna banka), 41

Ljubljanski Zvon (The Ljubljana Bell), 46

Ljubljanske novice (Ljubljana News), 7

Lončar, Dragotin, 53,77,78

Lovšin, Evgen, 109

Lunder and Adamič shooting (190845-64

Magyars, 15,37,47,66,71,75; Magyarization, 16; Compromise of 1867, 22; Hungarian-Croat Compromise (1868), 23; Hungary and Yugoslav Conference of 1870, 23-24,25; Declaration of Rijeka and Zadar, 49; Slovene

parties and, 63,67; and Bosnian annexation, 68,70,90; and Balkan Wars, 90-91

Mahnič, Anton, vi, 29-33 passim, 80; anti-liberalism, 29,31,33, 41,44,45

Majar, Matija, 16; and Maribor Program, 20

Maria Theresa (Habsburg Empress), 6

Maribor Program (1865), 20-21

Marmont, Maréchal, 9; ruler of Illyrian Provinces, 8

Masaryk, Thomas, 74,83; and Slovene intellectuals, 53-54; and treason trials (1909), 71-72; and Albania, 94

Masarykites (Masarykovci), 53-54,55,56,100,116; and cultural Yugoslavism, 61,74,76-79,84, 87-88

Metternich, Prince Clemens Lothar, 10,11,14

Miklošič, Fran, 14,15

Miletić, Svetozar, 25

Mitteleuropa, 59-60

Montenegro, 36,69,90,91,97,100

Mrazović, M., 23,25

Muršec, Josip, 14

Napoleon, 7,9; Illyrian Provinces, 8

Napredna misel (Progressive Thought), 84

Naprej (Forward), 54

Narodna napredna stranka (National Progressive Party) (See Liberals)

Narodna odbrana, 112

Naši zapiski (Our Notes), 53,55, 74,78,85

Nastič, George, 70-71,72
National Progressive Party (Na-
rodna napredna stranka) (See
Liberals)
National Radical Youth (Narodna
radikalno dijaštvo), 82,83,107
"Non-historic" nation, 3
Novak, Janže, 104-105

October Diploma (1860), 19-20
Old Slovenes (staroslovenci)21,
26,27
Omladina (Youth), 82,107
Orthodoxy, 37,38,94,97,98;
opposed by Clericals, 33-34,
101; and Slovene Liberals, 48;
Orthodox culture, 75

Palacky, František, 17,45
Panslavism, 66,67,70; and
Illyrism, 11-12; among Slo-
venes in 1860's, 23; and
Slovene Liberals, 46-47; Neo-
slavism, 47-48,50,80-82,100;
congresses, 47,80-81; banking
ventures, 47-48,50
Parliament, Vienna, v,15,21,29,
40,41,63,114
Peter I (King of Serbia), 49,64
Plut, Milan, 112-113
Pohlin, Marko, 6
Poles, 35; and Neoslavism, 80,
100
Ponikvar, Adolf, 108,109
Prague Slav Congress (1848, 16,
18
Prepeluh, Albin (Abditus), 52,
77-79,80; concern for peasants,
55-56; and Serbia, 59; Yugo-
slavism, 59
Preporod (Renaissance),
106,107,109,110,111,116;

Preporod movement, 99,102-
112; founding and organization, 102-103; contacts in
South Slav lands, 103; arrest
and trial, 104-105; break with
older generation, 106; and
socialism, 111; Illyrism, 110-
111
Prešeren, France, 11,42,46,74,
75; Romantic poetry, 11;
views on Slovene language and
culture; 11,12,12; revival of,
82,83,84,87
Pressburg, Treaty of (1805), 7
Protestantism, 33-34
Prijatelj, Ivan, 76,85
Prussia (See Germany)

Rački, Franjo, 48,49
Rdeči prapor (See Delavec)
Reformation, 5,36; Catholic
Reformation, 6
Reichspost, 70-71
Renner, Karl, 58
Rerum novarum, 32
Revisionism (Socialist), iv,53-54
Revolution of 1848, 13,14-18;
German nationalism, iii; and
Slovene students, 105
Rimski Katolik (The Roman Ca-
tholic), 29,41
Roman Catholic Church, vi;Con-
cordat of 1855, 18,21; Catholic
politics, 29-30; Catholic con-
gresses, 30; Papal Proclamation
of Infallibility (1870), 44,48;
position regarding socialism,
52; Leo XIII and Christian So-
cialism,31-33;Western Christian
civilizing mission, 75,79-80
Romania, 99-100
Rostohar, Mihajlo,83-84,85,86,88

Rudolf (of Habsburg, 1273), 4
Russia, 23,26,33,66-67,81; and
Slovene Liberals, 45-47; Russian
Socialists, 57; and Slovene Socialists, 61; and Bosnian annexation, 69; and Neoslavism,
80; Austro-Russian rivalry, 90;
and Balkan Wars, 90-91.92,93,
100,101
Russo-Turkish War (1876-78),
26,64

Sardinia (See Italy)
Sazonov, Sergej, 48
Schmerling, Anton, 19
Serbia, 26,45,47,49,61,99;
"Yugoslav Piedmont", 59,94;
and Bosnian annexation, 65,
69; and Balkan Wars, 62,90-91,
97,100; and Albania, 98; and
Preporod, 103,104-105,111;
Plut and, 112-113
Serbs, iv,73,76,86; Declaration
of Zadar, 49; excluded from
trialist program, 96
Seton-Watson, R. W.,iv
Slomšek, Anton Martin, 13,17,18
Slovan, 42,46
Slovenci (Slovenes), 3
Slovenci in Jugoslovani (Slovenes
and Yugoslavs)(Cankar speech),
114-115;
Slovene, concept of, 3,4,9;
Slovenec (The Slovene), 29,65,
93,95,97,98
Slovenes,v,vi,vii,3,5,6,8,14,16,
26; in Italy,v,22; in Hungary,
iii,22; schooling, 6; peasant
emancipation, 6; population
figures, 118
Slovenes, classes, 3,4; peasant

demands in 1848, 17; growth
and prospering of middle class,
41-42; Clericals and peasant
support, 42; workers, 51-52;
middle class students, 108
Slovenes, cultural awakening, 6,
7-13; Alphabet War, 120
Slovenes, education, appeals for
Slovene university, 15,43,78;
advances in elementary schooling, 27; Liberals and "national"
education, 43; and Preporod,
103; student strikes, 103-104;
student organizations, 106-107;
Germanization in schools, 108-
110
Slovenes, Germanophiles, 16
Slovenes, language, 3; first book,
5; Latin alphabet, 5; work of
Pohlin, 6; Zois Circle, 7; first
newspaper, 7; under French administration (1809-1813), 9;
Kopitar's grammar, 10;
Prešeren's views on, 11-13; used
in theater, 13; appeals for use
in schools and administration
(1848), 18; publishing societies,
19; promotion of language
rights, 19; Liberals and, 42-44;
nature of a nation, 75; and
Illyrism and Panslavism, 81
Slovene People's Party (Slovenska ljudska stranka) (See
Clericals)
Slovenia, v,3; concept of, 7
Slovenija (1848 political organizations), 14,15
Slovenija, first Slovene political
journal, 15
Slovenska ljudska stranka (Slovene People's Party) (See Clericals)

Slovenska matica, 19,83
Slovenski narod (The Slovene Nation), 23,42,65,81; anticlericalism, 44-45; anti-Germanism, 46,65
Slovensko društvo (1848 political organization), 14,15,17
Slovensko drustvo (Liberal club of 1890), 40
Socialists (Yugoslav Social Democratic Party/*Jugoslovanska socialnodemokratična stranka*), iv, 63,65,72-74,75,79,84,102, 116; party founding and ideology, 51-62; working class centers, 51-52; leaders, 52-56; national question, 56-60; democratic federalism for Austria, 58,69,73; "principle of personality", 58; Yugoslavism, 58-62; and Bosnian annexation, 68-69; 1909 Tivoli Conference, 60,61; treason trials (1909), 71-72,73-74; and Illyrism, 76-79,89; and Balkan Wars, 91-95 passim, 99-100; Albania, 94; Cankar and, 114
Socializem, 32 (See J.E.Krek)
Sokols, 47,103
Šorli, Ivo, 86
The Southern Slav Question and the Habsburg Monarchy, vi
Starčević, Mile, 95
Štokavian, 11,12,82,83,84
Stolypin, Piotr, 47
Strossmayer, Josip, 44,48,49
Styria, 3,16; language of, 6; and Illyrism, 12,20; election to diet, 41; mining districts, 51; 1908 Slovene-German conflict, 64-65
Šuklje, Franjo, 41

Šuštersic, Ivan, 31-32,39,44,65, 67,72,95-98,100
Taaffe Coalition, 27,29,30,40,41
Tabors, 22-23,26
Tavčar, Ivan, Liberal leader, 41-42; and anti-clericalism, 44
Tivoli Program (1909), 60,61,73-74,76-78,89,115
Tansleithia (Hungarian part of Habsburg Empire after 1867) (See Magyars)
Treason trials (1909) 70-71, 82, 90,94,107
Treaty of Bucharest (1913), 100
Trialism, 37-38,61,66-67,68,72, 79,80,95-97,98
Trieste, iii,3,14,49,52,59,112; lost to France (1809), 7; German designs on,33-35; as Southern Slav port, 48; workers of Austrian Lloyd, 51; Socialists in, 58
Triple Alliance, 45,93
Triune Kingdom (Croatia, Slavonia and Dalmatia), 16,66
Trubar, Primož, 3; religious reformer, 5,6
Tuma, Henrik, 55,74,78; concern for peasants, 55-56; Yugoslavism, 59-60,61,62,100; on Austria as economic unit, 59-60
Turks, 50,61; Turkish invasions, 5,36; and Bosnian annexation, 65,69; and Balkan Wars, 90-93, 99-100
Ultramontanism, vi,29-30,44
Unified Slovenia (*Zedinjenje Slovenija*), 15,16,17,18,22,23,24, 26,95
Ušeničnik, Aleš, 30,31,88,101
Vienna (Also seeAustria), vii,19, 31,54,68,71-72,90,99,113

Veda (Knowledge), 76,83,84,85, 116; and Neo-Illyrism, 85-89; questionnaire, 86-89

Versuch einer Geschichte von Krain unter der übrigen südlichen Slawen Oesterreiches, 7

Vodnik, Valentin, 3,7; "Ilirija Oživljena," 9

Vošnjak, Bogomil, 85,86,88

Vraz, Stanko, 74,75,82,83; Illyrism, 12; and 1848, 16; revival of, 82,84,85,87

Vseslovenska ljudska stranka (All Slovene People's Party) (See Clericals)

Vzajemnost (Solidarity), 114,116

Winden, 3

World War I, vi,31,47,51,89,109, 111

Young Slovenes (*mladoslovenci*), 21,22,26,42,43,55

Yugoslav Conference (Ljubljana, 1870), iv; Sisak meeting, 23-24; Ljubljana meeting, 24-25

The Yugoslav Idea and the Slovenes (*Jugoslovanska ideja in Slovenci,* 1907) 59

Yugoslavia, v,vii

Yugoslavism (political), vii,26, 75; Yugoslav idea, 9; in 1848, 15-18; in 1860's 23-25; and Slovene Liberals, 48-50; and Slovene Socialists, 58-62; cultural Yugoslavism, 75-89; during Balkan wars, 97-98; and Preporod, 102,103,109-111; Cankar and, 114-116

Zagreb, 52,58; congress in 1848, 16; treason trials (1909), 70-71,72,82,107; university, 78,89

Zarja (Dawn), 116 (Also see *Delavec-Rdeči prapor*)

Železnikar, Fran, 51

Zois, Žiga, 6; Zois Circle, 6,7,9,10

Zupančič, Oton, 103,111

EAST EUROPEAN MONOGRAPHS

The *East European Monographs* comprise scholarly books on the history and civilization of Eastern Europe. They are published by the *East European Quarterly* in the belief that these studies contribute substantially to the knowledge of the area and serve to stimulate scholarship and research.

1. *Political Ideas and the Enlightenment in the Romanian Principalities, 1750-1831*. By Vlad Georgescu. 1971.

2. *America, Italy and the Birth of Yugoslavia, 1917-1919*. By Dragan R. Zivojinovic. 1972.

3. *Jewish Nobles and Geniuses in Modern Hungary*. By William O. McCagg, Jr.

4. *Mixail Soloxov in Yugoslavia: Reception and Literary Impact*. By Robert F. Price. 1973.

5. *The Historical and Nationalistic Thought of Nicolae Iorga*. By William O. Oldson. 1973.

6. *Guide to Polish Libraries and Archives*. By Richard C. Lewanski. 1974.

7. *Vienna Broadcasts to Slovakia, 1938-1939: A Case Study in Subversion*. By Henry Delfiner. 1974.

8. *The 1917 Revolution in Latvia*. By Andrew Ezergailis. 1974.

9. *The Ukraine in the United Nations Organization: A Study in Soviet Foreign Policy, 1944-1950*. By Konstantin Sawczuk. 1975.

10. *The Bosnian Church: A New Interpretation*. By John V. A. Fine, Jr. 1975.

11. *Intellectual and Social Developments in the Hapsburg Empire from Maria Theresa to World War I*. Edited by Stanley B. Winters and Joseph Held. 1975.

12. *Ljudevit Gaj and the Illyrian Movement* By Elinor Murray Despalatovic. 1975.

13. *Tolerance and Movements of Religious Dissent in Eastern Europe.* Edited by Bela K. Kiraly. 1975.

14. *The Parish Republic: Hlinka's Slovak People's Party, 1939-1945.* By Yeshayahu Jelinek. 1976.

15. *The Russian Annexation of Bessarabia, 1774-1828.* By George F. Jewsbury. 1976.

16. *Modern Hungarian Historiography.* By Steven Bela Vardy. 1976.

17. *Values and Community in Multi-National Yugoslavia.* By Gary K. Bertsch. 1976.

18. *The Greek Socialist Movement and the First World War: The Road to Unity.* By George B. Leon. 1976.

19. *The Radical Left in the Hungarian Revolution of 1848.* By Laslo Deme. 1976.

20. *Hungary Between Wilson and Lenin: The Hungarian Revolution of 1918-1919 and the Big Three.* By Peter Pastor. 1976.

21. *The Crises of France's East-Central European Diplomacy, 1933-1938.* By Anthony J. Komjathy. 1976.

22. *Polish Politics and National Reform, 1775-1788.* By Daniel Stone. 1976.

23. *The Habsburg Empire in World War I.* Robert A. Kann, Bela K. Kirily, and Paula S. Fichtner, eds. 1977.

24. *The Slovenes and Yugoslavism, 1890-1914.* By Carole Rogel. 1977.